Blindsided

Best wishes
in applying these
principles! ji

Here is what people had to say about Jim Harris' previous book, *The Learning Paradox*.

"*The Learning Paradox* is a rich in depth exploration of the major issues facing today's organizations. But it's more than that – it's filled with stories and examples that evoke curiosity, laughter, and true learning. Long after I put the book down, I found myself thinking about many of the lessons Jim Harris describes so well."
   – Margaret J. Wheatley, Author *Leadership and the New Science*

"*The Learning Paradox* deals with the challenges of incessant change and helps make sense of the confusion, emerging trends and technologies. With profound insight, the book presents practical, proven strategies, tools, tips and techniques for individuals and organizations to thrive in today's fast changing business environment. I highly recommend you read the book – it had the same impact on me that Alvin Toffler's *Future Shock* did in 1971."
   – Larry Wilson, Author *Play to Win*, founder of Wilson Learning & Pecos River, coauthor
      of *The One Minute Sales Person* and *Stop Selling Start Partnering*

"Syncrude is the largest oil sands operation in the world. In a technically advanced and continually evolving business such as ours, it's vitally important for our people to constantly learn, change and adapt to uncertainty. In *The Learning Paradox*, Jim Harris' message is clear, concise and powerful."
   – Eric P. Newell, Chairman and CEO, Syncrude

"In *The Learning Paradox*, Harris offers a strikingly insightful and coherent organizational learning strategy for businesses in this rapidly changing world."
   – Hunter and Amory Lovins, Co-authors *Natural Capitalism*, Founders Rocky Mountain
      Institute

"Jim Harris has written a credible, well-reasoned book on the modern learning environment. In particular, I found his treatment of the impact of the Web on business/new economy thinking to be very insightful."
   – Dr Bill Richardson, Vice President and General Manager, Sun Educational Services,
      Sun Microsystems

"If I were told that my people and I could read only one business book during the next year I would, in a heartbeat, choose Jim Harris' *The Learning Paradox*. It communicates so very clearly not only the key issues we face, but also the solutions we need for survival. This book is priceless."
   – Lou Pritchett, retired Vice-President, Sales, Proctor and Gamble

How to spot

the next breakthrough

Blindsided

that will change

your business forever

J I M   H A R R I S

CAPSTONE

First published 2002 by

Capstone Publishing Ltd (A John Wiley & Sons Co.)

8 Newtec Place

Magdalen Road

Oxford OX4 1RE

United Kingdom

http://www.capstoneideas.com

Jim Harris encourages readers to send him feedback. E-mail him at jimh@jimharris.com or visit http://www.jimharris.com

British Library Cataloguing in Publication Data

A CIP catalogue record for this book is available from the British Library

ISBN 1-84112-242-4

Typeset by

Forewords, 109 Oxford Road, Cowley, Oxford

Printed and bound by

T.J. International Ltd, Padstow, Cornwall

This book is printed on acid-free paper

Grateful acknowledgement is made for permission to reprint excerpts from the following works:

From the Introduction to *Reframing*. Copyright © 1982 by Richard Bandler and John Grinder. Reprinted by permission of Real People Press.

"The Internet Economy and Its Impact on Local Economic Development" by David R. Kolzow and Ed Pinero. *Economic Development Review*, Winter 2001. Reprinted by permission.

"eLearning Hype Cycle Diagram" by Gartner Inc. Copyright © 2000. Reprinted with permission.

Excerpt from the "Big Idea" column in *Saturday Night Magazine*. December 2, 2000. © Alan Cross and Brain Dead Dog Productions. Reprinted by permission of the author.

Excerpt from "Blind to Change" by Laura Spinney from the *New Scientist*. November 18, 2000, page 28. Reprinted with permission.

The Seven S Model © 1979 by McKinsey and Company. Reprinted with permission.

Excerpt from *The Internet Bubble* by Anthony Perkins (New York: Harper Business, 2001). Reprinted with permission.

Excerpt from "Sharing Power" by Bruce Upbin in *Forbes* November 27, 2000. Reprinted by permission of Forbes Magazine © 2001 Forbes Inc.

Excerpt from "Quality of Working Life Survey, 2000." Institute of Management and the University of Manchester Institute of Science and Technology. Reprinted by permission of Les Worrall.

Powers of Ten on pages 75–6 reprinted by permission of Roy Williams, Caltech Center for Advanced Computing Research.

DVD Movie Download graph on page 157. Reprinted by permission of Worldwide Packets.

Reprinted by permission of Harvard Business School Press. From *The Loyalty Effect* by Frederick F. Reichheld. Boston, MA 1996, p. 51. Copyright © by Bain and Company, Inc., all rights reserved.

Courtney Love. "Courtney Love Does the Math." Salon.com. This article first appeared in Salon.com, at http://www.Salon.com. An online version remains in the Salon archives. Reprinted with permission.

Music files downloaded graph on page 25 reprinted by permission of Condé Nast, 2002. From *Wired*, September 2001. Copyright © by Condé Nast. All rights reserved.

To Lee-Anne McAlear, my wife.
She inspires my soul.

Strategic Advantage Mission Statement

We work to change the world
by changing ourselves and by helping our clients change.

Strategic Advantage is a learning and teaching organization. We study emerging trends and technologies and their potential impact on businesses. We are committed to advancing the understanding and practice of cutting-edge leadership and assist our clients – individuals and organizations – to achieve the greatest possible security within a dynamic and changing marketplace.

Contents

Introduction

CHALLENGES

- Are business issues increasingly complex?
- Is decision making more difficult?
- Are the negative consequences of wrong decisions greater than ever before?
- How can you be sure that your organization arrives at the best decisions?
- How can you ensure that you are ready for new entrants, or competitors coming out of left field?
- Are meetings efficient or do they drift away from the "real issues"?
- Are decisions delayed due to lack of consensus?
- Is it increasingly difficult to allocate scarce resources?
- Does decision making degenerate into antagonistic confrontations between different departments, where issues are decided through political maneuvering?
- Does ongoing conflict and politics wear staff out?
- How can you be sure that strategic planning focuses on the most important issues?
- Do decision makers in your organization assume the future will be like the present or past?
- Could your corporate approach to product development be improved?
- Do you proactively solicit timely, reliable feedback from employees and customers?
- Does the product development process get product and services to the market fast enough?

Good questions are better than good answers.
David Hurst, author

CAUTION

Paradox is essential to this book. For every case cited there is an opposing case. Do not swallow anything you read here whole. Debate it, talk about it with your team or group, and see if it applies to your company.[1] There is no "silver bullet" or panacea. The value of this book is in helping you arrive at the answers to these questions. It is meant to provoke thought. What works today may not tomorrow. What works for a manufacturer may not work for a service-based company. The cases cited in *Blindsided!* are meant to serve as examples and to stimulate thinking.

Following each chapter are questions to provoke you to ask how the material applies to your situation, department or organization as a whole. A good question is worth a thousand answers.

Albert Einstein was holding an exam for his university students when a teaching assistant rushed up to him and said, "Dr Einstein, there's been a terrible mistake. This exam is exactly the same as last year's! All the questions are the same!"

"Yes, I know," replied Einstein. "But this year all the correct answers are different."

The questions for business remain the same, but the answers are different. How can we better serve our customers? How can we add new value with our products and services? How can we increase margins? Increase customer satisfaction? Increase employees' growth and development? Shorten cycle times? Better align stakeholder interests? Eliminate non-value-added activity? The questions remain constant but the answers change.

People viewing the same situation can have radically different interpretations. There is an expression, "You don't read a book, the book reads you." In other words, the way you interpret a book highlights your perception. It is not that one interpretation is right or wrong, but that perceptions vary. It is important to use the examples in *Blindsided!* to help stimulate discussion with colleagues and to discover applications of the material within your organization.

TARGET AUDIENCE

This book is written for decision makers in organizations who are trying to cope with relentless change. Between 1992 and 1996, I represented Stephen Covey in Canada teaching *The Seven Habits of Highly Effective People* to clients. Covey takes complex concepts and explains them in ways that everyone can understand and relate to. His work is simple without being simplistic. *Blindsided!* seeks to do the same. It is my hope that senior executives will read *Blindsided!* and think, "These are exactly the critical issues that we are dealing with." At the same time, frontline workers reading the book will understand why change is not only inevitable, but also absolutely necessary to embrace in order to increase job security.

PART I

This book is divided into three sections. Part I provides examples of companies getting blindsided and highlights the reasons why this is occurring with increasing frequency.

CHAPTER 1

Blindsided!

Why are companies blindsided? Why is it occurring with increasing frequency? What are the consequences for organizations that are blindsided?

Polaroid filed for bankruptcy protection on October 12, 2001. The icon of instant photography was blindsided by the rapid rise of digital photography. Kodak's sales have slid over 20 percent from 1996 to 2001. Traditional photography companies with long, proud histories were blindsided.

Microsoft was blindsided by the rapid rise of the Web. Netscape's initial public offering (IPO) valued the company at $2 billion on its first day of trading. Goldman Sachs downgraded Microsoft's stock, citing concerns that the software giant would become irrelevant in the Internet age. Netscape's browser was being downloaded at a rate of one million copies a month. All of this happened before Bill Gates held his famous turnaround event in December 1995 announcing that Microsoft was serious about the Web.

Finally, the United States was blindsided on September 11, 2001 when two commercial airliners were deliberately crashed into the World Trade Center in New York, killing over 2,800 people. The effects were catastrophic causing billions of dollars damage. The resulting cancellations of travel plans pushed four airline carriers into bankruptcy, and many others to the brink. The event pushed the US economy into a deeper recession.

Old, established companies are being blindsided. New economy companies are being blindsided. Financial markets are being blindsided. Whole industries and even societies are being blindsided. Why is this occurring? How can you identify early warning signs that your company or industry is about to be blindsided? What systems and structures can you put in place to prevent this happening to your organization? Finally, knowing all this, how can you take advantage of this information to blindside your competition?

The key to avoid being blindsided is increasing the speed of recognizing and responding to change. This book will present a series of tools, techniques, and strategies to help decision makers in organizations identify trends earlier and respond faster. The new tools presented in this book will help leaders build consensus within organizations where there is conflict, chaos, and confusion.

We are experiencing more change than ever before: organizations are changing and many are suffering from initiative fatigue. Companies restructure and reorganize. Technology is changing at a dizzying rate. Individuals feel overwhelmed by their work. At times it seems impossible to keep up with the changes. Yet the rate of change is accelerating. The chart below shows the number of years it has taken 25 percent of the households in North America to adopt different technologies.[1]

Technology	Number of years for 25% of North American households to adopt
Electricity	46
Car	44
Phone	35
TV	26
PC	15
Cellphone	13
Web	<7

The Web is becoming the infrastructure of the new digital economy, accelerating the rate of change to Internet speed. Because the Web eliminates traditional barriers of time and distance, it accelerates the adoption of new technologies. The Web is both the product and the delivery medium. Here is how many years it took different technologies to reach 10 million customers:

Technology	Number of years for 10 million customers to adopt
Radio	20.0
TV	10.0
Netscape	2.3
Hotmail	1.5[2]
Napster	1.0[3]

It took radio 20 years to reach 10 million customers, but Napster only 12 months. In a *Time* magazine article, Bert Roberts, chairman of US telco MCI, revealed that the 75 million phone numbers registered in 1995 equaled the total number of phone numbers distributed from 1876 to 1956.[4] Internet access is growing even faster. The Web connected as many people in five years as the phone company did in 100, and Internet traffic is quadrupling every year.

Because of the speed of change, companies will have to employ new strategies and tools to keep up with, let alone stay ahead of, the change in the business environment. Here's a simple fact: 80 percent of the technology we will use in our day-to-day lives in just 10 years hasn't been invented yet. Some people don't

> *It's not the strongest of the species, who survive, nor the most intelligent, but the ones most responsive to change.*
> **Charles Darwin**

believe this. The Web was born with the release of *Mosaic* in 1993 or *Netscape* in 1995. E-commerce is expected to grow to $6.78 trillion by 2004![5] Job security for individuals and market share security for organizations is now based on learning, changing and accepting uncertainty.

The speed of change is accelerating – this means that companies will get blindsided faster than ever before and with increasing frequency.

"The Internet runs on dog years," the saying goes, and it's true.[6] A staggering 95 percent of Sun Microsystem's revenue comes from products that were not commercially available just 18 months ago. Bill Gates in *Business @ the Speed of Thought* writes, "In three years every product we make will be obsolete. The only question is whether we'll make them obsolete or if someone else will." If knowledge and information have a half-life of between nine months and three years, we will have to employ new ways to accelerate learning. Learning is the only sustainable competitive advantage.

Because of the dot.com bust and the fall of the NASDAQ composite index, some people dismiss the Internet boom as being all hype. There are, however, many companies that have experienced explosive growth and profit. For example, the following table shows the growth of online sales by Dell Computers:

Dell online sales	($m/day)	
March 1997	1	
February 1998	4	
February 1999	14	25%
January 2000	40	
September 2001	50	50%

Dell is an Internet company, because 50 percent of its sales come over the Web. In 2001, Dell was the only large computer company to make a profit. The Internet makes processes and interactions very efficient by stripping away activities that don't add value. The amount of slack that exists in most industrial processes is staggering.

Here's a provocative question: Can a company appear healthy and yet be dead?

Think back to learning how to drive a car. When I was taught how to drive, I was told to keep 10 feet of distance from the car in front for every 10 miles per hour of speed. So at 60 m.p.h. we're supposed to keep 60 feet behind the car in front. Imagine a driver on the highway at 60 m.p.h. Suddenly a fog descends on him so he can only see 10 feet in front. If you were to measure the vital signs of both the driver and car at that point, you'd find both were healthy. But I argue that in reality the driver is dead because sooner or later he will come to a bend in the road, an oncoming car, a stopped vehicle, or a cliff and won't be able to respond in time.

Driving at high speed in fog is a metaphor for organizations today. Companies used to have five and ten-year strategic plans, stable industries, and predictable customers. Today, however, whole industries are being turned completely upside down in two years. Seemingly healthy companies that can't recognize and respond quickly to change may be dead but not know it yet.

If you are driving at 60 m.p.h. with only 10 feet of visibility there are two things you can do: one is to slow down to 10 m.p.h. But can we slow down in our organizations today? No. We are being exhorted to go faster and faster. The other thing you can do is increase your response time sixfold.

Increased speed requires decreased response time. How can individuals and organizations recognize change sooner, understand it better and predict its impact more accurately?

Radar is a powerful metaphor for an early recognition system. The farther out the radar can see, the earlier the warning. However, the value of early warning is not great if you can't tell the difference between a flock of geese and a fighter jet. In other words, how accurately you "see" and evaluate the threat is just as important as how early you perceive it.

In an age of perpetual change, it's no longer the big who devour the small, but rather the quick that eats the slow.
Business maxim

Increased speed also requires increasing the speed of responding to change. How can organizations respond faster to the changing market, consumer preferences, and technological trends? The metaphor here is reflexes.

Recognition and response. Radar and reflexes. Just trying harder won't work. Organizations have to put in place systems and structures that are guaranteed to increase the speed of recognition and response. This book will present interviews with executives from leading companies worldwide and provide insight into what strategies, tactics and approaches create the fastest responses.

Blindsided! is not just for organizations. It also presents tools, techniques, and strategies for teams and individuals to recognize and respond to change faster.

Being blindsided strikes fear in the hearts of senior executives. Microsoft didn't see how the rise of the Web would threaten its future until three years after *Mosaic* was introduced. It was not until Netscape's IPO valued the company at $2 billion on the first day of trading that Microsoft really took note.

The major record labels didn't see the MP3 file format coming and were blindsided by Napster. Detroit automakers didn't see Japanese car companies coming. Sears and K-Mart were blindsided by Wal-Mart.

THREE TYPES OF ORGANIZATIONS

There are three types of organizations – those crashing into brick walls, those swerving to avoid brick walls, and those out in front building brick walls for their competitors. The principles outlined in *Blindsided!* can be used not only to prevent your organization from being blindsided, but to blindside your competitors.

BLINDSIDING AFFECTS MOST ORGANIZATIONS

The digital era is changing the competitive landscape of most industries. By creating new relationships with customers, while radically lowering costs, many companies and whole industries are at risk of being blindsided. The best prevention is to understand and embrace these new principles, and put systems and structures in place to increase the speed of organizational recognition and response.

There are many instances in which leaders, companies, industries, financial markets, or even countries have been blindsided. In 2001, Kodak and Polaroid, the traditional leaders in the field of photography, experienced declining revenues. These companies defined their products and services around film, film development, chemicals for film development and photographic paper. Few of these are essential if consumers adopt digital photography.

Polaroid filed for bankruptcy protection on October 12, 2001. Founded in 1937, the company grew to reach sales of $2.3 billion in 1994 and was the number one maker of instant cameras worldwide. Polaroid's business slid 18.4 percent between 1996 and 2000, but the company really began to falter in 2000 when competition from one-hour photo developing shops and digital cameras began to take its toll.

At its peak in 1988, Kodak employed 145,300 people, but in the early 1990s began divesting itself of non-core businesses such as healthcare and chemicals to focus on photography. In 1997, the company laid off 20,000 people and another 7,500 in 2001. By 2002, the company will have shed roughly 74,000 employees, half the workforce of 14 years earlier. The company's sales peaked at $20 billion in 1992 and dropped to $14 billion in 2000.[7] Kodak expected sales to decline by 6 percent in 2001.[8]

The effects of the digital tidal wave on companies has spread to a number of different industries. For instance, over 50 percent of Dell Computer's sales and and 90 percent of Cisco's occur on the Web. Dell, through its direct sales model, has become the largest computer vendor worldwide, blindsiding its competitors. Napster facilitated over one billion music file transfers in its first 12 months of operation. More than 70 percent of all stock trades at TD Waterhouse, the second largest discount brokerage globally, are done over the Web. E*Trade, Schwab, and TD Waterhouse blindsided the brokerage industry, forcing even Merrill Lynch, one of the largest brokerage firms in the world, to begin offering

Internet-based trading. Being blindsided threatens most organizations and industries.

MARKET VALUE LOSS

The worldwide financial markets have been blindsided by a loss of market value greater than any other time in the world's history.

On March 24, 2000 Cisco edged out Microsoft to become the most valuable company in the world. Cisco ended the day with a market capitalization of $579.2 billion, slightly ahead of Microsoft's $578.2 billion, and was valued higher than General Motors, Ford, Sears, Boeing, American Express and Dow Chemical combined. This led some market commentators to speculate that Cisco might become the first company in the world with a trillion dollar market capitalization. But Cisco enjoyed this pinnacle for only a brief period.

From the NASDAQ composite index peak of 5,048.62 on March 10, 2000 to its low of 1,387.06 on September 21, 2001, the market lost a staggering $6 trillion in market capitalization – equivalent to roughly 60 percent of the US gross domestic product. The decline dwarfs all previous market downturns.

In this period, five companies stood as bell weathers of the new economy – Cisco, Microsoft, Intel, Oracle and Nortel Networks, which collectively lost over one trillion dollars in total value. That's what the entire market was worth in 1980.

As Anthony Perkins, the Chairman and Editor-in-Chief of *Red Herring* magazine points out in his book, *The Internet Bubble*:[9]

By March 9, 2000, 378 Internet companies were publicly traded, with a collective market capitalization of $1.5 trillion – amazing considering this was supported by only $40 billion in total annual sales; most of which was concentrated in the hands of a few companies such as Qwest, AOL, and Amazon.com. And most incredibly, 87 percent of those 378 Internet companies had yet to even show a quarterly profit.

Between Spring 2000 and July 2001, 300 Internet companies laid-off a total of over 31,000 employees. And 130 dot.com companies have closed down altogether. By December 22, 2000, the total market capitalization of public Internet companies had plummeted by 75 percent – meaning over a trillion dollars of value had evaporated in under one year. A staggering 211 out of the 378 public Internet companies that *Red Herring* follows had seen their stock prices crater by more than 80 percent. Former high-flyers such as DoubleClick, priceline.com and Red Hat – once considered to be core Internet holdings – were now threatening to become penny stocks. And it wasn't just the under-performers that had taken a serious whack in price. Even Internet brand names such as eBay (down 72 percent), Amazon (down 77 percent) and Yahoo (down 84 percent), had seen their stock prices pounded from their 52-week highs.

This plummet in market capitalization was one of the biggest and fastest destructions of wealth in peacetime.

Some people feel that the technology slump of 2000–2001 came out of nowhere. Companies that were lauded by Wall Street as visionary were completely blindsided. How could this have happened?

Founded in 1984, Cisco's sales grew from $1.5 million in 1987 to $22.3 billion in 2001. But on April 16, 2001, Cisco warned that third-quarter earnings would be 30 percent below the previous second quarter results. Cisco also said it was cutting about 8,500 jobs.

"This may be the fastest any industry our size has ever decelerated," said CEO John Chambers, "which has required us to make difficult business decisions at an unprecedented speed." Cisco wasn't the only company caught off guard. It seems everyone in the high-tech sector was blindsided. Since the market crash of 2000, everyone has admitted that they were living in a fog. Former Nortel Networks CEO John Roth said, "Given the poor visibility into the duration and breadth of the economic downturn and its impact on the overall market growth in 2001, it is not possible to provide meaningful guidance for the company's financial performance for the full year 2001."[10] On July 26, 2001, JDS Uniphase, the world's biggest supplier of fiber-optic components, announced a loss of $50.6 billion for its year-end, the largest loss in US corporate history. The company also announced it would cut a total of 16,000 jobs by 2002, or 55 percent of the 29,000 people it employed worldwide at the start of 2001. As telcom companies profits plummeted in 2001, so have the profits of their suppliers.

TELECOM MELTDOWN

The effects of what *Business Week* labeled the "telecom meltdown" are being felt worldwide. Between 1996 and 2002, telcos worldwide assumed nearly $650 billion of debt.[11] Analysts estimate that more than $100 billion in junk bonds will end up in default or restructured as a result of the meltdown. And the ripple effect on other technology sectors has been profound with phone companies buying networking equipment to route Internet traffic, computer servers for Web hosting, software to enable services, and fiber optics to provide bandwidth services.

In 1996, deregulation of the telecom industry in the US and Europe opened up markets to competition at the same time as demand for new Internet and wireless services was exploding. Opportunities for telcos appeared limitless. Established players began spending wildly on networks that would carry voice and data, while upstarts emerged, offering high-speed lines at low prices. In 1999 and 2000, telecom equipment companies couldn't fill orders or hire workers fast enough. Mergers and acquisitions were rampant. Telco share prices continued skyrocketing as investors bet on the business of building the Internet. But promise turned to peril as profits vanished, revenues slumped, and stocks plummeted.

According to the Commerce Department, in 2000, US spending on communications equipment totaled $124 billion, or 12 percent of business spending on equipment and software, and accounted for 25 percent of the rise in business spending. When a jet lands, it reverses the thrust of its engines to come to a standstill. The effect of telecom spending is working in the same way. After boosting spending 25 percent per year between 1996 and 2001, US telecom companies slashed it and led the whole US economy into a recession. The job cuts in 2000 and 2001 exceeded 200,000.

Company	Job cuts
Nortel Networks	49,000
Motorola	30,000
Nokia	22,000
AT & T	20,000
Lucent	18,500
Ericsson	17,000
Alcatel	15,000

JDS Uniphase	14,000
360 Networks	9,000
Cisco	8,000

As of August 2001, the Standard & Poor's Communications Index had fallen for nine of the previous 12 months and lost 55 percent of its value. This compounded a 56 percent decline in 2000.

In 2002 and 2003, bankruptcies and mergers will sweep the industry. In Europe, British Telecom, France Telecom, Deutsche Telekom and The Netherland's KPN may need to find merger partners to be able to afford the construction costs of new networks. In the US, AT&T, WorldCom and Sprint are weakened to the point where they may become takeover targets.

MICROSOFT BLINDSIDED BY WEB

Microsoft was blindsided by the rise of the Web. Netscape *Navigator* was being downloaded at a rate of one million copies a month and on November 16, 1995 Goldman Sachs downgraded Microsoft stock because of Internet concerns. Until December 7, 1995 it looked like Microsoft would become irrelevant in the Internet Age. Netscape, Sun Microsystems, Oracle and IBM were rewriting the rules of computing. Net startups such as Lycos, Yahoo! and Hotmail were multiplying with dizzying speed and were rushing to create new value and lay claim to market leadership in areas where Microsoft was doing nothing.

In the early 1990s, Marc Andreessen was an undergraduate at the University of Illinois, making $6.85 an hour writing computer code for the National Center for Supercomputing Applications. He and fellow student Eric Bina became intrigued by the Internet. Although it had potential, it lacked a simple graphical user interface (GUI), an intuitive way for people to unearth the vast amount of information stored on the world's interconnected computers. In a manic burst of coding in the winter of 1993, Andreessen and Bina wrote the basics of a graphical Web browser called *Mosaic*. Almost overnight, their work turned the Web into the business and pop culture phenomenon it is today.

In times of rapid change, experience could be your worst enemy.
J. Paul Getty

Mosaic was the first GUI for the Web. Users could download the browser for free. By the fall of 1994, it had become the tool for three million Web surfers and was growing at a rate of 600,000 new users per month.

Technical merit seldom determines who wins and loses the competitive race. First movers are market makers. Progress is more important than perfection. And *Mosaic* was first.

Venture capitalist and entrepreneur Jim Clark, founder of Silicon Graphics, contacted Andreessen early in 1994. Using $5 million of Clark's capital, they founded Netscape with the idea of becoming the Microsoft of the Internet.

Every year Bill Gates appoints technical assistants who become his eyes and ears in Microsoft and within the technical community at large. The technical assistant works to identify new trends or technologies that might impact Microsoft or change the course of technological development.

In February 1994, Gates' technical assistant, Steven Sinofsky, returned from Cornell University where he saw students accessing the Web using *Mosaic*. He sent an e-mail to Gates and his other technical staff entitled, "Cornell is Wired." In April 1994, Microsoft's top executives pored over a 300-page briefing on the Internet by Sinofsky; they debated the importance of the Web and how much Microsoft should invest in it.

David Marquardt, a member of Microsoft's board of directors and a venture capitalist in California, attended an April 1994 board meeting and was amazed at how little Microsoft was investing in the Net and he raised the subject. Gates' response was that the "Net was free. There was no money to be made there. Why is that an interesting business?"

In early 1995, Microsoft management was intensely focused on *Windows 95*. Originally scheduled for release in December 1994, it would finally be released in August 1995. Microsoft was scrambling to complete *Windows NT* for the corporate market, finishing video servers for Interactive TV, and programs for set-top boxes. Government regulators were probing Microsoft's anti-competitive practices. But perhaps most importantly, Gates and other senior executives had already committed to developing Microsoft Network (MSN), a proprietary online service to compete with America Online (AOL).

Planning for MSN began in 1992, and Gates approved bundling the service with *Windows 95* in 1993. In 1993, AOL was perceived to be a far larger threat than the Internet.

By November 1994, *Mosaic* accounted for 60 percent of all Web traffic. In

December, Netscape launched its first commercial Web browser, *Navigator*. In four months, with no advertising and no sales in retail outlets, a stunning six million copies of *Navigator* were in use. By the spring of 1995, 75 percent of Web surfers were using *Navigator. Mosaic's* share had plummeted to 5 percent.

By May 1995, Gates was sounding the Internet alarm. He issued a memo titled, "The Internet Tidal Wave," declaring that the Net was the "most important single development" since the IBM PC. "I have gone through several stages of increasing my views of its importance. Now I assign the Internet the highest level."

Benjamin Slivka, who was in charge of *Internet Explorer*, wrote his own alarm in May titled, "The Web is the Next Platform," warning that the Web had the potential to supersede *Windows*. In June 1995, Microsoft held another retreat focused on the Internet. Gates gave a talk on his memo and Slivka's scheduled 15-minute talk lasted more than an hour. At one point, Slivka proposed that Microsoft give away software on the Net, as Netscape was doing. Gates dismissed the idea saying, "What do you think we are, communists?"

On August 8, 1995, Netscape's spectacular IPO sent a shock wave through the consciousness of the business world. On the first day, the stock offering, which was priced at $25, rose in trading to $75 – valuing the company at over $2 billion. Amid the subsequent blaze of publicity, no one could ignore the power of the Web.

Finally Gates had had enough. On December 7, 1995 he staged an all-day program for analysts, journalists, and customers to show that Microsoft had every intention of playing and winning in the new medium. This was the beginning of a complete about face.

Microsoft's Internet Platform & Tools Division was created in February 1996 and by July had grown to 2,500 employees. And Microsoft changed its strategy mid-stream on MSN. Microsoft forged a deal with AOL to have its *Internet Explorer* as its primary Web browser, in return for putting AOL in *Windows 95*, ending the exclusive edge for MSN.

NAPSTER

In June 1999, an 18-year-old named Shawn Fanning studying at Northeastern University e-mailed a little program called Napster to 10 of his friends. The program allowed his friends to swap digital music files, called MP3s, across the Web.

In its first 18 months, Napster attracted more than 50 million people who downloaded its software, threatening the profitability of the $40 billion-a-year music industry. In February 2001, the service facilitated over 2.3 billion song transfers.

Here's a chart of the number of downloads of Napster software:

Napster's growth (millions of software downloads)

November 19, 1999	1
February 29, 2000	5
April 30, 2000	10
June 15, 2000	15
July 13, 2000	20

Napster's growth was exponential. In July 2000, the Recording Industry Association of America's (RIAA) court case against Napster began to get widespread publicity. And what was the effect?

August 30, 2000	38
December 23, 2000	50
February 15, 2001	62

The RIAA's (1999–2001) court cases actually drove Napster usage to all-time highs. The number of users who downloaded the software nearly doubled between July 13 and August 30, 2000!

While there were 62 million downloads of Napster software by February 15, 2001, Eric Garland of BigChampagne, which analyzes peer-to-peer (P2P) networks, pegs the actual number of users between 10 and 25 million.

Throughout *Blindsided!*, you will find sidebars like this one with a screened background. These explore a topic relevant to the text in greater depth, but if you are already knowledgeable about the background information on that topic or are not interested in it, you can skip any sidebar without sacrificing any understanding of the text.

WHAT IS MP3?

During the early 1990s, two scientists, Dieter Seitzer and Heinz Gerhauser, working at the Fraunhofer Institute in Germany, oversaw the development of the MP3 file format. The MP3 file format was finalized in 1997, allowing for the compression of music files by eliminating all the frequencies and sounds that the human ear can't hear. Before MP3, file sharing across the Internet was impractical because music files were so large. A typical four-minute song was 40 megabytes (MB) in size.[12]

MP3 compresses audio using the principle that some sounds are masked. During loud sounds, the human ear cannot hear weak ones. When an organ is not playing you can hear the breathing in the piping; when it is booming you will never hear the breathing because the sound is masked. It is therefore not necessary to code all sounds.

With MP3, the higher the quality of sound reproduction, the larger the file size. The chart below shows the size of a four-minute song using various compression qualities. The bitrate is the number of times the music is sampled per second. The greater the bitrate, the higher the sound quality. A four-minute song digitized from a CD without compression takes 41.3 MB, while a CD quality MP3 (192 bitrate) is only 5.6 MB and excellent CD quality (128 bitrate) is 3.8 MB. An FM quality MP3 of the same song takes up less than 2 MB. Basically, files can be compressed to one-tenth to one-twelfth the size of an uncompressed CD file.

Bitrate	Quality	Download speed (kbyte/minute)	Size (MB)
1411	CD	10584	41.3
192	Perfect CD quality MP3	1440	5.6
160	Perfect CD quality MP3	1200	4.7
128	Excellent CD quality MP3	960	3.8
112	Near CD quality MP3	840	3.3
96	Near CD quality MP3	720	2.8
64	FM Quality MP3	480	1.9
32	AM Quality MP3	240	0.9
16	Shortwave Quality MP3	120	0.5

Source: Fraunhofer IIS

How Napster Worked in 2000

Once someone downloaded the Napster software and installed it on their computer, they could log onto Napster's central server. All the songs on their hard disk then became visible to anyone else logged onto Napster and all the songs on everyone else's hard disk were visible to them. Napster served as a central directory for all the songs of everyone logged on to the service. At the peak of Napster's popularity there were never fewer than 500,000 songs available for download.

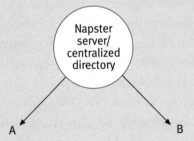

Figure 1.1 Napster architecture.

You could search for your favorite song, and if you had a high-speed Internet access (cable or DSL) connection to the Internet you could download a song in less time than it would take to play it. Napster is one of the reasons we have seen an explosion in broadband access.[13]

While Napster's directory was centralized, when downloading, you would connect directly to someone else's hard disk; this is called peer-to-peer architecture (P2P), and worked as shown in Figure 1.2.

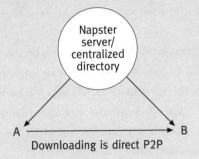

Figure 1.2 Peer-to-peer downloading.

By downloading directly from someone else's hard disk there are few bottlenecks in the system. If all downloads had to go through Napster's server the system would have crashed or at least slowed down as usage soared exponentially. In other words, Napster was designed to scale (grow quickly).

P2P PHENOMENON IS MORE THAN TECHNOLOGY – IT'S BEHAVIOR

The P2P phenomenon has been driven not just by technology, but also by the attitudes and behavior of the Net Generation. The "Net Generation" or NetGen is the first generation to grow up from birth with computers and the Web for the majority of their adult lives – anyone born after 1975.[14]

What music industry executives don't understand is that the spending behavior of the Net Generation has been irreversibly changed by the Napster phenomenon.

One venture capitalist admitted, "My eight-year-old son has never had any interest in business. When the court order came to shut down Napster he was really upset."

When his older teenage son could no longer find his favorite songs on Napster because of the removal of copyrighted songs, he and a group of friends would each contribute $1, buy a CD, digitize the songs and e-mail them to each other to load onto their MP3 players. While the recording industry successfully forced Napster to close, it has been unsuccessful in preventing file sharing. Napster has changed forever the value proposition of music in the minds of the Net generation.

Demographic differences in behavior are one of the reasons organizations will continue to get blindsided. Who is closest to the future? The 18-year-old who listens to MP3s or the 65-year-old CEO who has never downloaded or listened to an MP3 file? Who does all the strategic planning in organizations? Who is most disenfranchised from strategic planning? Is it any wonder organizations only change incrementally?

To a 65-year-old CEO the behavior and attitudes of the Net Generation are completely alien. Without any understanding of this generation, recording industry executives are making decisions that are out of step with the attitudes and behaviors of people under 35. This increases the likelihood of the industry being blindsided.

One way to avoid this is to create systems and structures that ensure interaction between different age groups. Jack Welch, former CEO of General Electric, instituted a process of reverse mentoring: a 30-year-old GE employee taught him how to use the Web. At Microsoft, technical assistants regularly brief Bill Gates on new trends that could affect the company. Some organizations have established shadow executive committees composed of individuals under the age of 30 who represent different functions. Decisions made by the executive committee are run by the shadow cabinet for comment before actions are taken.

RIAA PROMOTED NAPSTER

The recording industry created its own worst nightmare. The media coverage that was generated by the RIAA taking Napster to court drove the new service to all time heights. Until the RIAA began legal action there were few, if any, media mentions of Napster. Napster remained popular among a very limited group of highly wired students, primarily on college campuses. Media coverage from the court cases informed the public about the possibility of sharing music files and accelerated the number of people downloading the Napster software. When heavy metal band Metallica launched its suit against Napster, coverage exploded until it reached 2,500 mentions in print articles in July of 2000 (see Figure 1.3). Had the music industry decided to take a different approach, it might have been better off.

NAPSTER ALTERNATIVES

The RIAA may have won the battle against Napster, but it has lost the war on file sharing. Some recording industry executives think that by eliminating Napster, the future of digital music is dead. Think again.

Napster began filtering copyrighted files in response to a court order on March 6, 2001 and immediately thereafter, the number of songs traded on the site plummeted as much as 95 percent, according to digital music research company Webnoize.[15]

While the RIAA focused on shutting down Napster, conventional wisdom was that other, under-the-radar file sharing services would never pose as great a threat because they were hard to use and didn't have a critical mass of users.

In Greek mythology the Hydra was a fierce, nine-headed water serpent. Hercules was instructed to kill it, but each time he chopped off one of its heads, two more grew in its place. The Hydra represents a persistent or multifaceted problem that cannot be eradicated by a single effort; difficulties and obstacles multiply in the course of accomplishing a task.

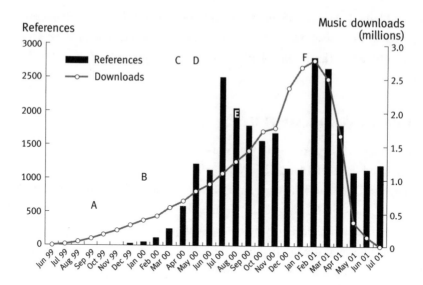

Figure 1.3 Napster media references and music file downloads

A	December 9, 1999	Recording Industry sues Napster
B	April 29, 2000	Metallica sues Napster
C	July 26, 2000	Federal Judge orders injunction on Napster
D	July 29, 2000	Appeal court blocks injunction
E	October 31, 2000	Napster and Bertlesman agree to partnership
F	February 12, 2001	Appeal court backs lower court ruling

Source: Webnoize, 2001 and Nexis.com.

Rather than kill file swapping, the RIAA's court victory over Napster has spurred the practice to new heights. There are now more than 90 file-swapping alternatives to Napster. Five of them have achieved critical mass and are growing significantly. Nine of the most popular alternative services are listed below and in August 2001 each had 283,000 to 2.3 million users, according to Jupiter Media Metrix, which measures Web traffic. All of these services had little traffic or did not even exist in February 2001.[16]

Napster's Achilles heel was that it had a central server and was a legal entity that the RIAA could take to court. At Napster over 200 company-owned servers connected to high-speed networks indexed user's file libraries and answered search requests. It proved to be a fast and reliable system capable of supporting millions of users. When the courts ordered Napster to filter out all copyrighted material, usage dropped significantly. At its peak in February 2001, Napster had 1.6 million simultaneous users, and by July 2001 it had fallen to 160,000. Shutting down Napster will not end music file sharing. The behavior of the Net Generation hasn't changed. Instead, file swappers have just moved to other services. And many of the new services don't have Napster's architectural or legal liabilities.

Post Napster unique users of alternative file-sharing services, February to November 2001 (US homes only)

Service	Feb (000)	Mar (000)	Apr (000)	May (000)	Jun (000)	Jul (000)	Aug (000)	Sep (000)	Oct (000)	Nov (000)
Morpheus	–	–	–	–	808	1,731	2,312	2,770	3,898	4,808
KaZaA	–	–	–	–	519	1,223	1,333	2,207	2,464	2,014
WinMX	–	–	–	–	653	1,005	1,244	1,389	1,365	1,723
Aimster	–	–	–	–	534	956	927	942	774	942
iMesh	–	–	428	474	928	942	970	964	769	858
BearShare	–	267	354	382	842	830	289	746	605	776
LimeWire	–	160	164	388	710	576	283	186	–	–
Audiogalaxy	–	550	457	978	722	462	308	2,068	2,050	822
Napigator	–	173	348	323	193	210	–	–	–	–
Totals	–	1,150	1,751	2,545	5,909	7,935	7,666	11,272	11,925	11,943

Source: Jupiter Media Metrix, January 2002

Until March 2002, Morpheus, KaZaA, and Grokster all used the same software to access the Fast Track Network (owned by KaZaA's parent company). By marketing independently, but operating interdependently, all three systems grew quickly. Users of any one system were able to search the hard disks of users of the other two systems. This guaranteed that individual users were more likely to find the popular music, videos, software, and movies that they were looking for.

On March 4, 2002, KaZaA barred Morpheus users from logging onto the Fast Track Network, as the result of a licensing dispute. In the same week Music City changed its name to Stream Cast Network and released a new version of Morpheus which uses the more decentralized Gnutella network for searching and file sharing. While traffic on the Gnutella network increased as a result, I believe that 75 percent of former Morpheus users migrated to using KaZaA in the following weeks. Searching and downloading are faster on the Fast Track Network than on the Gnutella network.

Three of the top six services are not even based in the US – Imesh is based in Israel, KaZaA in Holland, and WinMX in Canada – and therefore US courts may have not jurisdiction.

Some of the most popular peer-to-peer file-swapping services – Aimster, BearShare, Freenet, Gnutella, iMesh, and Morpheus – have no central content index like Napster. The content is indexed and maintained by the users connected to the network. Therefore it is questionable whether the RIAA can shut down these services. As of October 2001, the RIAA had begun legal proceedings against the services listed above.

KaZaA

KaZaA is quickly becoming the most popular P2P music file sharing on the Web. The Dutch company owns the Fast Track network that allows over a million users to swap media files free of charge. KaZaA has a number of unique features that highlight the direction in which P2P file sharing will continue to evolve. KaZaA allows users to search and download all types of media – music, videos, photos, and documents.

Once the KaZaA software is installed on a user's computer, it doesn't interact with KaZaA except to request on-screen advertising. Unlike Napster, KaZaA has no centralized server that could be easily shut down by the courts. The Recording Industry Association of America launched a lawsuit against KaZaA and other P2P music sites in the fall of 2001.

KaZaA's decentralized approach involves selecting the most powerful computers with the fastest connections logged onto the system at any time and assigning them to serve as search hubs or "supernodes," with each connected to an estimated 250 other users. Supernodes build an index of the media files being shared by each peer connected to it. When a user logs onto the KaZaA network, his computer will connect to a supernode. When a user performs a search it will check the nearest supernode first, which replies immediately. It then searches all other supernodes. As a result of this decentralized but interconnected architecture, searches are just as fast as with a centralized directory.

KaZaA is more powerful than Napster was because of its decentralized architecture. With Napster, users downloaded directly from each other's hard disks. If the donor logged off the network or shut down their computer before the download was complete, the recipient was out of luck and had to begin the download all over again. KaZaA resumes broken content streams by finding another source for the same file. If another source isn't available the software will monitor the network until the requested file becomes available. The network speeds up downloads by finding a list of peers with the desired file and then coordinates the download from a number of computers, relieving any one peer from serving the entire file.

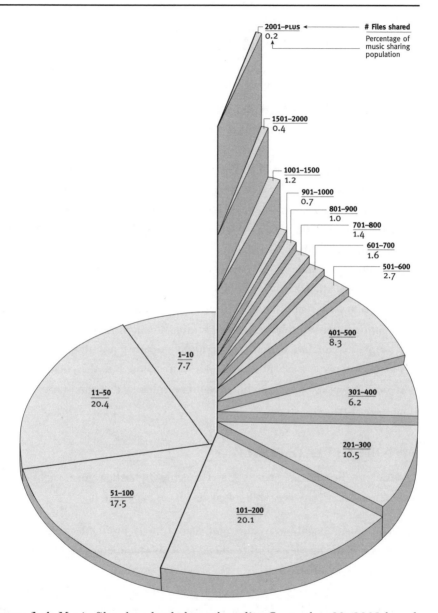

Figure 1.4 Music files downloaded: week ending September 20, 2001 based on 25 million users. As we have taken the mid-point in every category for estimating (i.e. in the 1–10 category we assumed the average user has five songs), the total number can be doubled from 5.29 billion to 10.58 billion. Source for data: BigChampagne (www.bigchampagne.com). This image was originally published in a slightly different form in *Wired* magazine. Copyright © 2001 Condé Nast Publications Inc. Reprinted by permission. All rights reserved.

FILE SHARING ACCELERATES

Rather than abating after Napster's demise, file sharing accelerated. Webnoize reported that the top four file-sharing systems – FastTrack, Audiogalaxy, iMesh and Gnutella – were used to download 3.05 billion files in August 2001,[17] greater than the 2.79 billion files downloaded using Napster in February 2001, at the peak of its popularity.

Because of the nature of P2P networks, no one can say exactly how many users there are – somewhere between 10 and 25 million. BigChampagne surveys P2P users' hard disks and analyzes how many MP3 files users have stored. Almost 2 percent of file swappers have over 1,000 MP3 files on their hard disk! (See Figure 1.4.) Given BigChampagne's analysis multiplied by 25 million users – there are somewhere between 5.29 billion and 10 billion MP3 files stored on users' disks!

The figure of 10 billion MP3 files being stored on users' hard disks may seem confusing given that over three billion files are transferred each month. The simple explanation is that users download many more files than they actually keep. A typical user will download a song, listen to it, then decide whether to keep or delete it. So an individual could download a thousand songs, but only keep a hundred.

HISTORY REPEATS ITSELF

An article by Toronto disk jockey Alan Cross highlights how the music industry's typical reaction to any new technology has been to oppose it:

> The music moguls were mad and scared. Sixty profitable years of selling music to the masses was threatened by a new technology that looked to put them all out of business.
>
> Another tiresome screech about the evils of Napster? Not quite. This end-of-the-world-as-we-know-it bleat came from sheet-music publishers at the beginning of the 1900s. A company called Aeolian introduced a mechanical piano that magically played popular songs using a roll of perforated paper. Sheet-music companies panicked: if people could get a machine to play for them, who would buy music paper? Then, before the music industry could organize an anti-Aeolian campaign, they were blindsided by the phonographs.

In the 1920s and early 30s the new enemy was radio. The industry panicked: if people could hear their favorite recordings on radio why would they bother to buy records? Until they realized that radio actually promoted record sales and entered into a licensing agreement with them.

Then in 1963 Philips introduced the audiocassette, and the industry faced the prospect of losing control of distribution. For the first time music fans had a simple, inexpensive way to make copies of their favorite songs.

In 1976 Universal and Disney sued Sony over the VCR, alleging that it allowed consumers to violate copyright by making unauthorized copies of TV shows and movies. It wasn't until January 1984 that the Supreme Court ruled five to four in favor of Sony thereby saving the now ubiquitous VCR from extinction.

The industry backed the compact disk, which was highly successful. But Digital Audio Tape (DAT) wasn't so lucky. It was effectively rendered stillborn by music-industry lawyers who successfully lobbied world governments to make copy-protection chips mandatory in all DAT players. What good was a tape machine that couldn't be used to make tapes?

In 1998 the Diamond Rio (the first portable MP3 player) liberated MP3 files from hard drives everywhere. Armies of lawyers sought to sue the bejesus out of the manufacturer, but a judge dismissed the case. (The Rio fell through a loophole in the Audio Home Recording Act that exempts hardware used for computer data.)[18]

The licensing and collection of royalties for music is handled by organizations, such as the American Society of Songwriters, Composers and Publishers (ASCAP), which represent songwriters and performers. Radio stations license the right to broadcast music from ASCAP. All-music radio stations can purchase a blanket license. Stations earning more than $150,000 pay a fee of 1.615 percent of annual gross revenue, while stations earning less, pay between $450 to $1,800 a year.[19]

ASCAP uses a complex formula to work out how much money each artist should receive per song. Payouts are calculated based on duration of the work, use of the work and frequency of play. Payments are divided between publishers and songwriters.

An average song lasts four minutes, and an all-music station will play 10 songs an hour – the rest of the time is announcer and commercials. With 24 hours a day that's 240 songs a day, 365 days a year, that's roughly a million songs a year. If the radio station has a $200,000 dollar budget it will pay $3,230 per year, or 0.3¢ per song. If an average of 1,000 people listen to the station the actual payment is three ten-thousandths of a cent per song per person.

A similar payment model could be developed for digital music, such that every time you listened to a song a small payment would go to the record company. As noted above, there is already a precedent for this model with songs played on the radio. Over time, the music industry may be forced to adopt such a model as a means for consumers to pay for music.

The recording industry has consistently resisted change. In June 2000 the major record labels sued MP3.com, a business committed to paying the recording industry. At MP3.com consumers could listen to tracks before buying using streaming audio – a technology which lets them listen to a song over the Web. Upon purchase, MP3.com would ship the CD and allow the consumer to immediately download the MP3s of songs they had bought from the company's database. Buyers could then listen to their newly purchased songs while the physical CD was working its way through the mail or shipped by courier. MP3.com argued that the consumer had already bought the CD and paid for the intellectual property and therefore this was not piracy. US courts ruled against MP3.com.

While the courts ruled this was illegal, from a practical standpoint the ruling was ludicrous. Once the consumer received the CD in the mail they could "rip" it themselves creating their own MP3s. Why not let consumers immediately begin listening to the music they've bought? Again it boils down to the issue of control.

Tim O'Reilly, editor of O'Reilly Networks, a Web site that rates P2P services says:

> I believe most people want to pay for what they use online. It sounds like an odd and contrary thing to say, but the biggest problem that we have right now with online music is there is no legitimate alternative. The music companies have basically stood in the way of any legitimate alternative. So they're getting what they deserve – that is, piracy, because there's no other way to do it.[20]

Napster has made it easy and instantaneous to get any music you want, when you want it. That ease of access does not exist with the current music labels.

INTERNET RADIO

Internet radio gives listeners control over music. They can listen to whatever they want, whenever they are logged onto the Internet. The days of suffering through weather and traffic reports waiting for a favorite song are over. Launch.com is an Internet radio station that puts the power back into the hands of the listeners. Anyone can become a DJ by creating his or her own radio station. Launch provides the music; users simply select the artists they want. They can listen to other people's stations and rate their choice of music. Launch.com has over 6.4 million registered users and offers two million stations.

Listeners can rank a song by sliding a rule from zero to 100, zero being "Hate It" to 100 being "Favorite." The higher the ranking, the more frequently the song will be played. Listeners can even click on a red X to skip a song they hate and never have to hear it again.

Another Internet radio, Live365.com gives its DJs the ability to upload MP3s and play them on their own radio station for everyone to hear. Live365.com also allows DJs to broadcast live from their computers, change play lists instantly, add live voice between songs and broadcast live talk shows or performances. The site has 40,000 private radio stations on its network and is visited by two to three million users each month.

WHAT IS PIRACY?

As a kid, I would listen to the top 500 songs of the year on the radio with a tape recorder ready, play and pause pressed. As the station would come out of a commercial break, I'd quickly release the pause button, listen to whether or not I liked the song and if I didn't, recue the tape. We called it "making tapes". The record industry calls it piracy. The only reason I cite this example is to show that this is not new behavior for kids who are long on time and short on cash. The difference is that today's kids don't make tapes; they swap music digitally.

In the past, consumers bought their favorite music on records, then on eight-track cassette, then had to repurchase it all again on audio cassette, and then on CD. Finally, consumers often only want to buy one song but are forced to purchase a whole CD . . . and music industry executives say it's consumers who are pirates.

The whole controversy over digital music has led a number of artists to call

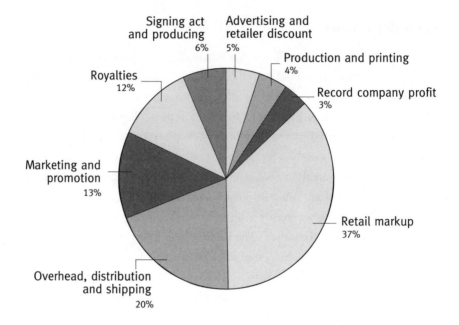

Figure 1.5 Compact disc cost breakdown. Source: *Billboard*.

the recording industry the pirates. Courtney Love, the singer from rock band Hole and the widow of Nirvana founder Kurt Cobain, argues that the industry "has been gouging artists for decades."[21] In a global industry that makes $40 billion a year,[22] the average recording artist in North America makes only $40,000 a year[23] and receives less than 6 percent of the cover price of the CD's sold. Love points out that the recording companies own the copyright on music, but book authors own their works and license first publication rights to publishers. When the contract expires, writers get their books back, but record companies own recording artists' copyrights forever.[24] Love argues that artists have been practically giving their music away under the old system, so they have little to lose from the public pirating their music.

"In a society of over 300 million people (North America), only 30 new artists a year sell a million records. By any measure, that's a huge failure," claims Love.

While a record contract may grant an artist a 12 percent royalty, musicians actually receive only a fraction of this. Out of their royalty musicians pay for the producer (3 percent); packaging costs (2.25 percent); promotional copies given away (1 percent); and the record company will hold in reserve 1.6 percent for returned goods, and various other charges, leaving the average musician with a royalty of 2.98 percent or 50¢ on a $17 CD.

So a band selling a million copies of its album only gets $500,000.[25] The artists' manager and lawyer will take a cut of this amount. The sum is further divided between members of a band. The sidebar by Courtney Love below highlights how artists feel about how the recording industry is currently structured.

File-sharing technology offers consumers convenience, ease of use, the option to sample music, portability, and instant gratification. Rather than address these issues and fully embrace the new technology, the recording industry has chosen to label all those who have as "pirates." And the industry has still not addressed the issues driving the change in consumer behavior.

COURTNEY LOVE

In March 2001, Courtney Love launched a counter-suit against her record label Vivendi Universal in an effort to get out of a contract that she believes to be unfair.

Today I want to talk about piracy and music. What is piracy? Piracy is the act of stealing an artist's work without any intention of paying for it. I'm not talking about Napster-type software.

I'm talking about major label recording contracts.

I want to start with a story about rock bands and record companies, and do some recording-contract math:

This story is about a bidding-war band that gets a huge deal with a 20 percent royalty rate and a million-dollar advance. (No bidding-war band ever got a 20 percent royalty, but whatever.) This is my "funny" math based on some reality and I just want to qualify it by saying I'm positive it's better math than what Edgar Bronfman Jr. (the president and CEO of Seagram, which owns Polygram) would provide.

What happens to that million dollars?

They spend half a million to record their album. That leaves the band with $500,000. They pay $100,000 to their manager for 20 percent commission. They pay $25,000 each to their lawyer and business manager.

That leaves $350,000 for the four band members to split. After $170,000 in taxes, there's $180,000 left. That comes out to $45,000 per person.

That's $45,000 to live on for a year until the record gets released.

The record is a big hit and sells a million copies.

So, this band releases two singles and makes two videos. The two videos cost a million dollars to make and 50 percent of the video production costs are recouped out of the band's royalties.

The band gets $200,000 in tour support, which is 100 percent recoupable.

The record company spends $300,000 on independent radio promotion. You have to pay independent promotion to get your song on the radio; independent promotion is a system where the record companies use middlemen so they can pretend not to know that radio stations – the unified broadcast system – are getting paid to play their records.

All of those independent promotion costs are charged to the band.

Since the original million-dollar advance is also recoupable, the band owes $2 million to the record company.

If all of the million records are sold at full price with no discounts or record clubs, the band earns $2 million in royalties, since their 20 percent royalty works out to $2 a record.

Two million dollars in royalties minus $2 million in recoupable expenses equals . . . zero!

How much does the record company make?

They grossed $11 million.

It costs $500,000 to manufacture the CDs and they advanced the band $1 million. Plus there were $1 million in video costs, $300,000 in radio promotion and $200,000 in tour support.

The company also paid $750,000 in music publishing royalties.

They spent $2.2 million on marketing. That's mostly retail advertising, but marketing also pays for those huge posters of Marilyn Manson in Times Square and the street scouts who drive around in vans handing out black Korn T-shirts and backwards baseball caps.

Add it up and the record company has spent about $4.4 million.

So their profit is $6.6 million; the band may as well be working at a 7-Eleven.

Of course, they had fun. Hearing yourself on the radio, selling records, getting new fans and being on TV is great, but now the band doesn't have enough money to pay the rent and nobody has any credit.

Worst of all, after all this, the band owns none of its work... they can pay the mortgage forever but they'll never own the house. Like I said: Sharecropping. Our media says, "Boo hoo, poor pop stars, they had a nice ride. Fuck them for speaking up;" but I say this dialogue is imperative. And cynical media people, who are more fascinated with celebrity than most celebrities, need to reacquaint themselves with their value systems.

When you look at the legal line on a CD, it says copyright 1976 Atlantic Records or copyright 1996 RCA Records. When you look at a book, though, it'll say something like copyright 1999 Susan Faludi, or David Foster Wallace. Authors own their books and license them to publishers. When the contract runs out, writers gets their books back. But record companies own our copyrights forever.

The system's set up so almost nobody gets paid.

Recording Industry Association of America (RIAA)

In November 1999, a Congressional aide named Mitch Glazier, with the support of the RIAA, added a "technical amendment" to a bill that defined recorded music as "works for hire" under the 1978 Copyright Act.

He did this after all the hearings on the bill were over. By the time artists found out about the change, it was too late. The bill was on its way to the White House for the president's signature.

That subtle change in copyright law will add billions of dollars to record company bank accounts over the next few years – billions of dollars that rightfully should have been paid to artists. A "work for hire" is now owned in perpetuity by the record company.

Under the 1978 Copyright Act, artists could reclaim the copyrights on their work after 35 years. If you wrote and recorded "Everybody Hurts," you at least got it back as a family legacy after 35 years. But now, because of this corrupt little pisher, "Everybody Hurts" never gets returned to your family, and can now be sold to the highest bidder.

Over the years record companies have tried to put "work for hire" provisions in their contracts, and Mr Glazier claims that the "work for hire" only "codified" a standard industry practice. But copyright laws didn't identify sound recordings as being eligible to be called "works for hire," so those contracts didn't mean anything. Until now.

Writing and recording "Hey Jude" is now the same thing as writing an English textbook, writing standardized tests, translating a novel from one language to another, or making a map. These are the types of things addressed in the "work for hire" amendment. And writing a standardized test is a work for hire. Not making a record.

So an assistant substantially altered a major law when he only had the authority to make spelling corrections. That's not what I learned about how government works in my high school civics class.

Three months later, the RIAA hired Mr Glazier to become its top lobbyist at a salary that was obviously much greater than the one he had as the spelling corrector guy.

The RIAA tries to argue that this change was necessary because of a provision in the bill that musicians supported. That provision prevents anyone from registering a famous person's name as a Web address without that person's permission. That's great. I own my name, and should be able to do what I want with my name.

But the bill also created an exception that allows a company to take a person's name for a Web address if they create a work for hire. Which means a record company would be allowed to own your Web site when you record your "work for hire" album. Like I said: Sharecropping.

Although I've never met any one at a record company who "believed in the Internet," they've all been trying to cover their asses by securing everyone's digital rights. Not that they know what to do with them. Go to a major label-owned band site. Give me a dollar for every time you see an annoying "under construction" sign. I used to pester Geffen (when it was a label) to do a better job. I was totally ignored for two years, until I got my band name back. The Goo Goo Dolls are struggling to gain control of their domain name from Warner Bros., who claim they own the name because they set up a shitty promotional Web site for the band.

Orrin Hatch, songwriter and Republican senator from Utah, seems to be the only person in Washington with a progressive view of copyright law. One lobbyist says that there's no one in the House with a similar view and that "this would have never happened if Sonny Bono was still alive."

By the way, which bill do you think the recording industry used for this act?

The Record Company Redefinition Act? No. The Music Copyright Act? No. The Work for Hire Authorship Act? No.

How about the Satellite Home Viewing Act of 1999?

Stealing our copyright reversions in the dead of night while no one was looking, and with no hearings held, is piracy.

It's piracy when the RIAA lobbies to change the bankruptcy law to make it more difficult for musicians to declare bankruptcy. Some musicians have declared bankruptcy to free themselves from truly evil contracts. TLC declared bankruptcy after they received less than two percent of the $175 million earned by their CD sales. That was about 40 times less than the profit that was divided among their management, production and record companies.

Toni Braxton also declared bankruptcy in 1998. She sold $188 million worth of CDs, but she was broke because of a terrible recording contract that paid her less than 35 cents per album. Bankruptcy can be an artist's only defense against a truly horrible deal and the RIAA wants to take it away.

Artists want to believe that we can make lots of money if we're successful. But there are hundreds of stories about artists in their 60s and 70s who are broke because they never made a dime from their hit records. And real success is still a long shot for a new artist today. Of the 32,000 new releases each year, only 250 sell more than 10,000 copies. And less than 30 go platinum.

The four major record corporations fund the RIAA. These companies are rich and obviously well represented. Recording artists and musicians don't really have the money to compete. The 273,000 working musicians in America make about $30,000 a year. Only 15 percent of American Federation of Musicians members work steadily in music.

But the music industry is a $40 billion-a-year business. One-third of that revenue comes from the United States. The annual sales of cassettes, CDs and videos are larger than the gross national product of 80 countries. Americans have more CD players, radios and VCRs than bathtubs.

Story after story gets told about artists – some of them in their 60s and 70s, some of them authors of huge, successful songs that we all enjoy, use and sing – living in total poverty, never having been paid anything. Not even having access to a union or to basic healthcare. Artists who have generated billions of dollars for an industry die broke and uncared for.

And they're not actors or participators. They're the rightful owners, originators and performers of original compositions.

This is piracy.

Published in Salon.com, June 14, 2001

DISTRIBUTION IN THE DIGITAL AGE

A typical CD costs about $17, of which distribution, shipping and store mark up account for more than $9.50.[26] By contrast, the cost to send a song over the Internet is close to zero. So P2P file sharing ultimately threatens music retailers, shippers, and companies that press CDs.

Not only does digital distribution eliminate 50 percent of the cost structure of traditional distribution, it is more convenient for consumers. By offering the opportunity to sample music before buying, it does not require consumers to buy a whole album or CD to get one song, giving users control.

Record labels were the gatekeepers, controlling the means by which music was distributed. But digitization threatens that power. Napster was like a canary in a coalmine, warning the record industry that the rules of the game have changed. The speedy emergence of alternative services after Napster's demise warns the industry that they cannot control this phenomenon through the courts, so they had better embrace it.

USER CONTROL

Napster and digital file sharing took off quickly not just because it was free, but also because it offered radical new value. The Napster revolution empowered music listeners, and broke the control that the record labels have on the production and distribution of music. Music lovers could select and listen to *any* music, *when* they wanted to, in *any sequence*.

Traditionally, record labels have not allowed consumers to buy a single song, but instead have worked to force consumers to buy a whole CD, audiocassette or record. A single song CD costs $7.50 and usually contains four songs, three of which are either 'B' sides or remixes of the first song.

Creative Lab's Nomad Jukebox[27] is an MP3 player that holds 20 gigabytes of MP3 files, equal to more than 250 CDs of music, more than 3,000 songs. This means that an individual can carry with them *all* the music they have ever loved during their lifetime with them *at all times*. Users can create play lists, random shuffle, etc.

The fact that music was free was not the only thing that drove users to Napster. It provided ease of use and the ability to find almost any song. Users can widely sample music. While radio stations allow sampling, the user is not in control of the play list.

Napster helped music lovers find old songs no longer sold in stores. And it created a worldwide community. For instance, an Indian working in the US will have a very limited choice of Indian music at his local music store. But Napster allowed him to download his favorite songs from someone in Bombay.

BERTELSMANN INVESTS IN NAPSTER

Thomas Middlehoff is chairman and CEO of Germany-based Bertelsmann, the world's third largest media company. In 1994, Middlehoff, then head of Bertelsmann's corporate development, met with Steve Case, the founder of then little-known AOL. Middlehoff was "blown away" by Case's vision of an online media empire, and proposed that Bertelsmann invest $200 million in AOL. The board eventually let Middlehoff invest $50 million. In October 2001, Bertelsmann's stake in AOL was worth $445 million (€500 million) and owned 49.5 percent of AOL Europe. Because of this and other successes Middlehoff was named CEO and chairman of Bertelsmann.

Just as Napster caught the recording industry by surprise, Middlehoff caught all the other recording labels by surprise by giving Napster a $60 million loan convertible into an equity stake in November 2000. To an industry that makes $40 billion a year, a $60 million investment is spare change.

WHY THE MUSIC INDUSTRY'S RESPONSE WILL FAIL

But Bertelsmann is facing a challenge changing the industry. The P2P revolution has shown that the recording industry will only change when forced to. In 2001 the music industry finally awoke to the fact that it had to embrace digital distribution. The five major record labels have launched two competing file-sharing services. Vivendi Universal acquired MP3.com and Sony launched Pressplay. AOL Time

Warner, EMI, BMG, and RealNetworks have launched MusicNet. However. file swappers will see both services as a step backwards for two key reasons:

- *Lack Napster's breadth of choice.* Neither service will offer all music. Pressplay will only offer music from two labels and MusicNet from three. Neither service will offer music from independent labels. Napster was convenient because it offered one point of access to all music.
- *Lack of portability.* Both services will place restrictions on users as to how they can use downloaded music. Songs downloaded from Pressplay or MusicNet will not play on anything except the PC that downloaded them. Fans won't be able to download them onto an MP3 player or even burn them to a CD. Both companies say they will eventually allow subscribers to shuttle songs to non-PC devices – once they figure out a way to avoid piracy. It's like buying a CD that you can only play on one CD player.

FIVE STAGES OF DEATH AND DYING

Individuals, organizations, and whole industries are blindsided because of the natural human tendency to ignore, deny or resist change that is perceived to be threatening. In her book, *Death and Dying*, Elizabeth Kubler Ross describes the five emotional stages an individual goes through when diagnosed with a fatal disease: denial, anger, bargaining, depression, and finally acceptance. It is only at the final stage that constructive responses emerge.

We all go through these five emotional stages when we experience any upsetting change or situation, or feel threatened or overwhelmed by change. Some of the tools presented in *Blindsided!* such as scenario planning, help executives move through these stages. When a previously identified scenario actually begins to occur, executives can respond faster because they have already been through the first four stages. By contrast, their competitors will refuse to acknowledge it, as the record industry did with respect to digital distribution for all of 1999, 2000, and most of 2001.

Hank Berry, the former CEO of Napster and partner at Hummer Winblad, the venture capital firm that invested $15 million in Napster, in an interview talked about the attitude of recording industry executives towards new technology:[28]

> Their position is that they are in control and, that they don't have an obligation to make that work [music] available in any way, shape or form other

than the way they want to. One executive said at a forum I was at, "Why do you keep talking about business models? We decide the business model and the consumer's job is to accept it."

I believe that this music executive's attitude exemplifies the reaction of most record industry executives to the P2P phenomenon in 1999–2001, and highlights the industry's deep denial. This executive felt that he and his industry peers were in control and could ignore the challenge posed by the Internet and Napster. This attitude guaranteed the industry would be blindsided and that the old distribution would eventually crumble.

HISTORY REPEATS ITSELF: P2P WILL AFFECT HOLLYWOOD

Movie executives take comfort in the fact that movie revenues grew to a record $8 billion in 2001. However, in 2001, only 18 million North Americans went to see a movie every week. In the late 1940s, before the TV boom, up to 60 million people a week went to the movies.[29] It is not safe to remain complacent. In 2001 over 70 percent of Hollywood's revenue came from the rental business. Remember, Hollywood studios opposed Sony's production of the VCR, suing Sony in a series of court cases that lasted almost a decade. The studios eventually lost in the US Supreme Court.

Another shift is currently occurring away from physical media (video tapes, and DVDs) to downloading or streaming videos across the Internet. Morpheus, and other P2P services that allow users to share full movies, will affect Hollywood. Television shows, video games, and feature films, some of which have yet to hit theaters, are being captured digitally, downloaded, and swapped on the Internet, with up to 500,000 videos and films changing hands every day, according to Andrew Frank,[30] chief technology officer (CTO) of Viant and a media and entertainment analyst.

The movies are posted on the Internet and traded just like digital music. They are captured in a number of ways: (1) "ripping" DVDs – breaking the encryption code and unlocking the digital video; (2) recording films in movie theater using a digital camera and then posting on the Web (you identify this as the method when you see people get up in front of the camera and block the screen); and (3) someone in the post-production process releases a copy – sometimes before the final cut.

But rather than resist the new technology as the music industry did, Hollywood studios have embraced it. In August 2001, five major studios – Metro-Goldwyn-Mayer, Paramount Pictures, Sony Pictures Entertainment, Universal Studios, and Warner Bros – announced an initiative that will let US broadband Internet users watch new and old releases for the cost of a pay per view movie ($3–5). The studios have also partnered with universities and colleges to allow students to watch first-run films, which are appearing in movie theaters, in their dormitories. Universities and colleges will serve as distribution partners, sharing in the revenue.

This strategy is particularly important because in 2000, 50 percent of North American movie-goers were under the age of 30. This is the Net Generation – they are highly computer and Net literate. Movie studios have no choice but to embrace digital distribution or risk being blindsided like the recording industry:

North America movie attendance by age in 2000

Age	Percentage
12–15	10
16–20	17
21–24	11
25–29	12
30–39	18
40–49	14
50–59	10
60+	8

Source: Motion Picture Association of America[31]

While the Hollywood studios sued Scour.com (a precursor to KaZaA) and successfully forced it out of business by scaring away investors, moviemakers have learned from the music industry's inability to stem the rapid rise of P2P file sharing.

With the rapid expansion of bandwidth (see Gilder's Law in Chapter 4), streaming full motion videos across the Internet will be as easy and as fast in 2005 as downloading a four-minute MP3 song is today. Rather than fight the flood, Hollywood has taken the more intelligent strategy in embracing a technology that will inevitably grow more prevalent.

By 2005, movies and television shows will be traded online as easy as

MP3s are in 2001. To watch *The Sopranos*, a cable subscriber is not going to need a subscription to HBO if they can get it online the next day.

The actions of the five Hollywood studios show that the executives have moved through the denial that gripped the record industry since Napster's launch, and has now moved to the final stage – acceptance. If you can't beat them, join them. Rather than have the Net Generation exchanging and watching films illegally, the industry has decided to embrace the technology, make its practice legal, and gain revenue from it.

Some people see things as either black or white. It's either all digital distribution or all movie theaters. It is not an either–or; it is an and. We will always have movie theaters because of the big screen experience and crystal clear images. But what will shift is the balance of how movies are being watched. Small shifts in an industry can have large impacts. If within the next few years people born after 1975 consume just 15 percent of their movies by downloading them over the Net – because this group represents 50 percent of the public that go to movie theaters, the impact on the industry will be significant. Movie theaters that are marginally profitable or break even now will eventually close. The changes will challenge video stores. Currently Blockbuster makes up to 30 percent of its profits from late charges. With digital distribution there are never any late charges. How will this affect Blockbuster?

CONCLUSION

Blindsided! focuses on systems and structures that decision makers can put in place to recognize and respond faster to change. The essence of W. Edwards Deming's work was that every organization is perfectly aligned to get the results it gets! The role of the leader is to put in place systems and structures that ensure the organization's capacity to recognize and respond to change quickly and accurately is always enhanced.

Blindsided! has relevance for all organizations, because the rate of change that individuals, organizations, and even societies face is accelerating. Individuals feel overwhelmed, and need a new set of tools, strategies and techniques for coping with change.

The next chapter will present additional case studies outlining how companies in a wide range of industries have been blindsided. These cases highlight why all decision makers in organizations need to be attuned to changes in the market.

REFLECTIONS

- What would be the early warning signs in your industry that would indicate your organization could be blindsided?
- What preventative measures could you develop to avoid being blindsided?
- What are the systems and structures that could be put in place within your company to avoid being blindsided?
- How could you accelerate learning within your organization? For yourself?
- In what ways is your organization operating in a fog? How would you know? What obstacles are impeding your ability to see through the fog? What tools/techniques might help?
- How could your organization benefit from reverse mentoring? (For example, GE's Jack Welch learning about the Web from a 30-year-old.)
- How could you organization understand the habits of demographic groups not represented among decision makers (i.e. the Net generation)?
- Among those who are involved in strategic planning for your organization, is there a cross-section of demographic groups represented? If you are a young company, do you have an experienced voice? Is there a surround sound of perspectives?
- What are the current or announced technologies that threaten your organization?
- Knowing what you know about your own organization, if you were your own competitor, how would you blindside yourself?
- What new technologies, processes, or systems have you initiated within the last year? Which of those can be quickly and easily changed or modified?
- What is currently being offered for free in other industries that could affect the expectations of customers in your industry?
- What radical changes have taken place in yout customers' environment? What are/might be the implications for you?
- What customer request has caused you the greatest incredulity? If you were to consider delivering it, what would have to change?

CHAPTER 2

Recognition and Response

How can companies avoid being blindsided? If technological changes are drivers ensuring that companies will be blindsided, is it only companies in high-tech industries that are at risk? What structural blind spots do organizations and individuals have that make them susceptible to being blindsided?

The significant challenge we face in organizations today is not **problem solving** but **problem seeing**. As managers we have become excellent problem solvers – that is, after all, how we became managers. However it is *problem seeing* and *opportunity perceiving* that will separate market leaders from losers.

Some of these structural blind spots are embedded in our thinking at such a deep level that we are unaware that they bias our perception of reality and doom us to continually fail. This chapter will outline some of these pathologies.

Amid all this change, the key to job security for individuals and market share security for organizations is based on learning, changing, and accepting uncertainty. Paradoxically these are what we fear the most.[1] Our security is based on embracing the very things we fear the most.

While the first chapter focused on case studies of companies and whole industries that have been blindsided, this chapter will discuss some of the reasons why companies are being blindsided with increasing frequency. The key to preventing it is faster recognition and response to change in the business environment. Recognition involves five processes. In the case of Napster and the music industry:

1. *Seeing/perceiving risk:* Digital music has the potential to completely reshape the music industry.
2. *Seeing/perceiving opportunity:* Rather than perceive this as a threat, see it as providing tremendous opportunities, such as cross marketing and selling music concert tickets with P2P because you can see what is on people's hard

disks in order to identify your customer base. By eliminating the retail channel and the need to physically produce CDs, digital music distribution, if embraced, could allow the industry to charge 50 percent less for music while increasing profit!

3. *Understanding the importance of the potential impact of the risk/opportunity:* Digital music has the potential in the long term to devastate the current retail channel, which takes 37 percent of the current industry revenue. It also shakes the industry's grip on the distribution channel and lowers the barrier to entry of new competitors. Musicians can use the Internet to distribute their music directly.

4. *Communicating throughout the organization:* Within a music company, communicating this reality to all employees is essential so they can perceive opportunities in the market, form strategic alliances and launch new products and services that take advantage of the new technology.

5. *Vigilantly monitor the situation.*

The first three processes may sound simple but can, in fact, be very difficult. Having never experienced the current business environment we are in, it is difficult, if not impossible, to instantly recognize danger signs. It is hard to understand the implications and importance of situations when we are experiencing them for the first time. How then can we prepare ourselves for possibilities before they occur? Scenario planning is a part of "seeing" potential futures so that if any of them do evolve, we have already prepared for them and can respond faster.

Response involves a number of processes:

1. *Generating options:*
    (a) Buy Napster (as Bertelsmann did).
    (b) Create our own digital service (Pressplay and MusicNet).
    (c) Brainstorm services to generate new revenue streams – direct advertising and selling concert tickets to fans who have a band's songs on their hard disk.

2. *Evaluating and selecting the best option.*

3. *Communicating throughout the organization.*

4. *Executing.*

5. *Monitoring the situation.*

HYPE CYCLE

The Gartner Group's Hype Cycle Model is a tool for recognition. This model looks at the market perception of different technologies as they mature, starting with a technology trigger, a rise to a peak of inflated expectations, a fall into a trough of disillusionment and then gradually a rise on a slope of enlightenment to a plateau of productivity (Figure 2.1).

While Gartner applies the hype cycle to new technologies – evaluating where they are in the cycle – the cycle can be applied to any new phenomenon. For instance, it can be applied to the rise and fall of the NASDAQ index, which is heavily weighted with technology stocks. The Web boom was born with Netscape's initial public offering, which on its first day valued the company at $2 billion. Because the number of shares in Web-based companies was limited, demand exceeded supply and the market experienced an incredible appreciation to the point where companies were trading at price earnings (P/E) multiples in the hundreds, a level that was clearly not sustainable. At this point on the Gartner hype cycle, the market reached a peak of inflated expectations.

The inevitable crash came as Anthony Perkins, editor of *Red Herring*, so

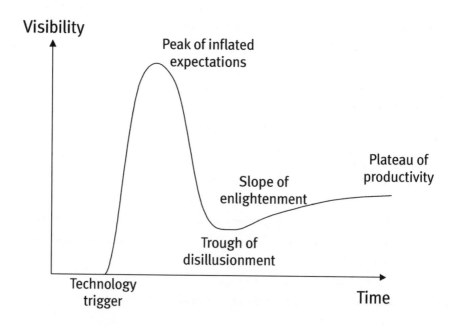

Figure 2.1 Hype cycle. Copyright ©2000 Gartner Group.

aptly predicted in his book *Internet Bubble*. The NASDAQ peaked at 5,048.62 on March 10, 2000 and dropped to its low of 1,387.06 on September 21, 2001. In the crash, companies that had negative cash flows, weak business plans, and little cash in the bank were driven to bankruptcy.

However, the market tends to overreact in both directions. We will now see the remaining companies, stronger for having gone through the downturn, succeed in the long term.

Here is a simple truth: Individuals using Net tools will not go back to old ways. We are:

- Not going to stop using e-mail and go back to snail mail.
- Not going to stop sending attachments and switch back to using couriers.
- Not going to stop surfing the Web.
- Not going to stop using digital photographs and go back to developing film.
- Not going to stop downloading music over the Internet.
- Not going to stop shopping online.
- Not going to stop video conferencing and Web casting.
- Not going to stop using wireless e-mail.
- Not going to stop using cell phones.
- Not going to stop downloading software over the Web.
- Not going to stop trading stocks over the Internet.
- Not going to stop getting news online.
- Not going to stop using eBay.
- Not going to stop the growth of e-commerce.
- Not going to stop the explosive growth of Internet banking and phone banking.

Just because many dot-coms have died doesn't mean the Internet is dead. Too many individuals and companies are now dependent on the new technology. Consider:

- 9.7 billion non-spam e-mails are sent every day
- eBay lists six million items on its site at any one time
- 3 billion songs were traded online in September 2001
- The world is short of 720,000 IT positions

American Airlines spends less than 10¢ to create an e-ticket compared with $12 for a paper ticket. In 2000, an estimated 10 percent of all airline tickets were sold online. By 2004, it will be 25–30 percent, estimates University of California professor Peter Sealey.[2]

The Internet has cut the average time it takes IBM to order supplies from vendors from 68 to 23 days. Internet efficiencies have saved IBM $7 billion since the mid-1990s, according to IBM chief information officer Phil Thompson. And it has only just begun.

"The bubble may have burst on Wall Street, but the Web-based revolution in core business processes is just beginning," said Ford CEO Jacques Nasser in 2001.[3]

WHY DO COMPANIES GET BLINDSIDED?

The principles discussed below explain why organizations get blindsided: Fitt's Law, ants' strategy, just noticeable difference, signal-to-noise ratio, critical tracking task, frequency of upheaval, increasing complexity, problems of context, law of inherent conflict, search for simple solutions, mistaking subjective feelings for objective reality, conventional wisdom, linear thinking, and problems with business theory.

FITT'S LAW

Fitt was a psychologist who watched Cuban women rolling cigars against their thighs. He noticed that as they grew more experienced, they took less and less time to roll the cigars. He plotted the relationship on a graph (Figure 2.2).

This is called a log-linear relationship. The time to roll a cigar decreased in a linear fashion as experience in rolling the cigars increased logarithmically (i.e. 1; 10; 100; 1,000; 10,000; 100,000) This is also known as Fitt's Law of Learning. In other words, we become more efficient at a task the more we perform it. It highlights the law of diminishing returns; say the initial improvement is 20 percent from the first time in performing a task to the 10th time. It now takes another 90 repetitions of the task to get an equal performance gain. To get the next equal performance gain requires 900 additional repetitions. Initially we are very bad at performing a task and therefore see major improvement very

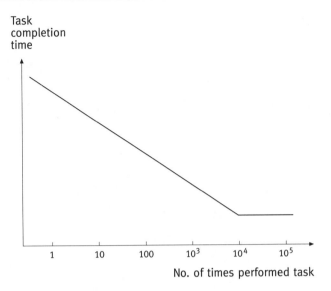

Figure 2.2 Fitt's Law of Learning.

quickly. Over time, though, we become quite efficient and it takes more and more refinement to improve the process.

Fitt's law demonstrates that by the time we become incredibly efficient at doing something we have invested a tremendous amount of time. When a new technology comes along this strength becomes a weakness. The new way of doing this is not yet proven or efficient and is easily disdained.

This explains the phrase, "Nothing fails like success." By the time an organization has perfected its systems and structures, it has invested tremendous energy and everyone in the organization is loath to change anything because of all the effort sunk into the status quo.

"The entire structure of a bureaucracy," says Seth Godin, author of *Permission Marketing* and *Unleashing the Idea Virus*, "whether corporate or government is to hope and pray that the system is going to stay exactly the same because it took them so long to set it up in the first place."

"Look at the 10 most popular pages on the Internet, including Amazon," says Godin. "They don't change for months at a time, because the executives have too much at stake to try new things and there's a culture that says, 'look we got this right, let's not change it'."

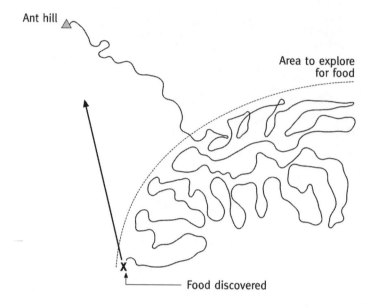

Figure 2.3 Ants' strategy for food discovery.

ANTS AND EFFICIENCY

Ants are fascinating. While the majority of ants are working efficiently, bringing food and water to the colony, a few ants go off to look for new sources. In Figure 2.3, an ant sets out from the anthill to forage for food in an unknown territory marked by the curved black line.

The ant sets off and takes a circuitous route to the area that is to be explored. Once inside the area, the ant begins laying down a very faint scent trail, which lets him remember where he has been. His seemingly random pattern allows him to very efficiently cover the area. Once the ant does find food, he uses a different strategy, which is to head straight back to the ant colony in a very direct route laying down a different trail to let others know that, "This is the way to food or water."

Once the new area has been identified, the colony sends out many workers to collect food using the direct route. Seen in this light, the strategy is very efficient.

The ants follow the principle *move and explore in a direction that you know least*. The principle is critical for businesses today. Send some people out to move in a direction that you know least. In other words, allow some individuals to explore new areas that individuals and the organization don't currently understand as being relevant or related to your business.

How can companies take advantage of opportunities they can't perceive? How can companies solve problems they can't yet see? Imagine how frustrating it would be to play a game in which the rules of the game were always changing. Working in today's business environment is like building a plane while flying it, which guarantees we will make mistakes.

This sounds impossible, but nature has a solution to this dilemma: evolution and infinite experimentation. Through genetic mutation, nature runs an infinite number of experiments. Most fail. Some genetic mutations, however, create a variation of a species more able to compete in the environment. Once a new species begins to thrive, it changes the ecological balance and affects every other species. Species most capable of adapting will not only survive, but thrive in the new environmental reality. This was the essence of Charles Darwin's work on the origin of species.

In *Complexity: The Emerging Science at the Edge of Order and Chaos*, Mitchell Waldrop writes about how very small differences at the molecular level can have profound impacts on the organism:

> At the molecular level every living cell is astonishingly alike. The basic mechanisms are universal. And yet a tiny, almost undetectable mutation in the genetic blueprint might be enough to produce an enormous change in the organism as a whole. A few molecular shifts here and there might be enough to make the difference between brown eyes and blue, between a gymnast and a sumo wrestler, between good health and sickle cell anemia.[4]

Why, then, don't companies take the same approach to the business environment? Seth Godin argues that "most of the books about change management and the way that most people go about it is wrong. Because change is everywhere all the time, we can't view it as a temporary thing that has to be survived, instead, it's a constant process of evolution."

Godin's book, *Survival's Not Enough*, looks at change in Darwinian terms; ideas that are successful get replicated and reinforced, while unsuccessful ones die off. Whereas species have to die out and become extinct, there is no such physical death in the world of ideas. Therefore ideas, or memes, evolve much faster than species do. Godin advocates "zooming," moving from one thing to another without the pain that many people associate with change, as the best way to win in this world.

Godin argues that companies should adopt a disciplined approach equivalent to mutation in nature – rapid experimentation. For instance, Websites, even the most popular, should have a policy of changing 10 percent of what Web visitors see. Analyze what happens, whether it works for better or worse, and use that knowledge to change it.

Using the analogy of the ants, companies should mandate a small percentage of staff to play, experiment, and create new products and services.

Throughout the Microsoft vs. Netscape saga, the market was proving the value of the Web. People were downloading Netscape's *Navigator* at a rate of one million copies a month before Microsoft's big turnaround announcement in December 1995. However, in 1993 and 1994, the Internet was an area that Microsoft as a whole, and senior executives in particular, had very little understanding about. What could Microsoft have done differently? Allow a few individuals to "play" as in the case of the ants.

The Chinese have an expression; it is easier to step on a dragon's egg than to step on a dragon. In other words, deal with small problems when they are small. Microsoft could have dedicated a small team of 50 programmers to work on Internet strategies for the company in 1993 or 1994 instead of having to dedicate 2,500 programmers in an abrupt about face. While Microsoft was able to do it, how many companies can afford to throw 2,500 people at a problem? As Stephen Covey says, the first virtue of leadership is humility, the second, courage. Gates at least has the humility to admit when he is off base. It is more important to be right than to hold onto old views. The second virtue is courage because we have to make decisions amid uncertainty, which guarantees we will make mistakes.

The earlier Microsoft executives had identified Netscape as a challenge, the smaller the price of catching up would have been. Microsoft today has the luxury of buying start-up companies that have developed unique technology quickly, rather than developing it in-house. This is an inexpensive form of research and development as the entrepreneur takes all the risk and once it is proven successful, Microsoft buys the company. Rather than have to try thousands of different ideas itself, Microsoft buys companies once they have reached a critical mass as start ups, and have proven that their business model and technology work.

JUST NOTICEABLE DIFFERENCE

A just noticeable difference is the amount of change over a given time that is so small we do not perceive the change. For instance, in 1977 Dr Clifford Saunders[5] began working for Bell Northern Research (BNR) as a design engineer. Design projects typically had five engineers and lasted for a year. In 1979 he went to work in Saudi Arabia for five years. When he returned he began working on design teams again, but he noticed a number of differences that had escaped others. By 1983, design teams had typically grown to 50 engineers. For the engineers who had been working in North America over the period of five years, the changes had been so gradual that they were not noticeable. Saunders, however, having been away for five years, noticed the differences immediately. If change in an industry is constant but occurs just below the threshold of a just noticeable difference, after a period of a year this cumulative change is exponential. The complexity of projects, design choices, and the number of personnel involved had grown exponentially, but the tools that the teams were using to make product design decisions and trade-offs had not changed. In Saunders' case, the design teams' decisions were still being made in discussion, using flip charts.

The Microsoft vs. Netscape case shows that when organizations are operating in a rapidly changing world, it is hard for individuals to notice that the continual incremental change over time is exponential.

SIGNAL-TO-NOISE RATIO

Radar has two phases. The first is a long-range, broad sweep. In this phase, the radar picks up all sorts of "noise" from birds and meteorological events, such as rainstorms, as well as "signals" from targets it is actually designed to identify, such as enemy airplanes. In the first phase, the radar has to be able to distinguish signals from noise.

Failure to separate signal from noise can have serious consequences. In the 1982 Falkland Islands war between Britain and Argentina, officers aboard the British ship *HMS Invincible* failed to alert other British warships about the first

Exocet missile attack during the conflict, although they had 19 minutes warning. One missile – fired from an Argentine plane first spotted on radar 180 miles away – hit the destroyer *HMS Sheffield*, killing 20 men and wounding 24. Senior officers aboard HMS Invincible dismissed a series of sightings as "spurious." The war was the Royal Navy's first encounter with low-flying, Exocet-carrying attack planes.[6] Argentinean planes flew so close to the water that British officers interpreted the weak signals the radar picked up as noise.

Once a radar system has separated a signal from background noise, the system moves into the second phase, involving "locking onto" or tracking the target. If the target is a plane, an anti-aircraft missile can be launched. Anti-aircraft missiles use infrared, or heat-seeking sensors, to "lock onto" the aircraft's jet engine.

A number of years ago, Saunders was working on a military design problem, "How can an aircraft avoid an anti-aircraft missile once it has locked onto the engine?"

One solution that his team developed was to create a diversionary signal stronger than the original signal. A hot flare is lit. The flare exits the plane right below the engine and gradually flies away from the plane. The anti-aircraft missile begins tracking the flare instead of the plane because its signal is stronger than the original engine signal.

Signal-to-noise ratio is a useful way of thinking about the problems executives face in strategic planning today. There are literally thousands of trends – new technologies, shifts in consumer behavior, products and services launched by competitors, mergers and acquisitions and new competitors being launched. The clamor can be overwhelming for executives responsible for strategic planning. Which company, technology, or trend will be successful in the long run? Which will have the greatest impact on your product, service and organization?

One way to think about all these small trends – new products, companies, and technologies – is as "noise". Hidden among this "noise" are a number of "signals" that will grow increasingly strong. Some of them will eventually become dominant. Sorting out which trends are noise and which are signals is tricky, as the case below will illustrate. The reason that executives cannot sometimes perceive a threat is that (1) it is buried in the noise of other trends; (2) there are other diversionary signals that are taking their attention – as in the case of the flare; (3) the concept of just noticeable difference; (4) the whole concept of paradigm paralysis – the mentality that "surely 6,000,000 lemmings jumping off a cliff can't be wrong."

The Microsoft vs. Netscape case highlights how the executive team of Microsoft confused the "signals" about the Internet with "noise." This in part was due to the fact that management's focus was intensely focused on *Windows 95*, MSN, *Windows NT*, software for video servers for Interactive TV, and programs for set-top boxes and the anti-trust investigation. It was not until *Windows 95* had been released that Microsoft really changed focus and Gates did his public 180-degree turnaround.

CRITICAL TRACKING TASK

It is important to understand how we as humans focus. We can only focus our attention intensely on a few items at the same time. Chinese acrobats awe audiences by spinning many plates on sticks at once. The best can spin eight plates, four in each hand.

The critical tracking task is the point at which a system is stable, but all the processing resources are taken up with the task at hand. For instance, if you had a piece of wooden dowel, like a broom handle that was ten feet long, you could balance it on your upturned palm. The pole would move so slowly that you could easily engage in other activities, such as talking with a friend, drinking coffee or answering the phone.

However, if you shorten the pole to six feet, the task of balancing it on your hand would become more difficult and would require more attention. Cut another foot or two off so that the dowel is only four feet long and you would not be able to do anything else: your entire attention would be focused on balancing the pole. You would have reached your critical tracking task. The system would be stable, but it would take up all of your processing capacity.

Saunders was once working on a project to design military helicopters that could fly so low to the ground they would avoid radar detection (Figure 2.4). Another criteria was that the helicopter had to go as fast as possible to escape enemy anti-aircraft fire. However, if the helicopter went too fast, it would require all of the pilot's concentration. If there were any problems he would not be able to focus on them, because all his attention would be taken by flying above high objects. So another design consideration was making the controls

Figure 2.4

easy to handle so the pilot could easily rise to avoid crashing into tall objects such as trees and electrical wires.

One principle in system design is to find the critical tracking task point and then back the system off to allow spare capacity to deal with other challenges.

In many organizations there is such a drive for efficiency that everyone is busy all the time. In other words, the organization strives to reach the point of critical tracking task where everyone's time is not only occupied, but stretched beyond capacity. The standard nine to five workday becomes eight to eight. However, if new challenges come along, where will the organization find time to research a new way of doing things? Some organizations work to become so lean, mean and efficient that there is no time for people to use the ants' strategy to explore new products and services, to investigate competitors, to better understand customers and to uncover their unarticulated needs.

FREQUENCY OF UPHEAVAL

A group of academics has studied the formation of sand piles:

> Imagine a pile of sand on a table top, with a steady drizzle of new sand grains raining down from above. The pile grows higher and higher until it can't grow any more and an avalanche of sand cascades down the sides of the pile. The resulting sand pile is self-organizing, in the sense that it reaches a steady state all by itself without anyone explicitly shaping it. It is also in a state of criticality, in that sand grains on the surface are just barely stable. The microscopic surfaces and edges of the sand grains interlock in every conceivable way, but are just as ready at any point to begin a landslide. So when a falling grain hits there's no way of telling what might

happen. Maybe nothing. Maybe just a few tiny grains, a medium sized avalanche or a full-scale avalanche that will take off one whole face of the sand pile. All these things do happen at one time or another. Big avalanches are rare and small ones are frequent. But the average frequency of a given size of avalanche is inversely proportional to its size.[7]

The implications for business are significant. While we cannot predict when major shifts will occur, such as the Web threatening Microsoft's business, we can predict the frequency. Minor shifts will occur frequently and major ones less frequently. What is important for executives to realize is that their understanding is only partial. Looking at the Microsoft memos, the sense of urgency increased over time, until December 1995 when Gates publicly stated that the Web was the most important development since the PC itself.

INCREASING COMPLEXITY

Our world is becoming increasingly complex. Globalization. Digitization. The Internet. Market fragmentation. Markets of one. As recently as 1993 marketers talked about mass markets and mass media. Today the buzz is one-to-one marketing, also known as mass customization, tailoring products and services to the taste of individual customers.

The rate of change is faster than ever before. For instance, it took 80 years, between 1876 and 1956, for the phone companies to install 75 million local lines in North America. A staggering 75 million local lines were added in North America in 1995 alone![8] *Mosaic* was released in 1993 giving birth to the Web. Netscape drove the Web to grow exponentially and today the company doesn't even exist, having being sold to AOL and Sun Microsystems in 1998 for $4.3 billion. The e-commerce revolution it spurred will continue and is estimated to grow to more than $6.8 trillion by 2004. Amazon.com, founded in July 1995, achieved $3.12 billion of sales in 2001.

Information available to us across the Web is doubling every nine months, and knowledge has a half-life. Microsoft assumes half the code that is written today will be thrown out in three years because the tools will be so much more powerful that it will be easier to recode than to edit.

Companies that were lauded as market leaders – Motorola, Polaroid, Sears, Sega, and IBM – are labeled laggards.

Business leaders are incited by management gurus to embrace various management theories. Excellence. Teamwork. Quality. Speed to market. Reengineering. Rightsizing. Customer focus. Benchmarking. Activity-based Accounting.

The stakes have never been higher and the expectations for performance have never been higher. Amid these challenges, how can leaders cope? The answer is: they can't if they employ the old methods of management. The change in the external business environment must be matched by change within the organization.

Systems are growing more complex. For example, each subsequent release of *Windows* shows an exponential growth in the number of lines of code. This increases the development time and the number of bugs that are uncovered during development, as the interaction of features and the potential for conflicts increases exponentially: *Windows 95* has 11 million lines of code, *Windows 98* has 18 million while *Windows 2000* has 34 million lines.[9] The rate of change is faster than ever before and it doesn't promise to slow down.

Albert Einstein said, "We cannot solve problems at the same level of thinking we were at when we created them in the first place." Or to use the Taoist maxim, fish discover water last. Or the Sufi wisdom, the eye cannot see itself. If our minds have blind spots, by definition we will not be able to perceive them with my own mind. Could it be that there are certain blind spots in Western management theory and practice that doom us to stay stuck? As Alcoholics Anonymous states: insanity is doing the same thing over and over again and expecting different results. An alcoholic is doomed to keep on repeating the same mistakes until he learns a completely new approach to life and work.

By definition, a complex situation is one in which no one individual can have all the information, insight, or necessary perspective required to resolve it. Yet, our organizations have a bias for action and demand solutions. So organizations try another approach, unaware that the very root of their problems is in how they perceive and attempt to resolve complex situations.

As the change impacting organizations is accelerating, it seems we have less time to deeply understand complexity and strategically plan. Executives and organizations are caught up in more competing priorities than ever before. As a result, decision makers are facing greater pressures and under more stress than ever before. The solution is to find better methods of decision making, rather than working longer or harder.

John Warfield, a retired George Mason University professor, has made a lifetime study of complexity. Warfield coined the phrase, "Law of Enforced Substitution." Put simply: most decision makers have a bias for action. After an initial study of the problem, there is a pressure within the decision-making group to agree on a course of action. However, if the situation is complex, by definition the course of action will only treat a symptomatic problem, not the root cause. In complex situations, problems are interdependent and tackling one problem, without concurrently tackling the other problems that exacerbate it, will not result in a satisfactory long-term

> *For every one individual hacking at the root of evil there are thousands hacking at the leaves.*
> **Henry David Thoreau**

solution. In fact, the solution may cause a seemingly unrelated problem in another area. After a period of time, the decision making group, recognizing their initial approach is not solving the situation, will decide on another course of action. The interdependent root causes of the complexity will remain unresolved as the group lurches from one decision to another.

Few individuals, groups and organizations have studied complexity and therefore don't understand the difficulty in coping with complex situations. We are condemned to go round and round the merry go round without even knowing it.

There are a number of limitations in perception, business theory, individuals, groups and organizations, that prevent us from effectively resolving complex situations.

SEARCH FOR SIMPLE SOLUTIONS

There is a deep yearning for the simpler times. Executives are under pressure and yearn for stability, security, peace, and tranquility. They are fatigued. They want a simple solution.

Our perception is also flawed because we find ourselves thinking, "If we could just get to the root problem. If we could just get the answer." It is this thinking that plays into the latest management fad of the day, or the Law of Enforced Substitution.

A complex situation, by definition, does not have just one root cause. Unless you argue that the complex situation is perpetuated by a lack of a systematic, scientific approach to resolve it.

Again the problem rests in our perception. It is the interplay of a number of factors that cause complex situations. In other words, our problem is that we think there is only one problem. This reductionism approach dooms many individuals and organizations to stay stuck in their problems indefinitely as stated by the Law of Enforced Substitution.

*To know and not to do . . .
is not to know.*
Proverb

Instead of thinking about a problem, we need to think of a "problem set," a cloud of problems that surrounds the issue or situation. In Interactive Management (IM), it is important to identify all the problems and to clarify them. This process is expansive, opening the minds of the participants to the scope and inter-relatedness of the factors. However IM doesn't just stop there. The process also sorts out which are the most significant problems.

LAW OF INHERENT CONFLICT

The law of inherent conflict states that resolving complex situations without the proper tools will always result in conflict. Often it will be an open battle of egos, as individuals strive to have their position adopted by the group. Or the conflict may simmer under the surface as those individuals who lose this time engage in rearguard action in subsequent meetings, raising the same problem again and again because the group invalidated their perspective when it adopted another approach. Groups adopt one approach because they have no other way of dealing with the complexity.

Individuals cannot realize or get at another root of the situation because of: (1) spreadthink, which is when each individual in the group is arguing to advance his/her understanding of the hierarchy of contributing factors; (2) contributing factors or problems may interact in ways which create other problems; (3) no effective way of resolving complexity, the group's solution will not get at the root of the situation. Therefore, the Law of Enforced Substitution will prevail.

Interactive management is a discipline for resolving complex situations.

The time is spent productively because it "harmonizes" each individual's perceptions, drawing out the collective wisdom of the group.

Harmonize is an appropriate word because traditional problem solving methodologies homogenize perception. That is, only one perspective is typically taken. IM takes into account all the perceptions of individuals in the group. This not only increases buy-in and reduces fighting, but also makes the end strategy far more effective.

We too often look for simple answers that do not adequately address the complexity of the situation at hand. Yet how can we maintain diversity without being overwhelmed by conflicting ideas, trends, and information? Interactive management does just that by respecting and maintaining the diversity of opinion and perception while at the same time creating a shared and collective understanding.

MISTAKING SUBJECTIVE FEELING FOR OBJECTIVE REALITY

In his paper, "How to Make our Ideas Clear" in 1878, Charles Sanders Peirce wrote:

> One singular deception, which often occurs, is to mistake the sensation produced by our own unclearness of thought for a character of the object we are thinking [about]. Instead of perceiving that the obscurity is purely subjective, we fancy that we contemplate a quality of the object, which is essentially mysterious . . .

In other words, when we confront a complex situation we confuse our own subjective feelings of frustration, and being perplexed, as being objective characteristics of the problem itself. Like a child being frustrated at not yet being able to ride a bike, the true deficiency is the child's lack of skill and not the impossibility of the bike riding itself. By labeling a situation as being "complex" we take no responsibility for looking at our own deficiencies. Have we individually studied the science of complexity? Have we taken time to understand how our perceptions limit us individually, in groups and in organizations? What corrective actions are we taking? What new ways of working are we employing on all three levels to take remedial action?

CONVENTIONAL WISDOM

Whole industries can be blindsided because everyone adopts "conventional wisdom." Everyone is blind to problems that the industry faces as well as new opportunities. It is often newcomers to an industry who really shake things up. For instance, why was it a student making $6.85 an hour and not Bill Gates who created *Mosaic*, then *Netscape*, thereby creating the Web as we know it and fundamentally changing the world?

Fish discover water last.
Taoist saying

During the late 1800s and early 1900s in Canada and the northern US, food was kept cold in iceboxes. There were numerous companies that went out to the lakes and rivers in the winter. Using saws, teams of men cut large blocks out of the ice, hauled them up onto horse-drawn sleighs, and dragged them to barns where they were insulated in hay. During the summer, small blocks of ice were chipped off and delivered door-to-door using horse-drawn carriages.

Think about the core competencies or skill sets required for the ice company: working with saws, working with horses, first aid would probably be helpful. There would be a barn acquisition department, a door-to-door sales force and an accounting department. And how would the company spend its research and development (R&D) budget? Most likely on trying to find better ways of cutting ice, insulating materials, and breeding horses that work better in cold weather.

But when refrigeration came along, none of the iceblock companies made it in the refrigeration paradigm. Why? Well, look at the core competencies required in the new paradigm: handling Freon gas, manufacturing and servicing compression motors, mass manufacturing, and wholesale distribution. The only competency that would remain would be accounting.

Every organization is perfectly aligned to get the results it gets.
Stephen Covey

Why is it so difficult for organizations to change? In the ice company, if you were a good saw-handler you became head of the saw department. The employee who handled horses best became head of horses and the best barn-buyer became head of barn acquisition. However, none of these skills were required in the new paradigm. The people most vested in the old way of doing business were running the organization. The strengths of the old organization, its people and its R&D, were the weaknesses in the new paradigm.

For many declining industries the contraction is slow. As business declines, the whole organization works to become more efficient and most are unaware that what is really required for long-term viability is new ways of working, completely new "paradigms" of their business.

LINEAR THINKING

Another problem in our perception is that in Western society we see things in very linear ways. In fact, companies are interconnected like ecosystems. What one department does affects the other.

For instance, the marketing department launches an initiative to attract new customers, but production is backlogged for six months, like the IBM Think Pad when it was released. While all the executives in marketing are getting bonuses for achieving their objective of raising awareness of the new product, customer satisfaction has plummeted as angry customers turn away from the company in frustration. Departments often plan and execute independently, even though what one department does affects another. We live in an interdependent reality. This is one of the functional blind spots of many organizations.

The sales department is rewarded by a campaign to increase the number of customers, but a large percentage of the new customers are poor credit risks. So while reps are enjoying bonuses, the account department is being chastised for plummeting productivity.

PROBLEMS WITH OUR BUSINESS THEORY

In Western management we have always had a "bias for action," the phrase Tom Peters made famous in *Search for Excellence*, in 1982. Our cultural bias is to do. We are unaware that the way we do things in dealing with complexity is in fact part of the problem. John Warfield, one of the founders of the field in resolving complexity, was talking with a prospective client who wanted to resolve a complex situation. The Ford Motor Company had been working to develop "Analytical Power Train" and some 700 engineers had been wrestling with the project for seven months without any success. So Warfield proposed a three-day

IM session with 15–20 people. The manager's response was, "We don't have three days to spare."

Warfield replied, "So let me understand, you have just told me that 700 people have been working without success for seven months. Is that correct?"

"Yes."

"But you can't spare 20 people for three days?"

"No."

"So if the 700 engineers work without success for another seven months, will you *then* be able to spare 15–20 people for three days?"

The manager got it and planned for the three-day workshop. In fact, the IM sessions were so successful that Ford established a permanent staff of IM experts and eventually spent over a million dollars consulting with Warfield and his associates.

In the quest for efficiency we are often ineffective. Rather than take the time to deeply understand and diagnose root cause problems, managers often rush in and treat symptomatic problems.

CONCLUSION

The above principles guarantee that organizations will continue to be blindsided. The only safety against the threat of being blindsided is to increase the speed of recognition and response to change in the market. This will require individuals and organizations to embrace new ways of working that accelerate the speed of recognition and response to change. The next chapter will highlight the laws that guarantee the rate of change will continue to accelerate.

REFLECTIONS

- How can your organization explore new business models and technology? Which new business model is the most provocative?

- What percentage of your revenue is allocated to research and development?

- What percentage of your personal and organizational time is spent on strategy?

- What percentage of current company revenues comes from products and services not commercially available 18 months ago? Three years ago? Five years ago? How could that timeline be shortened further?

- What strategies do you have in place to gather competitive intelligence? Is everyone in your organization charged with capturing competitive intellignce? Are they compensated for doing so? What structures do you ahve in place to house that intelligence and how is it shared across the organization?
- List the ways in which your organization can better distinguish "signals" from "noise"?
- Is creativity the purview of the elite few in your organization or is it truly a strategic competency expected of everyone? List ways that creativity can be embedded/encouraged/rewarded.
- List the ways in which your organization recognizes failure as a necessity. How could you encourage quick identification of misfires and reward the learning and subsequent enriched application?
- How could you mitigate failures (i.e. reduce their cost) without reducing experimentation?
- Why do employees resist change? At what phase of the change process are your employees experiencing the greatest challenge and what can be done to pre-empt that challenge?
- How can you improve your own perception of change? If you have any negative perceptions of change, what experiences contributed to that? What systems and structures have you implemented to counter these experiences?

CHAPTER 3

Laws Shaping the Future

What is driving the relentless speed of change that individuals and organizations are experiencing? Do these drivers ensure that it is inevitable that companies, industries, and whole societies will continue to be blindsided? If technological change is one of the drivers ensuring organizations will be blindsided, is it only companies in high-tech industries that are at risk? What tools help see through the information fog?

A number of laws are driving change in society. These laws guarantee that organizations will continue to get blindsided; therefore it is important to understand them. The rate of change in society is continuing to accelerate: it is inevitable that individuals, organizations, industries, nations, and even the world as a whole will be blindsided with increasing frequency.

In *Telecosm*, George Gilder argues that abundances and scarcities govern and define each age. Businesses and whole societies are optimized to conserve what is scarce and waste what is abundant.

But as the world changes and what was once abundant becomes scarce and/or what was once scarce becomes abundant. To remain successful, businesses and society as a whole must realign with the new reality. The scarcities are immediately apparent – such as the oil crisis of 1973 – but new abundances often go unnoticed and unappreciated for their potential. So, for instance, the Web offers incredible opportunities for companies to lower the cost of transactions, shorten cycle times, enter into one-to-one relationships with customers, and increase the quality of services to customers. But decision makers, who don't perceive the opportunities that the Web presents and take advantage of them, risk their company being blindsided. Organizations that don't reoptimize their systems and structures to conserve what is scarce in the new environment, while taking advantage of what is abundant, risk being blindsided.

The trends outlined in this chapter highlight new abundances and scarcities. The laws listed below guarantee that certain resources that were scarce in the past will be increasingly abundant in the future. To succeed, individuals, organizations and society as a whole must question how these laws will alter their operations and business model.

New abundances enable new businesses to spring up and blindside businesses that were optimized to conserve resources that were formerly scarce. As new abundances emerge, new business models become highly feasible. Nature abhors a vacuum and it is only a matter of time before someone somewhere perceives this new opportunity and takes advantage of it.

The most successful companies are continually adjusting to fully exploit resources that are abundant while economizing on those that are scarce.

Despite the volatility in equity markets in 2000 and 2001, e-business is here to stay, and far from slowing down, the pace of this revolution will only intensify.[1] Technology will continue to be the driving force of change in all industries for the foreseeable future. The effects of this technological change can be understood as a series of laws. Below are 12 technological laws that can help individuals and organizations make sense of the fast pace of change. The final law, the "Environmental Imperative," will affect every organization, individual, and society. I will discuss each law in detail, but here they are in brief:

An invasion of armies can be resisted, but not an idea whose time has come.
Victor Hugo

- *Moore's Law* – Computer processing power will double every 18 months.
- *Metcalfe's Law* – The value of a network is proportional to the square of the number of people using it.
  - *Reed's Law* – Groups form within networks, whose value rises exponentially within the network.
- *Gilder's Law* – Bandwidth is growing three times faster than computing power.
- *Coase's Theorem* – The drive to seek the lowest possible transaction costs determines corporate activities and structures.
- *Information explosion* – The volume of new information is doubling every year.

- *Expanding storage capacity and falling cost* – Hard drive costs will continue to drop exponentially while doubling in capacity annually.

- *The wireless explosion* – 3G technology will make Internet access available to wireless devices and open up new business and marketing opportunities.

- *Schumpeter's Law of Creative Destruction* – Old companies and industries will be swept aside by outsiders using new technologies.

- *de Geus' Law of Learning* – "The only sustainable competitive advantage is the ability to learn faster than your competitors."

- *Law of wasted time* – On average only 3 percent of the elapsed time for a corporate process is needed to actually complete the process.

- *The power of peer-to-peer (P2P)* – The potential of distributed computing, decision making and organization.

- *The environmental imperative* – For the last 200 years the human economy (GNP within nations) has been growing. But we need a new economic measure, Gross Earth Product (GEP) to measure the health of the ecosystem. GNP can no longer rise at the cost of GEP falling. Every business will have to work to ensure GEP no longer falls.

The remainder of this chapter will explore each law in depth and give examples of how each will impact organizations. If you already understand them and their implications for organizations, you can skip to Chapter 4.

MOORE'S LAW

Moore's Law states that the number of transistors on a computer chip will double every 18 months while staying at the same price point. As microprocessors become dramatically smaller, cheaper, and faster, the price–performance ratio rises exponentially. The demand for computers increases because all sorts of new applications become economically feasible. Moore's Law will continue to remain in force until at least 2014.

We are not far from seeing the day when we can put 2 billion transistors on a chip that operates at speeds of up to 30 GHz
Craig Barrett
CEO Intel

The social impact of Moore's law is that the rate of change we are experiencing in organizations will continue to accelerate. The power and speed of supercomputers today will be the speed and power of everyday computers in just 10 years.

I predict that we will use an audio user interface (AUI) by 2007 to interact with our computers rather than a graphical user interface (GUI). Like Jean-Luc Picard of *Star Trek: The Next Generation*, we will talk to our computers.

Traditional economics assumes inputs such as land, machinery, and labor change incrementally. But the microchip industry invalidates traditional economic theory. By doubling power every 18 months at the same price point, the semiconductor industry is creating a non-linear future. If I can buy the power of today's supercomputer on a $300 chip in 10 years, what will the market size be for chips? And how will this affect your industry – enabling new competitors to enter?

If the rate of change inside an organization is less than the rate of change outside, the end is in sight.

Jack Welch

Moore's Law has had a profound effect on organizations. While the computational power at employee's finger tips has increased exponentially, management methods have only changed incrementally: computing power is widely distributed in many organizations but decision making power is not. In other words, the power of computers, of technology, the explosion of information and knowledge has not been matched by a corresponding increase in empowerment or implementation of new organizational structures to release more human potential within organizations.

BACKGROUND ON MOORE'S LAW

In 1965, Gordon Moore, co-founder of Intel, predicted the number of transistors per computer chip would double every year for 10 years while staying at the same price point. He revised his prediction in 1975, suggesting the pace would slow to a doubling every two years, but the ingenuity of engineers has kept it doubling every 18 months. Moore's Law has held constant for over 35 years and promises to continue until at least 2014. This implies a 100-fold increase every 10 years and 10,000-fold increase every 20 years.

In 1961 the chip industry put four transistors on a chip; by 1971 the number had risen to 2,300; by 1982 there were 134,000; and by 1991, 1.2 million. The Pentium 4, first released in 2000, had almost 42 million transistors and ran at up to 2 gigahertz.

The number of transistors per chip has increased by shrinking circuits, from 10 microns wide in 1971 to 0.13 microns in 2001 (1/1000th the width of a human hair!). In June 2001, Intel announced that it had produced a chip using a 0.02-micron technology (20 nanometers – roughly four times wider than a singe atom). Intel predicts that 0.02 manufacturing process will be viable by 2007, enabling microprocessors to contain a billion transistors running at 20 gigahertz.

As the circuits shrink so does the distance that electrons have to travel, increasing circuit speed, reducing power consumption, and increasing battery life.

By 2014, physics may limit the continuation of Moore's Law. Until then the Semiconductor Industry Association predicts that chip performance will continue to increase.[2] But even the laws of physics won't stop computers from becoming more powerful while falling in cost. Once Moore's law fails, computer makers will begin producing PCs with multiple processors.

Blue Gene

On August 22, 2001, IBM announced plans to complete "Blue Gene" a computer capable of 1,000 trillion calculations per second (1,000 teraflops or one petaflop).[3] It will be used to help map the human genome, understand the intricacies of DNA and proteins, and find cures for diseases such as Alzheimer's disease, cystic fibrosis, and cancer.

With approximately one million processors, Blue Gene will be more powerful than the next 500 largest computers in the world combined. The US$100 million computer will be operational by 2005.

Since Blue Gene can be used to tackle any problem where huge data sets need to be broken down and mapped to many processors, any logistic application such as airline schedules and warehouse distribution programs could also stand to benefit from the technology.

A corollary to Moore's Law is the continual miniaturization of computers. In 2001, the largest computer produced by IBM was a supercomputer at the Lawrence Livermore Laboratory in California that delivered 12 trillion calculations per second and took up two basketball courts of space (2,760 square feet). By contrast Blue Gene will deliver one petaflop (1,000 trillion operations per second) and be just less than 2,000 square feet in size.

Hardware based on microprocessors continues to go down in price, notes Gordon Moore, "in some instances, 100,000-fold in 15 or 20 years. That means that wherever electronics is appropriate, the electronic solution is going to be the one that eventually dominates."[4] Microprocessors will begin to affect all sorts of industries.

Miniaturization

As digital technology continues its relentless miniaturization, consumer electronic products will increasingly be multifunctional. French manufactured Archos Jukebox Multimedia allows you to record, store, and playback MP3s songs, videos, or photographs. This three-in-one unit can be used as a Dicta-phone, to record a concert, or as an external hard disk for back up or storage. All this for $399 with a 10 gigabyte hard drive; by 2003 it will come with a 30 giga-byte hard drive.

METCALFE'S LAW

Metcalfe's Law is named after Robert Metcalfe, founder of 3Com and designer of the Ethernet protocol for computer networks. Metcalfe's Law states that the value or usefulness of a network grows in proportion to the square of the number of people it connects, because that is the number of possible directions of commu-nication.

As the number of people connected to the Internet grows incrementally, the value of the Web increases geometrically. Gartner Dataquest estimated that there were 403 million individuals worldwide connected to the Internet in 2001. In North America alone, Gartner Dataquest forecasts Internet users will grow to 190 million active users by 2004, up from 110 million in 1999. World-wide, the number will grow to 604 million in 2004.

The cost of the network however increases linearly in relationship to the number of users added.

Metcalfe's Law suggests people are "pulled" to join these networks as they expand. In the language of new economics, this is a virtuous or self-reinforcing cycle. The more people who hook up to the Internet the greater its value. The greater its value, the more people feel compelled to hook up to it.

This law also means that the first company achieving critical mass in a market can set the standard and potentially make billions. This explains the success of Netscape, Hotmail, Amazon, and Napster. Netscape captured 80 per-cent of the browser market by August 1995, just months after its release in 1994. [5] Launched in 1996, Hotmail had more than 100 million users worldwide in May 2001, a tenfold increase from 10 million users in 1997 when Microsoft bought it.[6] A staggering 62 million individuals had downloaded Napster's soft-ware by February 2001, just 19 months after its release.

One of the keys to Metcalfe's Law is that while the cost of building a net-work lags behind its value, once it reaches critical mass the opposite is true: value increases faster than cost. This explains why phenomenon like Netscape, Hotmail, Amazon, eBay, and Napster reach flashpoints where they literally "take off." *This has an important implication for companies wanting to avoid being blindsided. Digital or Net-based threats have to be taken seriously while the phenomenon is still small because once a new trend achieves critical mass it can explode. The threat remains small until it reaches a "flashpoint." If a company waits until the flashpoint, it may be too late.*

Metcalfe's Law also affects how many users are willing to pay for high-speed access. With the increase in Internet users, corporate transactional sites, and new applications, the value of the Web increases geometrically, increasing the willingness of users to pay for high-speed access.

It explains how the Internet reduces costs by increasing efficiency of communication. If there are 10 buyers and sellers, the number of possible buyer–seller contact points is 102 or 100. If you add 10 more people to the network the total number is now 202 or 400. While the number of users has doubled, the value of the network has quadrupled.

Metcalfe's Law applies to data as well. The more people that can access data, the more valuable the data becomes and the more people will access it. In other words, data sharing adds value to data. It creates more interactions and generates derived data that can also be shared. For these reasons, data sharing is becoming an Internet phenomenon. (See Goldcorp case study in Chapter 7.)

Reed's Law

Reed's Law is a variation of Metcalfe's. David Reed is the former vice-president of research and development for Lotus. Metcalfe's Law states that the value of the network is the potential number of connections each person attached to the network can make, approximately N^2.

Reed talks about *group forming networks* (GFNs), which are groups of like-minded individuals that support a common interest, such as interest groups, clubs, meetings, communities. These groups are subsets of the larger community. The more people who are members of a larger community, the more vibrant the subgroups will be, the greater their membership, the greater value for like-minded individuals, the more the overall community will grow. This creates a virtuous cycle.

Group or community tools and technologies such as user-defined mailing lists, chat rooms, discussion groups, buddy lists, team rooms, trading rooms, user groups, market makers, and auction hosts, all allow groups and users to coalesce and to organize their communications around a common interest, issue, or goal.[7]

Reed notes that traditional telephone and broadcast/cable network frameworks do not support groups, but the Internet does.

GFNs create a new kind of connectivity value that scales *exponentially* with N. Briefly, the number of subsets that can be formed from a set of N members is $2^N - N - 1$, which grows as 2^N. Thus, a network that supports easy group communication grows in value exponentially with N.

This means that the value of Reed's Law grows faster than Metcalfe's Law. Reed's Law explains the success of eBay.

GILDER'S LAW

Gilder's Law, coined by futurist George Gilder, states that bandwidth is growing at least three times as fast as computing power. While computers double in power every 18 months, telecommunications power doubles every six months and will continue to do so until at least 2020. Fiber optics has 10 billion times the capacity of copper wires or wireless.

A corollary to Gilder's Law is that the cost of bandwidth in networks is halved every year. This reduction is driven by innovations in fiber-optic network transmission, wireless and compression technologies. Gilder's Law has as dramatic an impact on communications as Moore's Law does on computing.

Gilder argues that the computer age is over because since 1970 the price per transistor with support circuitry has dropped from around $7 to less than a millionth of a cent in 2002. Gilder argues that we are entering a new era driven by the collapsing cost of bandwidth. Innovations driving the increase in bandwidth are occurring three times faster than the innovation driving the increasing computational power.

Wavelength division multiplexing is a new fiber-optic technology allowing many different colors of light, or frequencies, each bearing a message, to be sent across a single fiber thread. Gilder notes that the fiber strands are "made of glass so pure that if it were a window you could see through 70 miles of it."[8]

A single fiber thread, the size of a human hair, can carry a thousand different wavelength streams of information. Each stream can carry about 10 billion bits a second. This means that the leading edge fiber technology can carry as much information in a second as the whole Internet carried in a month in 1999.

In 2001, a single, hair-thin fiber in an optical network can simultaneously stream 400,000 DVD movies. With the largest cable in 2001 containing nearly 900 such fibers, you can see how a previously unfathomable amount of information will pulse through the Internet.[9]

In 1999, the total monthly traffic of the entire Internet averaged a petabyte (1015 bits or 1,000,000,000,000,000 bits of information or 1,000,000 gigabytes). (To understand the size of a petabyte, see Data Powers of Ten sidebar below.) By March 2001, total Internet traffic had burgeoned to 20 petabytes a month. Gilder points out that the newest fiber-optic technology can convey a petabyte a second. He argues that this is not futuristic, because this technology has been fully demonstrated and tested. It's practical technology that will be deployed by 2003. So Gilder argues that the total traffic that is carried across the Internet in a month will be able to be transferred in a single second – two to three years into the future.[10]

The stumbling block to the bandwidth economy really exploding, according to Gilder, is "The last mile problem," which he describes as a "terrible jungle of regulations and byzantine special interests." While the Internet is a global communications system, within the United States, 50 different state public utilities commissions regulate it. Gilder argues that there should only be one national body within the US regulating the Internet. (See Ca-botics case study in Chapter 5.)

Gilder's Law promises to reduce the price of communication close to zero. Just as Moore's Law has reduced the cost of a transistor to virtually nothing, so Gilder's Law will reduce the price of sending a megabyte of information to virtually nothing, and that will open new opportunities and accelerate the growth of global commerce. For instance, it could increase the trend of North American companies outsourcing white-collar work, such as accounting, to firms based in India.

By 2006, there will be 31.1 million US households with high speed Internet connections: 15.7 million cable connections, 10.5 million DSL, 4.5 million satellite, and the balance by other means, according to a Yankee Group study.[11] This is a steep rise from 9.3 million high-speed connections at the end of 2001.

Gilder's Law and the explosive growth of high-speed Internet access is a significant driver of online growth. A study conducted by MediaOne noted that households with cable Internet connections averaged 22.5 hours of online usage per week, versus just 4.7 hours for those households with a dial-up connection.[12] Cable users connected to the Internet surf ten times more than their dial-up counterparts. A *Wall Street Journal* survey confirmed that speed is the primary factor determining time online: 65 percent of respondents said that increased speed would increase usage.[13]

COASE'S THEOREM

Ronald Coase, a University of Chicago economics professor, won the 1991 Nobel Prize in economics. In *The Nature of the Firm*, Coase observed that the drive to seek the lowest possible transaction costs is what determines corporate activities and structure. When transaction costs are high (i.e. when it costs a lot to do things in the open market), companies tend to take on many diverse tasks, as it is more efficient to do work "in-house." When transaction costs fall, companies tend to focus on their core businesses, outsourcing non-core activities. As electronic networks and market places arise, transaction costs of open-market interactions plummet, enabling increasingly focused and specialized firms.

Refining Coase's theorem, Douglass North, the winner of the 1993 Nobel Prize in economics, and John Wallis found that:

> . . . fully 45 percent of America's GNP in 1970 consisted of transaction costs. These costs are comprised to a great extent by expenses related to the gathering, retaining, and exchanging of information. North estimates that this percentage has increased since then.

By understanding and using the appropriate technologies to exploit the opportunities for business-to-business transactions, companies will be able to provide services at a reduced cost and with increased revenue. B2B eCommerce cuts companies' costs in three ways. First, it reduces procurement costs, making it easier to find the cheapest supplier and cutting the cost of processing transactions. Second, it allows better supply-chain management. And, third, it makes possible tighter inventory control, so that firms can reduce their stocks or even eliminate them. Through these three ways, B2B eCommerce reduces firms' production costs by increasing efficiency or by squeezing suppliers' profit margins. The result of these reduced costs and therefore barriers to entry is increased competition and lower prices for consumers.

Companies such as GE and Walmart, for example, have realized cost savings of as much as 30 to 40 percent by conducting their purchasing and customer relations functions on the Internet. Recent statistics also reveal a dramatic increase in consumer purchases of tickets and goods online, and a growing reliance on the Internet for banking and other personal and business transactions via the Internet. This is happening at a fraction of the cost and faster than similar transactions in the off-line world.[14]

As the Web significantly reduces the cost of transactions, it will facilitate the rapid rise of new forms of commerce between companies. Revenue from business-to-consumer (B2C) e-commerce will grow to $454 billion in 2004 and business-to-business (B2B) e-commerce will expand to $6.3 trillion in 2004. Worldwide, total e-commerce will grow to $6.78 trillion by 2004, according to Forrester Research.[15]

The interaction of Moore's, Metcalfe's, and Gilder's laws creates a new business environment in which companies taking advantage of the Internet and other technologies can reduce their costs by more than 50 percent. This gives companies embracing the new technology a radical advantage over those that don't.

While many people initially saw the Web as a way of increasing sales, the reduction in transaction costs will have an even larger impact.

INFORMATION EXPLOSION

We are living in an information fog. The number of books published annually has been climbing steadily. In 1947, the first year *Books in Print* began collecting data, there were 85,000 titles in print in the US from 357 publishers. In 2001, with lower production costs due to desktop technology, there were 2,275,148 titles in print from 69,205 publishers. And there are more than 120,000 new books published every year. To put it another way, there were more books published in the last decade than ever published in the history of the world. Consider these surprising facts.[16] In the US there are:

- 58,873 magazines, newsletters, catalogs, e-zines, and serials (yearbooks and annuals)
- 12,932 radio stations (AM, FM commercial, and FM educational stations)
- 12,484 TV stations (UHF/VHF commercial, educational, and low-power stations)

Add to these the fact that:

- On an average day in 2000, 10 billion non-spam e-mail messages were sent worldwide and by 2005 it is predicted to grow to 35 billion e-mails a day.[17] By the end of 2001 there were more than one billion e-mail boxes.[18]
- White-collar workers will spend 30–40 percent of their time managing documents by 2003, up from 20 percent in 1997.[19]
- In early 2001, the public Internet, the source of half of the information workers use, exceeded 550 billion pages and was growing at a rate of 7.3 million new pages every day![20]
- Information available across the Web is doubling every 2.8 years.[21]
- Even within companies, information overload can be overwhelming. Oracle, for instance, has more than 10 million Web pages on its Intranet.[22]
- In part, the number of people connected to the Web is driving this explosion of information. Alvin Toffler coined the phrase PROsumer – everyone connected to the Internet is a potential producer *and* a consumer.[23]
- Gartner Dataquest estimated that there were 403 million individuals connected to the Internet in 2001 and this is predicted to grow to 604 million in 2004. In North America alone, Gartner Dataquest forecasts Internet users will grow to 190 million active users by 2004, up from 110 million in 1999.

DATA POWERS OF TEN
• **Bytes** (8 bits)
– 1 byte: a single character
– 10 bytes: a single word
• **Kilobyte** (1000 bytes)
– 1 kilobyte: half a typewritten page
– 10 kilobytes: an encyclopedic page

- 100 kilobytes: a low-resolution photograph
- **Megabyte** (1,000,000 bytes)
  - 1 megabyte: a small novel or a 3.5-inch floppy disk
  - 2 megabytes: a high-resolution photograph
  - 5 megabytes: Shakespeare's complete works or 30 seconds of TV-quality video
  - 10 megabytes: a minute of high-fidelity sound or a digital chest X-ray
  - 50 megabytes: a digital mammogram
  - 100 megabytes: 1 meter of shelved books
- **Gigabyte** (1,000,000,000 bytes)
  - 1 gigabyte: a pickup truck filled with paper or a movie at TV quality
  - 2 gigabytes: 20 meters of shelved books
  - 20 gigabytes: a good collection of the works of Beethoven or a VHS tape used for digital data
- **Terabyte** (1,000,000,000,000 bytes)
  - 1 terabyte: all the X-ray films in a large hospital or 50,000 trees made into paper and printed
  - 10 terabytes: the printed collection of the US Library of Congress
- **Petabyte** (1,000,000,000,000,000 bytes)
  - 2 petabytes: all US academic research libraries
  - 20 petabytes: production of hard-disk drives in 1995
  - 200 petabytes: all printed material or production of digital magnetic tape in 1995
- **Exabyte** (1,000,000,000,000,000,000 bytes)
  - 5 exabytes: All words ever spoken by human beings
- **Zettabyte** (1,000,000,000,000,000,000,000 bytes)
- **Yottabyte** (1,000,000,000,000,000,000,000,000 bytes)

By Roy Williams Clickery[24]

The Deep Web

The "deep" Web is a reservoir of Internet content that is 500 times larger than the known World Wide Web, according to BrightPlanet,[25] a private Internet content and search company. This untapped reservoir consists of hundreds of billions of searchable documents that cannot be retrieved by traditional search engines such as Google, Yahoo!, and Excite.

Search engines obtain their listings in two ways. Authors either submit their own pages for listing, or the search engines use automated spiders or crawlers to scour the Web and index static pages. As the Web's growth exploded and database technology became more advanced, more organizations chose to store and transfer Internet information using database-driven designs, not static pages. A direct query must be posed to an individual database in order to retrieve its content. The results of each direct query create a new "real time" Web page. Traditional search engine crawlers cannot identify, catalogue or retrieve information from a database without a direct query, so the information never gets indexed.

Bright Planet uses the metaphor of a fishing trawler. Searching the Web today is like dragging a net across the surface of the ocean. The content identified is only what appears on the surface and the results are indiscriminate. The information is there, but is hiding in plain sight beneath the surface of the Web. Bright Planet has estimated that the largest search engines individually index, at most, 16 percent of the surface Web.[26] What this means is that by using a single search engine, Internet searchers are searching only 0.03 percent, or 1/3000th, of the complete content available to them via the entire deep Web. Some fascinating facts about the deep Web:

- The deep Web contains 7,500 terabytes of information, compared to 19 terabytes of information in the surface Web.
- The deep Web contains nearly 550 billion individual documents compared to the one billion of the surface Web.
- More than 100,000 deep Web sites presently exist.
- Sixty of the largest deep Web sites collectively contain more than 750 terabytes of information, sufficient by themselves to exceed the size of the surface Web by 40 times.
- The deep Web is the largest growing category of new information on the Internet.
- Total quality content of the deep Web is at least 400 times greater than that of the surface Web.
- Deep Web content is highly relevant to every information need, market, and domain.
- More than half of the deep Web content resides in topic specific databases.
- A full 95 percent of the deep Web is publicly accessible information – not subject to fees or subscriptions.

Volume of New Information Doubles Each Year

More unique information will be created in 2001 and 2002 than is accessible from the entire 300,000 years of human history combined, according to the eye-opening study *How Much Information?* by the School of Information Management and Systems at the University of California, Berkeley. The total amount of information that was created and remains accessible in the entire human history from caveman until 1999 totaled 12 exabytes (10^{18} bytes – see sidebar above on powers of ten). The world will collectively create 12 exabytes of new information in 2002. The study shows the amount of unique information is doubling every year (see Figure 3.1).

The study estimated that the total amount of information available for access in 1999 was 12 exabytes. This is not the total amount of unique information ever created (because some has been lost in history). The chart below shows the impact of doubling new unique information every year.[27]

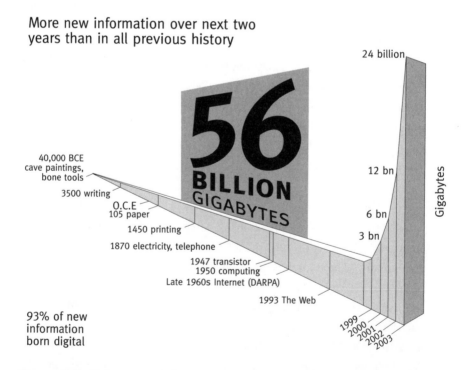

Figure 3.1 Unique new information doubles annually (1999-2003). Adapted from EMC © 2001.

Year	Unique info produced (exabytes)	Total unique info (exabytes)
1999	1.5	12
2000	3	15
2001	6	21
2002	12	32
2003	24	56

So in 2000, there were 15 exabytes of existing legacy content. The amount of new content produced in 2001–2 is predicted to be 18 exabytes.

The Berkeley study is the most comprehensive analysis of the world's digital and non-digital data volume to date. Researchers looked at a range of media and recording methods, including print, broadcast, film, letters, e-mail, and the Internet, and used 1999 as the base year to determine the rate of information generation.

"What we are seeing is a phenomenal boom in the production of information," said Hal Varian, dean of the school and co-author of the study. "One interesting finding is the degree to which individuals, rather than organizations, are responsible for generating data. We not only have mass production of information, but also production of information by the masses." The Berkeley researchers noted several key trends:

- There were 1.5 exabytes of information created in 1999 – the equivalent of 250 megabytes of information for every person on earth. The amount of unique information created will double every year until 2010.
- The bulk of unique information is created and stored by individuals. Original documents created by office workers account for over 80 percent of all original paper documents. Hard drives in stand-alone PCs account for 55 percent of total storage shipped each year.
- The democratization of data is quite remarkable. It is currently technically possible for an average person to access virtually all recorded information. Only copyright issues pose a barrier. Once we have a means to digitally pay for access to copyright material, accessing all information will be a reality.
- Photographs and X-rays account for 99 percent of all original film documents.
- Digital information is driving the boom. Not only is digital information the largest type of data produced, but also traditionally non-digital items –

such as books, music, films, and medical records – are being digitized at a rapid pace. In 1999, more than 93 percent of the unique information produced was digital. While unique content in print and film is hardly growing at all, optical and magnetic storage shipments are doubling each year.

- Varian feels that significant advances have to be made in information management before mankind can fully benefit from the information explosion. "Will we drown in a sea of information, or can we develop tools to help us swim?" he asks.

- "The difficulty will be in managing this information effectively," adds Varian. "This is no easy task. Our ability to store and communicate information has far outpaced our ability to search, retrieve and present it." Information management is one of the major challenges of the 21st century.

Item	Titles	Terabytes
Books	968,735	8
Newspapers	22,643	25
Journals	40,000	2
Magazines	80,000	10
Newsletters	40,000	0.2
Office documents	7,500,000,000	195
Cinema	4,000	16
Music CDs	90,000	6
Data CDs	1,000	3
DVD-video	5,000	22
Total		285

Source: How Much Information?[28]

MANAGING INFORMATION OVERLOAD

So how are companies developing radar to see through the information fog? Three companies in the $1.6 billion online news and information service market offer powerful new tools to gain insights into competitors and new trends: LexisNexis, Factiva, and Dialog.

LexisNexis is a global provider of information to legal, corporate, government, and academic markets. Launched in 1973, LexisNexis indexes 2.9 billion documents from more than 31,000 sources including newspapers, magazines, trade journals, industry newsletters, tax and accounting information, financial data, public records, and company data.

With 1.8 million customers, and 40 percent market share, LexisNexis is the leader of on-line news and information. LexisNexis offers a wide range of products, delivery mechanisms, and search tools.

I used Nexis to research this book and found it to be invaluable. It is the most powerful research tool I've ever used. I was able to track down what I was researching instantly. The service can generate alerts, allowing organizations to proactively track competitors' announcements, key personnel, and suppliers. As such, it is a key tool in competitive intelligence and a means of coping with information overload.

In 1999, Dow Jones Interactive and Reuters Business joined forces to announce Factiva, combining content from both services. On July 31, 2001, the company launched Factiva.com, which provides access to 145 million documents from 8,000 sources in 22 languages from more than 118 countries. And Factiva is adding almost a million new articles a week. While the volume of Factiva's content pales in comparison to LexisNexis', the service's primary focus is on business, consolidating business publications – such as the *Wall Street Journal* and newswires such as Reuters and Dow Jones. Factiva has the second largest market share and is the fastest growing. Factiva's emphasis is on customization, by allowing customers to construct personal pages that display news based on their favorite subjects, companies, or publications. Factiva.com can also e-mail topical articles directly to subscribers.

"It's the relevance of information and not the volume of it," that counts according to Clare Hart, CEO of Factiva.com. She says Factiva.com can be used as a form of radar to help companies prevent themselves from being blindsided. "If you're capturing the information internally and externally, and organizing it and categorizing it, and using enabling technology so that people can gain access to just the relevant information, then that's your radar, that's the radar that's going to help you make better informed decisions about your business, and your strategic planning, and I firmly believe it's going to give you a competitive advantage going forward."

Factiva is unique in providing information in 22 different languages. Factiva has a translation desk in London where the top business stories are translated into English abstracts. Hart says the translation feature is ideal for companies who want to track foreign-based competitors. She uses a hypothetical example of Motorola and Nokia. From Illinois, Motorola could find out what's being written about Nokia in the local Finnish press.

While Factiva is a paid service and guarantees quality of translation, Google, the most popular Internet search engine, offers free translation. When you conduct a Google search some of the documents that come back may be in other languages. Next to these articles you will see a "translate this" button. Click on it and the document will be translated into English. While the technology is still in its infancy and accuracy is only around 70 percent, it shows how the technology will advance in the future.

I predict that by 2010 we will have universal real time translation, where you will be able to translate written documents from major languages instantly.

Dialog is an information service focusing on scientific and engineering information, such as medical and pharmaceutical research. The content has more than 12 terabytes of information consisting of six billion pages of text and three million images. Dialog's Profound is a business intelligence service that provides access to breaking and archived news as well as market research reports and economic analysis. LexisNexis, Factiva, and Dialog all offer an alert service.

New Tools, New Solutions

You cannot solve an exponentially growing problem with a method that is improving in a linear fashion. Our current tools for managing information are failing. Given that more than two-thirds of all unique information created annually is in the form of office documents, which reside on individual users' hard disks, new forms of knowledge management are required. I predict that peer-to-peer information searching methods will be a rapid growth area in knowledge management.

EXPANDING STORAGE CAPACITY AND FALLING COST

The doubling of hard disk capacity every year worldwide is driving the information explosion. Between 1993 and 2000, the cost of data storage dropped by 90

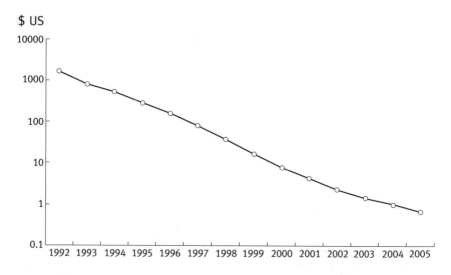

Figure 3.2 Hard drive cost per gigabyte. Source: IDC, October 2001.

percent.[29] As of fall 2001, a gigabyte of storage costs less than $5 and it is predicted that this will drop to 66¢ by 2005.[30]

Every year hard drive costs plummet and average capacity increases (Figure 3.2). The impact of this law is that every year it becomes cheaper to digitize images, movies, music, and information. As costs fall, all sorts of new applications become economically feasible. This in turn impacts industries in new ways. For instance, by 2006, video on demand over the Internet will be a large portion of Hollywood's revenue. This will change the whole ecosystem of movie distribution.

> *In 25 years, you'll probably be able to get the sum total of all human knowledge on a personal device.*
>
> **Greg Blonder**
> **Former Chief**
> **Technology Officer,**
> **AT&T**

WIRELESS EXPLOSION

An increasing variety of devices will connect people to the Internet. Europe and Asia are far ahead of the US in the wireless revolution. At COMDEX 2001 in Las Vegas, Jeff Hawkins, the inventor of the PalmPilot, and founder and Chairman of Handspring asked, "What is the most successful computational device?" His answer: the cellphone.

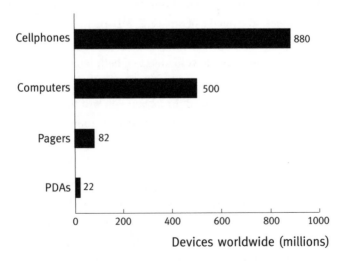

Figure 3.3 Devices worldwide (in millions). Sources: Intel for computers; Handspring for all other figures.

As shown in Figure 3.3, as of October 2001 there were 880 million cellphones in use worldwide, 500 million computers, 82 million pagers (including Research in Motion's [RIM] Blackberry) and 22 million handhelds personal digital assistants (PDAs – such as PalmPilot, Handspring Visor, and Compaq iPAQ). Many people feel that as computing devices become smaller they do not offer as much functionality as full-sized desktops. The most important application for people is being able to keep in touch with others. To do so you need to know how to reach them. Handspring is launching the Treo in 2002 – a three-in-one device: cellphone, PDA running the PalmPilot operating system, and a two-way pager such as the RIM Blackberry. As an always-on device, users will be able to access the Internet.

In 2000, only five million North America wireless customers were connected to the Web by their cellphone, Blackberry, or PDA. However, this will grow by 73 percent a year to 84 million in 2005, according to IDC. Business users will account for 49 million in 2005.[31]

The emergence of these Internet-enabled devices threatens the personal computer's monopoly as a computational device. This in turn threatens Intel and Microsoft 's duopoly. This highlights how even market leaders have to pay attention to shifts to avoid being blindsided.

The development of Third Generation (3G) cellphone technology is driving the wireless Web. This technology will allow users to connect to the Internet and send e-mail messages at speeds of up to 2 MB per second by 2004. This high-speed access will give users real time access to news, weather and even allow MP3 and video files to be downloaded to a cellphone.

Wireless devices equipped with 3G and Global Positioning System (GPS) create new opportunities. Stuck in traffic? Soon you will be able to download a map or even streaming video that will point out a clear route to your destination.

In 2001, drivers received traffic reports by listening to radio. Stations monitor traffic using helicopters. However, these have limited use when roadways sprawl over hundreds of miles. Some municipalities have video cameras posted on highways allowing drivers to log onto the Internet and see where traffic is snarled before leaving home or the office. However, with 3G GPS-enabled cellphones, traffic flows will be measured by how fast cellphones are traveling along the freeway. By 2006, drivers will be able to access real-time on-demand traffic services to determine where traffic is tied up.

Other applications will abound. Walk past a coffee shop and receive an electronic coupon to get a free muffin with a regular coffee. So how are we going to prevent our cellphones from becoming walking, talking spam cans? Through permission marketing. Permission marketing is when users give permission to certain individuals, or organizations to contact them based on user-defined criteria. Those who do not respect users' time will have their communications blocked. (See eLert discussion in Chapter 6.)

Japan's dominant cellphone provider, NTT DoCoMo, is leading the way with its innovative i-mode service, which allows users to download e-mail, play games with other i-mode users, and even sing karaoke. Launched in February 1999, i-mode had more than 28 million users by October 2001. In 2001, 63 percent of Japanese owned a cellphone, but only 20 percent owned a computer.[32] This means that more Japanese have the capability to access the Internet through their cellphones than through a computer.

A young Japanese programmer in 2001 created an application like AOL's instant messaging, which allows a DoCoMo user to contact a predefined list of friends. Have nothing to do on Friday night? Just instantly e-mail 30 friends to see who would like to go to the movies with you.

Asia will be the first to fully adopt the 3G technologies, mainly because the licenses have been cheaper. European licenses sold for $106 billion, leading analysts to hypothesize that the roll out of 3G services will be stalled as European carriers struggle to get out from under the heavy debt they have assumed. In October 2001, the British Telecom and Deutsche Telekom announced a deal to share the $17 billion cost of implementing 3G infrastructures.

US telcoms will try to stall the massive 3G expenditures by adopting 2.5G technologies as an interim solution. Each of the 12 US 3G licenses is expected to sell for $25 billion at auction.

SCHUMPETER'S LAW: CREATIVE DESTRUCTION

Joseph Alois Schumpeter (1883–1950) was an Austrian-born economist who remained in relative obscurity until the early 1980s, his work being eclipsed by that of better-known John Maynard Keynes. In 1982, *Forbes* ran a cover story on Schumpeter's works, which brought them to prominence. Schumpeter wrote about "perennial gales of creative destruction" to describe the process in a capitalist economy whereby old, inefficient companies and industries are swept aside by entrepreneurial outsiders employing innovative new technology. Today the phrase enjoys widespread use.

In *Capitalism, Socialism, and Democracy* (1942) Schumpeter argued that an entrepreneurial capitalist society provides a better living for people, but that the economic disequilibria it produces, the creative destruction, and the resulting inevitable waves of industry-wide unemployment would ultimately erode the political support for democracy and lead the public to demand socialism, preferring its economic stagnancy to the challenge and uncertainty of a capitalist economy.

Peter Drucker's father was a contemporary and friend of Schumpeter. In Drucker's opinion Keynes and Schumpeter are the two greatest economists of the twentieth century.[33] Drucker argues that successful organizations are "destabilizers" that are "organized for innovation." Like Schumpeter, Drucker defines innovation as "creative destruction."

Successful entrepreneurs break rules, and reject old assumptions to remake industries. "The entrepreneur," Drucker writes, "has to slough off yesterday and to render obsolete what already exists and what is already known. He has to create the future." In so doing, renegade entrepreneurs create unheard-of opportunities, build radically new businesses, tear down old truths, business models and even whole industries, revealing a brighter future than ever imagined.

In *The Living Company*, Arie de Geus points out that the average life expectancy of giant multinational corporations is between 40 and 50 years. One-third of the 1970 *Fortune 500* had ceased to exist by 1983. Some were acquired while others merged, or were broken into pieces.[34] Smaller firms have an even shorter lifespan, and across the northern hemisphere the average corporate life expectancy is well below 20 years:

> Of 1984's top 50 UK companies, around one-fifth had passed on by 1995. Of the 1974 list, 25 percent had ceased to exist, and 1965, nearly half. Of the 30 original constituents of the FT Ordinary Share Index in 1935, only nine survived in 1995. US death rates are even higher: nearly 40 percent of 1983's *Fortune 500* had dematerialized in 1995, 60 percent of 1970's, and of the 12 companies comprising the Dow Jones Industrial Index in 1900, GE is the sole substantial survivor.[35]

While it would seem that the UK's greater corporate longevity is a sign of economic stability, a study by Donald Hicks, a professor of political economy at the University of Texas, has interesting implications:

> Hicks was contracted by the state to examine the past and future of Texas's manufacturing base. Hicks pored over 22 years of sales-tax returns – including those of defunct businesses – to trace individual companies as they made their way into and out of existence. His most striking finding: the "half-life" of new businesses had been cut in half since 1970. That is, a group of companies founded in, say, 1985 took only half as long to have its ranks depleted by 50 percent as a group born in 1970 did. A process of attrition that used to take five years now took less than two. More surprising still, the Texas city whose businesses had the shortest life expectancy – Austin – had the fastest-growing job base and the highest wages. The counterintuitive lesson: high business-mortality rates are good for economic health.[36]

Hick's findings are counter-intuitive. Rather than being a negative, the US's higher rate of corporate mortality shows that there is more creative destruction occurring. The message is that speed of change is of the essence and that complacency kills. Even in rapidly expanding industries there is little job security. Computer software was the fastest-growing industry sector worldwide between 1980 and 1995, growing 30 percent compounded annually in real terms. Yet, even in this explosive industry there is no security. *Information Week* annually ranks the 500 most innovative corporate users of information technology. More than half the computer companies on the 1995 list did not appear on the 2000 list![37]

Other consultants and academics have created their own terms for Schumpeter's creative destruction. Clayton Christensen, author of *The Innovator's Dilemma* (1997) talks about "disruptive innovation" and "disruptive technologies." Nearly every disruptive innovation in history succeeded, according to Christensen, because it provided a larger population of less-skilled people with a product or service that was faster, cheaper, easier, and more convenient to use. The disruptive technology replaced a product or service that was available from expensive specialists typically in centralized and inconvenient locations. For instance:

George Eastman's camera made amateur photography widespread. Bell's telephone let people communicate without the need for professional tele- graph operators. Photocopying enabled office workers to do things that historically only professional printers could do. On-line brokerages have made investing so inexpensive and convenient that even college students now actively manage their own portfolios. Indeed, disruptive technologies have been one of the fundamental mechanisms through which the quality of our lives has improved. In each of these cases, the disruption left con- sumers far better off than they had been.[38]

A key to Christensen's notion is the *empowering* aspect of disruptive tech- nology. Desktop publishing (DTP) has displaced typesetting because it empowers end-users to publish their own material. (This is in part why there is such a rise in unique published information). (See the information explosion section above.)

Powerful disincentives prevent large, well-run companies or whole indus- tries from embracing disruptive technologies. In attempts to defend market share and grow revenues and earnings, large companies have a bias for what Christensen calls "sustaining technologies" which: (1) improve product perfor- mance; (2) are valued by mainstream customers; (3) focus on existing, mainstream markets; and (4) offer high profit margins. Sustaining technologies reinforce the status quo and others quickly match improvements by one com- petitor. These incremental changes rarely precipitate the failure of leading firms.

The most threatening challenge to dominant companies or industries are "disruptive technologies" that: (1) have lower performance than the existing ones, but are typically cheaper, simpler, smaller, and more convenient to use; (2) are valued by the least profitable customers; (3) are first commercialized in emerging markets; and (4) offer a relatively low profit margin. Companies that focus on "disruptive technologies" blindside industry leaders.

Using Christensen to analyze Napster vs. the music industry

In the case of Napster and its successors, digital music is not of interest to the bulk of the music industry's current customers. The majority of people still buy CDs and don't have portable MP3 players or MP3 players in their homes or cars.

Using Christensen's analysis, industries fail because they focus exclusively on core customers, ignoring customers at the fringes.

Typically new technologies offer inferior quality, and dominant industry players therefore dismiss them. The technologies, however, improve and eventually steal core customers.

The largest percentage of revenue from a CD goes to retailers, the music industry's largest distribution partners. Napster threatens this relationship. This is a powerful barrier to the industry embracing digital distribution.

Napster threatens to eliminate profits in the industry. One of the reasons for Napster's explosive growth was that for most of 1999, 2000, and 2001 there was no legitimate mechanism to pay for consuming electronic versions of music. A number of possible business models may eventually emerge: (1) electronic per use tolls, which means that every time I listen to a song I pay a small amount for the privilege; (2) licensing fee – like software I will buy the music once and be able to use it as often as I want.

From an industry executive's perspective, the energy, resources, and risk required to create profitable digital music initiatives seems so large and the revenues so small that it would seem crazy to pursue a strategy of digital music distribution. This emergent market doesn't solve the music industry's growth needs. In fact, from the music industry's perspective it threatens their profits.

Failure is an intrinsic part of innovation. This inherent unpredictability is in striking contrast to the level of predictability expected in the annual planning cycle of large corporations. Indeed, sound marketing and product strategy is the hallmark of corporate strategists and planners.

In *Competing for the Future*, Gary Hamel and C.K. Prahalad argue that companies must decide if they want to be rule-makers, rule-takers, or rule-breakers. Rule-makers are the incumbents that built the industry – good, well-managed businesses that enjoy market share leadership (Xerox, IBM, Merrill Lynch, Sears, British Airways). They are the protectors of industrial orthodoxy. Rule-takers work within the industrial way of doing business (Avis to Hertz, US Air to United Airlines). Avis' "We try harder" slogan sums up this group's strategy. Rule-breakers are architects of radical industry transformation by jettisoning industry rules (Canon, Body Shop, IKEA, Charles Schwab, Virgin Airlines, and Southwest Airlines). These are revolutionaries; radicals that create new wealth and long-term success.

It's not the strongest of the species who survive, nor the most intelligent, but the ones most responsive to change.
Charles Darwin

Hamel and Prahalad argue that planning, by definition, is bound by the old rules. Whereas strategy is revolutionary and the key ingredient is imagination.

Very few organizations have the courage or discipline to practice creative destruction with respect to their own products and services. It is literally too terrifying. Intel is one of the few companies that completely obsoletes its own products with new ones.

Intel has multiple development teams working concurrently, leapfrogging each other. As one team developed the 586 (known as the P5 or Pentium) another team was developing the 686 or P6 (Pentium Pro). As soon as the Pentium went into production, the majority of the design team went onto design the next generation of chip (Pentium II). As soon as Pentium Pro was released, the majority of the team went on to work on the Pentium III. The company continues to use this approach, known as concurrent engineering. Intel's strategy is to always make its own products obsolete. The result has been an explosion of the market. Radical technology breakthroughs have allowed Intel to continue to double the power of its microprocessors every 18 months, and have ensured Intel's security and success.

DE GEUS' LAW OF LEARNING

Arie de Geus, author of *The Living Company*, worked for Royal Dutch/Shell for 38 years in the planning department and was involved in the scenario planning exercises Shell ran in the 1970s. He coined the expression: "The only sustainable competitive advantage is the ability to learn faster than your competitors."[39] A corollary is the expression "When the rate of external change exceeds the rate of internal change, disaster is imminent" – a favorite of Lou Pritchett, author of *Stop Paddling and Start Rocking the Boat.*

PROCESS WASTE: THE THREE PERCENT RULE

As a general rule, only 3 percent of the elapsed time for a corporate process is needed to actually complete the activity. The "three percent rule" is one of the key concepts in cycle time reduction according to James Wetherbe of the FedEx Center for Cycle Time Research.

INSURANCE CLAIMS

The Learning Paradox highlights a case about insurance companies:[40] completing a claim may actually take a few hours but for most insurance companies in 2001 it took weeks or months to pay claims. Typically, insurance companies' internal processes are paperbound, linear processes with multiple hand-offs. The majority of the time a claimant's file is either waiting in someone's in-box or out-box, or in transit between boxes. Because of multiple hand offs, files get lost, have to be found, and then have to be expedited.

Companies are slaves to their internal processes: systems and structures govern performance. It is unreasonable to expect fast claims payment from a bureaucratic, paper-based, linear payment process. One company, Progressive Insurance, reengineered its internal processes so that over 50 percent of claims are paid within eight hours of an accident. To get this exponential improvement in performance required:

- Questioning the value of each step in the process:
    - unnecessary steps (which may have been valid historically)
    - automating every step possible using technology
    - approval limits – why does buying $1.19 of paperclips require a manager's signature?
- Eliminating hand-offs by using technology to move from a linear process to a concurrent one – so that work occurs in parallel. This requires thinking about the overall processes, a discipline known as systems thinking.

Multiplier Effect of these Exponential Laws

The convergence of these laws of exponential growth is creating the "Net effect" – an unprecedented compound multiplier effect that will bring radical new technological innovation.

We don't sell insurance anymore. We sell speed.
Peter Lewis
Progressive Insurance[41]

These laws create a new marketplace where transaction costs are reduced not incrementally, but exponentially. With the Internet and other technologies, businesses can reduce costs in certain areas by more than 50 percent.

P2P LAW OF DISTRIBUTED COMPUTING (MOORE'S LAW × GILDER'S LAW)

The combination of Moore's Law and Gilder's Law has led to an explosion of distributed computing. With bandwidth growing exponentially and becoming less expensive, there is now the option to do really distributed computing for the first time, because you can do the processing wherever it is optimal.

A number of industries employ powerful supercomputers: investment brokerages use them to model and anticipate market fluctuations; aerospace engineering firms run simulations of air flows through turbines; medical researchers use them to model the human genome; and meteorologists use them to predict weather patterns. Traditionally, companies in these industries bought or rented time on supercomputers.

The largest commercial computer sold by IBM was to NuTec Sciences in December 2000 to be used for genomic research. Genomic research maps human genes and identifies variations linked to diseases. NuTec's supercomputer, which clusters 1,250 servers and can process 7.5 trillion calculations per second, is the fastest computing system outside a government agency. The fastest machine is the ASCI White at the Lawrence Livermore National Laboratory; it does 12.3 trillion calculations a second.[42]

In 2001, a typical supercomputer that can process five teraflops (trillion calculations per second) costs more than $100 million. Intel believes that it can create a 50 teraflop virtual supercomputer costing only $1 million a year to run. In other words, Intel's "virtual" supercomputer will be able to process 10 times more calculations per second at 1/100th the price. The price per teraflop for a traditional supercomputer is $20 million versus $20,000 for the P2P virtual supercomputer. This represents a savings of $19,980,000 – incredible by any standard. This 1,000-fold price performance difference is going to drive P2P computing.

Napster has highlighted how peer-to-peer (P2P) file sharing can be used to perform computational intensive calculations, applications, and simulations using the idle processing power of computers distributed throughout a company, or the Internet as a whole. Analysts estimate that all the computers linked to the Internet offer a combined processing power of 10 billion MHz and 10,000 terabytes (trillion bytes) of storage.[43]

Intel saved $500 million in hardware costs between 1990 and 2000 by using an application called NetBatch. Intel developed the application, which sits on more than 10,000 engineering workstations around the world. When a designer is ready to test part of a new chip layout, his workstation uses

NetBatch to find all the other machines on the network that are idle, whether they are in Ireland or China or the US, and feed the job to them. As a result, Intel's workstations are now used 80 percent of the time, up from 20 percent[44] before the company deployed NetBatch. As a result of using its computational power more efficiently, Intel estimates that it has cut eight weeks off the development time for a new processor.

Other companies have developed similar technology:

> Since 1999, J.P. Morgan has been simulating trades in interest rate derivatives on 250 PCs in its London offices. It had always used powerful Sun workstations for such risk modeling, but it was getting too expensive. With the cheap new muscle added, J.P. Morgan can do complex calculations that were prohibitively expensive and time-consuming, such as running a trade through scenarios for both interest rate fluctuation and market volatility, rather than looking at just one variable at a time.[45]

Since 1997, the scientific project Search for Extraterrestrial Intelligence (SETI) has been using P2P computing to generate almost 88 million sets of calculations analyzing data received from the Arecibo radio telescope with its P2P project SETI@home. In October 2001, SETI@home was installed on over 3.3 million computers in 226 countries worldwide, donating more than 752,000 years of computer time combined. Dr David Anderson, the program director, contends that the network was rated at 25 teraflops and had cost just over $500,000. (In contrast, IBM's ASCI White supercomputer is rated at 12 teraflops and costs $110 million.) The only real costs incurred by the SETI project were software development. Participants voluntarily install the client on their computers. Once installed, SETI uses the spare, unused computational cycles of the client computer to analyze assigned packets of data and send completed results back to SETI.[46]

In April 2001, Intel, the American Cancer Society, the National Foundation for Cancer Research (NFCR), Oxford University, and United Devices announced the goal of creating the world's most powerful collaborative computer, through what they called the Philanthropic Peer-to-Peer Program. The program aims to get six million personal computers downloading the P2P software and installing it on their computers as a first step in finding new drugs and a potential cure for leukemia, the number one cause of childhood death by disease in the developed world.

It is estimated that office workers use as little as 20 percent of their available PC power. Intel estimates in 2001 there are 500 million PCs across the globe connected to the Internet. The resulting "virtual computer" will be capable of more than 50 teraflops of computational power.[47]

Once the client is installed on the computer, the idle computing resources will be used to analyze molecules for possible treatments for leukemia. The program sends information to a computer server at United Devices' Texas headquarters, which then passes the data on to Oxford.

Oxford hopes to screen 250 million molecules. Project NFCR scientists estimate that this will require 24 million hours of calculations, something that was previously unimaginable. The collaborative effort promises to save three to five years in the design of anti-cancer drugs, according to Dr Sujuan Ba, science director for the NFCR, meaning medicine will get to the market faster. The program will eventually expand to other forms of cancer and illness.

P2P is more efficient than prior computing models (mainframe, minicomputer, stand alone PC, workstation, client/server) because it uses simple, everyday computers and harnesses them together to get mainframe-like performance.

P2P is a force multiplier. Though each individual computer is not as large or powerful as a supercomputer, the sheer number of computers and ability to simultaneously perform calculations makes the distributed computer that much more effective than the stand alone supercomputer.

---

eBAY

eBay is an example of the P2P phenomenon. While many dot-coms have gone bust in 2000 and 2001, eBay.com is thriving, profitable, and continuing to attract new users. It is the world's largest online marketplace and the only online auction site listed in *Red Herring*'s top 100 companies most likely to change the world[48] and the top 20 global Web sites.[49] Company executives boast they can increase revenues 50 percent annually, to $3 billion by 2005. In 2001, the company achieved over 200 million unique page views per day.

eBay's secret: it has few fixed costs, no inventory, no sales force, and no warehouses (unlike Amazon.com). In 2000, eBay facilitated $8 billion in transactions making it the sales leader for any pure Internet company. Amazon.com, Ubid.com, and Yahoo! have not been able to grow sales or revenue as fast as eBay.

eBay is driven by Reed's Law. The site helps its members to set up specialized auction communities on its Website as buyers and sellers of many kinds of collectibles, art, and other easily tradable special interest goods. As eBay membership grows, the value of being part of one or more of eBay's GFNs (group forming networks) grows exponentially. This in turn attracts more like-minded people to join eBay to access the communities.

If I live in a little town in the Australian outback, it's highly unlikely that there will be other local philatelists (stamp collectors) who focus on British stamps between the years of 1847 and 1852. The Internet, however, creates a community among people of like interest, who otherwise would not be able to meet. Through the people behind the site, and the site itself, eBay has created the phenomenon of location-less P2P commerce.

Because eBay creates communities of like-minded individuals, members stay on the site longer than when surfing other sites. Nielsen, for example, reports that in September 2001, visitors to Amazon.com spent an average of 6 minutes and 38 seconds on the site, while eBay visitors averaged 37 minutes and 15 seconds.[50]

More than six million items are for sale on eBay, which charges each seller a small fee, ranging from 30¢ to $3.30, to list an item, then collects $1.25 to 5 percent of the final sale price. The number of registered users climbed to 34.1 million in July 2001, doubling from 15.8 million in 2000. International versions of eBay, in 12 languages, represented 14 percent of net revenue in 2001.

In August 2001, eBay facilitated the sale of a $4.9 million jet, setting a record for the highest known sale price for any single item ever achieved on a consumer-to-consumer (C2C) online marketplace.

INTERSECTION OF FIVE TRENDS

The intersection of the above trends will create new threats to existing business models and opportunities for those willing to take advantage of them. Take, for instance, the intersection of wireless, miniaturization, bandwidth, digital photography, Napster (P2P), and eBay. Your teenage daughter wants to see how big the line up is to buy Britney Spears tickets. So using her email-enabled cellphone she puts out a bid, "Who will tell me how big the line up is for the lowest price?" And bids come back. She picks the lowest one and, if it seems reasonable, approves it. The teenager

Online communities, rich content . . . And commerce – meaning the automation of transactions – provide a successful Web infrastructure
Michael Dell[51]

in the line up at Ticketmaster takes a digital photo and emails it to your daughter using a 3G (third generation) cellphone with high bandwidth. Your daughter realizes her fatal mistake: she should have camped out overnight to get her tickets because she will never get one now – the line-ups are humongous. So what to do? She puts out another bid, asking who will video the concert and broadcast it live to her using their high bandwidth 3G wireless phone – at the lowest price. Because of new compression technology by 2004 video streaming of live events will be feasible. She takes the lowest bid, calls 15 girlfriends, and they all watch the live concert from your large-screen TV at home. Fathers might not find this exciting until they realize they could do the same with hockey, football, and baseball games that are blacked out in their local area. These examples highlight a trend identified by Alvin Toffler: the rise of the "PROsumer."[52] Digital technology empowers individuals to produce content that was once the exclusive purview of television networks – and the Internet allows for wide, instantaneous distribution. Thus people consume content in new ways.

Impact of Information Overload and Rate of Change

Information overload and the rate of change driven by these laws is having a negative impact on people's lives. The *Quality of Working Life 2000 Survey*[53] of executives' and managers' experience, conducted every year since 1997, is the most comprehensive research into managers' working lives ever carried out in the UK.

A staggering 82 percent of respondents feel deluged by data and are suffering from "information overload." The report concludes that information overload is now a fact of managerial life.

Three-quarters of respondents said working longer hours was the only way to deal with their workload. Sixty-four percent said that long hours were a part of their organizational culture and 55 percent said their employer expected it of them.

Les Worrall and Cary Cooper, the authors of the research, note that given the changing business environment and the scale of organizational change in any year, 70 percent of UK managers will be affected by major organizational restructuring.

Managers indicated that the nature of the work they do and the demands placed upon them had changed considerably, and that in a majority of cases they had received little training to help them cope with these changes:

- 76 percent said interpersonal skills have become more important as the use of positional authority to manage has become far more difficult.
- 60 percent said they were spending far more time dealing with organizational politics.

The impact of cost reduction-driven restructuring has increased managerial overload and pressure, and has resulted in managers working long hours. In the 2000 survey, Worrall and Cooper found 40 percent of UK managers work in excess of 50 hours a week but that this varies by seniority. While 62 percent of directors work more than 50 hours per week, this declines to 24 percent for junior managers.

In 2000, 88 percent of managers rated home more important than work – but despite this, they are working longer hours than ever before.

- 79 percent think that longer work hours are having an adverse affect on their social life and leisure time.
- 77 percent of respondents with dependent children think it adversely affects their relationship with their children.
- 72 percent of managers with partners think it adversely affects their relationship with their spouse/partner.
- 65 percent of managers feel long working hours adversely affects their health.
- 59 percent think it adversely affects their productivity.
- 57 percent feel it adversely affects their morale.

The longer managers work, the greater the adverse impact they report. While 47 percent of managers who work 35–40 hours per week feel that the hours they work affect their health, this rises to 81 percent for those working more than 60 hours a week. Of those working 60 hours a week, 93 percent say it affects their relationship with their children, 90 percent say it affects their social life and 80 percent say it affects their productivity. But they keep on doing it!

ENVIRONMENTAL IMPERATIVE

A final law to highlight is the environmental imperative. Economists focus exclusively on the economy to measure financial health. But there is a more important economy at work, the earth economy. Instead of just focusing on GNP (gross national product), economists need to also focus on a new measure of success, GEP or gross earth product.

We cannot have an ever-increasing GNP if it is at the cost of an ever-falling GEP. If the earth economy goes bankrupt, the human economy will soon follow. If fish stocks on the east coast of Canada and the US plummet, it represents a bankruptcy in the earth economy. Bankruptcy in the human economy will soon follow as all fishing and canning activities halt. This occurred in the early 1990s. The earth economy is primary and the human economy is derivative.

The good news is that as the economy becomes more digitally based, the impact on the environment decreases. In the case of Napster vs. the recording industry, reproducing songs digitally involves no physical resources in terms of plastic for CDs and cases or fossil fuel for transportation.

IMPACT OF THESE LAWS ON ORGANIZATIONS

All organizations are at risk of being blindsided because of the above laws. While some people might think it is only companies and industries in the high-tech area that are affected, nothing could be further from the truth. These laws, and the material in this book, applies to decision makers in all companies and all industries.

Music labels were blindsided. Hollywood is threatened with being blindsided. Airlines are threatened. Telephone companies are at risk. Retailers are threatened. Even farming – one of the oldest professions – is at risk.

While cases will be cited extensively in later chapters here are just two quick examples from industries that one might think were immune to being blindsided by the above laws: clothing retailing and farming. One of the – if not the – fastest growing clothing retailer worldwide, Zara of Spain, is using technology to profitably grow its business – blindsiding its competition. And even farming is being affected as new technology promises to greatly increase yields.

So companies that do not perceive their businesses being built on technology are at risk of being blindsided.

Of course, companies that have built their business on technology know that their competitive advantage is always at risk because of changes in technology. As Andy Grove, the Chairman of Intel, says, "Only the paranoid survive." While this may seem harsh, and I don't want to promote paranoia, companies in high-tech fields must continually scan the horizon for new trends because of the incredible rate of change within technology-driven industries. In this field more than any other, successful companies cannot rest on past success; they must instead continually cannibalize their own positions before someone else does.

CONCLUSION

These laws guarantee that change will continue unabated, and in fact, will continue to accelerate. But many people are overwhelmed by the amount of change today. Often people's reaction to this is fear and a sense of being overwhelmed.

In *The End of Work*, Jeremy Rifkin predicts the elimination of all white-collar work by 2010. This adds to people's fear.

I agree with Rifkin's premise that white-collar work, as we know it, will disappear. However, what will appear in its place are new forms of white-collar work.

In 1850, more than 60 percent of the North American working population was employed in agriculture. Today, less than 2.7 percent of the workforce is engaged directly in farming.[54] If you go back to the newspaper editorials at the time of farm mechanization you would read the same predictions about the end of work.

A similar decline has been experienced in the manufacturing sector. Between 1970 and 2000, the proportion of workers employed in manufacturing fell from 24.6 to 13.2 percent in the US, a decline of almost 50 percent.[55]

The North American economy survived both the shift away from agriculture and manufacturing. In 2000, the North American market experienced the lowest unemployment levels ever. In fact, businesses had a terrible time hiring, as the labor market was so tight. Rifkin's thesis fails to take into account the incredible adaptability of people and of the economy. My belief is that once people understand the inevitability of change, they won't fear or resist it as much.

In my last book, *The Learning Paradox*, I presented a simple fact: 80 percent of the technology we will use in our daily lives in just 10 years hasn't even been invented yet. Job security for individuals and market share security for organizations is therefore based on learning, changing, and accepting uncertainty. Paradoxically what we fear most as adults is learning, changing, and uncertainty. Hence the title of the book – *The Learning Paradox*: our job security is now based on the very thing we fear the most.

The laws outlined above guarantee that change will continue unabated. In fact it will likely accelerate. If we know that change is inevitable, rather than fear it, a more useful strategy is to ask: "How can I better cope with the rate of change personally?" I try to answer this question in the final chapter. From an organizational point of view it is more useful to ask, "What systems and structures can we put in place to identify new trends as early as possible? What processes can we put in place to ensure we make the best decisions within teams to realign our organization with the new reality as it evolves?" These questions I will seek to explore in the remaining chapters.

REFLECTIONS

* How could the laws discussed in this chapter affect your
    – Organization?
    – Current products and services?
    – Current business model?
* How could your organization take advantage of these laws?
    – How could your competitors?
    – How could these laws enable non-traditional competitors to enter your markets?
* How can you cope with information overload?
* How might your organization benefit from the use of competitive intelligence tools such as LexisNexis?
* List the products and services currently perceived to pose an insignificant threat that could evolve to blindside your organization.
* How might the following affect your organization, and how might you take advantage of them?
    – 3G wireless networks?
    – Unlimited free bandwidth?

- What might prevent your organization from creating new products and services which, over time, might cannibalize existing ones?
- In what ways does your organization encourage employees to maintain a healthy work–home life balance? If you are a leader, what is your example in this area?
- How could your human resource policies better reflect the fact that intellectual capital is key?
- What impact will technology have on your organization? Your work personally?
- How quickly can the organization respond once a new threat is identified?
- How do you ensure that your organization attracts and retains the best people?
- What percentage of activities does your organization engage in that your customers might consider add no value? Discuss with your department. What practical strategies can be implemented to reduce this?
- What percentage of employees' skills and talents do you feel the organization utilizes? How could the organization unleash greater potential?
- What percentage of the work you do could be done by someone who reports to you? What would you have to change to redress that balance?
- Describe the balance between short-term and long-term focus within your organization. How could the balance be improved?

CHAPTER 4

10S Model

Why do change initiatives typically fail? How can organizations increase the chance of having initiatives succeed? Do organizations typically take on too many or too few change initiatives? What are the highest leverage activities for leaders?

Organizations are far more complex than we typically think. Decision makers who want to bring about change in an organization have to understand its interdependencies – and know that they will have to work on many different levels to bring about lasting change. The 10S model is an integrated, holistic, and strategic approach to organizational change. To highlight how the model works, I will use the example of Napster and the recording industry, and Jack Welch's drive to implement Six Sigma within General Electric.

McKINSEY'S 7S MODEL

The foundation of the 10S model began with the 7S model developed by McKinsey & Company. In June 1979, Robert Waterman of McKinsey published "Structure is Not Organization," an internal paper by and for the professional staff of the firm. It argues that "organizational change is really the inter-relationship between structure, strategy, systems, style, skills, staff and . . . superordinate goals,"[1] and that organizational effectiveness stems from the interaction of these factors.

The greatest leverage factor to bring about change in a particular organization will be dependent on the specific situation. The model is shown in Figure 4.1.

STEPHEN COVEY'S PRINCIPLE CENTERED LEADERSHIP

Stephen Covey used McKinsey's 7S model as the basis for *principle centered*

Figure 4.1 McKinsey's 7S model. © Copyright 1979 McKinsey & Company.

leadership. Covey made a finer distinction with staff by breaking it into self and people. He renamed "superordinate goals" as "shared vision and principles" and added an eighth S – stakeholders (customers and suppliers) outside the company. He then divided the model into four levels, personal (self), interpersonal (people), managerial (style and skill), and organizational (shared vision and principles, systems, structures and strategy). A fifth level was implied by the stakeholders' streams outside the organizations.

CHANGES TO THE MODEL

As form follows function, strategy must be based on an analysis of an environmental scan. What new technologies will affect the organization in the future? What new products and services will be enabled by suppliers' innovations? What is the hierarchy of needs of our most profitable customer segments? How are these needs changing? What are their most important articulated needs that are not being met by anyone in the market? What are our customers unarticulated needs – i.e. needs that they can't even express? What are their fears and frustrations, which we can turn into valuable new products and services? What is the SWOT (strength, weakness, opportunity, and threats) analysis regarding competition? This is the environmental scan outside the organization.

Keeping all of McKinsey's 7Ss, and adding Covey's enhancements of self and stakeholder needs, creates a 9S model. To this I would like to add a

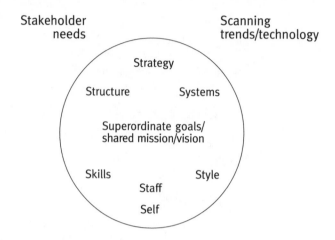

Figure 4.2 The 10S model.

tenth S – scanning trends and technology. This involves techniques such as scenario planning, trend analysis, technology, and competitive intelligence.

To determine strategy, individuals, and organizations should begin with stakeholder needs and environmental scanning (Figure 4.2).

There are many traditional tools for diagnosing stakeholder needs, such as force ranking customer needs and focus groups. There are also new techniques for unearthing customers' unarticulated needs. (See "Aligning Organization with Customer Needs" in Chapter 8.)

Similarly, there are all sorts of tools and techniques for scouting future trends and technology: competitive intelligence, SWOT analysis, attending trade shows and conferences, usability labs, scenario planning, and listening to customers, suppliers, and users of your products and services, and those of your competitors. *Blindsided!* will explore some of these in greater depth later.

STAKEHOLDER NEEDS

Stephen Covey has a great definition of stakeholder as any group that would be hurt if a business were to fail. So employees, shareholders, suppliers, the communities where a company operates, even the government to whom the company pays taxes, are all stakeholders.

So who are the stakeholders of the recording industry? Obviously the recording artists, employees, suppliers, retailers, customers who buy music, and even the governments that collect taxes.

What are the articulated needs of each group? Articulated needs are those that customers are conscious of and can therefore talk about. Unarticulated needs are often harder to determine because consumers don't know what they don't know. While consumers can't articulate in the positive the product or service they want, they can discuss their fears and frustrations. Companies can then turn these into positive benefits of a product or service. For instance, many drivers fear turning into another vehicle in their blind spot. A solution might be a sonar system that warns drivers when something is in the blind spot. Before it was invented, most consumers would not have suggested this as a feature because they couldn't imagine it. It is therefore up to individuals and organizations to uncover customers' fears and frustrations and create new features, products or services to address these concerns.

The articulated and unarticulated needs can be force ranked or prioritized. By force ranking customer's needs, an organization can discover what is truly important for them and invest the time to make sure it does this for customers better than any other company in the market.

To make this a little bit more complex, there are also different market segments that will have different hierarchies of needs. A company can do a competitive analysis in the market to find out which needs are not being met.

Those who used Napster, and now the alternative services such as Morpheus, are computer savvy and typically have high-speed Internet connections.

Focus groups with former Napster users showed that individuals loved the service because it offered "selection beyond the mainstream, instant gratification, and a community of unbiased peers who are not trying to sell them something."[2] Most importantly it offered them control. Rather than having to buy a whole CD, they could download a single song. They can sample music before deciding to keep it. They can sample a wider range of songs than ever before. Consumers have access to songs that are unavailable in record stores.

In other words, Napster provided new value to consumers that the traditional method did not. The current music industry does not allow for instant gratification, user control (choose to put the song on any device), or sampling.

If there is a popular song you want to have, the music industry currently forces you to buy the whole CD.

Another discontented group is recording artists. Courtney Love's position on the music labels exploiting artists represents a widespread discontent and presents a serious challenge for the industry. Up until now the five major labels have controlled access to the means of music distribution. With the advent of the Internet, however, musicians can distribute music directly to fans. Once a means of collecting royalties is in place, will musicians need the labels? In interdependent relationships, it is a danger sign if any stakeholder feels exploited. If circumstances change, and the balance of power shifts, as it will with the Internet and the music industry, that shift will threaten those who exploited their power in the prior situation.

When there is dissatisfaction within one stakeholder group, a shift in technology that changes the playing field can allow for the dam of ill will to break.

Even government is a stakeholder in a business, and can cause serious problems for a company if it is left feeling dissatisfied. (See sidebar below on Coca-Cola and transfer pricing.) Many people's reaction to this statement is that it is really stretching the definition of a stakeholder and the value of stakeholder analysis. But when any stakeholder is threatened, the risk of the organization being blindsided is increased. The case below highlights how Coca-Cola sold almost $C1 billion a year of soft drinks between 1990 and 1997 but claimed to make next to no profit. Using a mechanism called transfer pricing, Coca-Cola transferred profits to Puerto Rico, a tax haven.

COCA-COLA AND TRANSFER PRICING

In 2001, Revenue Canada, the country's tax agency, concluded a four-year investigation of Coca-Cola Bottling, the Canadian subsidiary of US Coca-Cola Enterprises. Tax authorities were investigating the company's transfer pricing between 1990 and 1997 with its Puerto Rican subsidiary. The concentrate used to make Coca-Cola sold in Canada during 1990–97 was made by Coca-Cola's Puerto Rican subsidiary and shipped to Canada. Coca-Cola was accused of charging inflated prices for its concentrate as a way of taking profits out of Canada to Puerto Rico, an American tax haven. Coca-Cola claims to have lost money or made only small profits for the entire period of 1990–97. In 1995, the Canadian operation turned its first profit since 1991, making $C4 million on pop sales of $C930 million. At stake in Revenue Canada's audit was more than $C100 million in back taxes.[3]

Transfer pricing is the establishment of a price for goods, services, or intangibles that cross borders between related parties. Since Canadian taxes are far higher than those in Puerto Rico, Coca-Cola organized its operations so that less income was taxed in Canada. Revenue authorities are naturally concerned that corporations may attempt to set transfer prices so that the highest profit is generated in the country where the taxes are the lowest to avoid paying taxes in Canada. The Canada Customs and Revenue Agency estimates that it has found more than $C1 billion dollars in unpaid taxes between 1998 and 2000 as a result of transfer pricing audits.

Coca-Cola's problems with tax authorities have not been limited to Canada. In the mid-1990s, the US Internal Revenue Service lost a highly complex case against Coca-Cola, which centered on how to calculate the value of its secret formula with its Puerto Rican subsidiary. Seventy million dollars was at stake.

Japan's National Tax Administration imposed ¥15 billion ($145 million) for back taxes on Coca-Cola's Japanese subsidiary in March 1994. Between 1990 and 1992 Coca-Cola (Japan) paid its US parent company ¥56 billion for the use of the Coca-Cola trademark and other intellectual property rights. Japanese tax authorities said the royalties were excessive in comparison with similar fees paid by Japanese subsidiaries of other soft-drink makers and that Coca-Cola (Japan) used the royalties to reduce its taxable income by 38 billion yen. Until 1998 it remained the largest ever transfer-pricing dispute in Japan. In February 1998, Tokyo tax authorities reduced the penalty by 10 billion yen.[4]

In its 2000 annual report, Coca-Cola mentioned that Japanese tax authorities collected an undisclosed amount of back taxes for a number of years, after reassessing the royalties that the Japanese subsidiary paid to US operations from 1993 to 2000.

SCANNING

Scanning involves scenario planning, conducting a Delphi (a technique), examining trends (social, political, demographic, technical, technology), using content aggregators such as Factiva, LexisNexis and Dialog, and competitive intelligence. These tools and techniques help

individuals and organizations develop "radar," helping them to see more clearly into the foggy future. These techniques will be discussed later in the book, but any one of these could have given the record industry earlier warning of the impending challenges it would face – and helped the industry respond faster to the challenge digital music would pose to its business model.

STRATEGY

Strategy is the means to achieve the corporate goals. The McKinsey paper points out strategy is not enough. Execution is essential.

"Form follows function," said architect Frank Lloyd Wright.[5] It is the same with the relationship between strategy, and systems and structures. Systems and structures should follow strategy. Once the environmental scan has determined the articulated and unarticulated interests of customers and the executive team has scanned the horizon, (using tools such as competitive intelligence, delphi, trend analysis, scenario planning) the organization needs to create strategies to respond to the evolving business environment. In the case of the recording industry, scenario planning would have alerted record industry executives to the dangers of compression technology such as MP3. Similarly, studying trends would have drawn attention to Gilder's Law and Metcalfe's Law highlighting the inevitability of the P2P phenomenon. Forewarned to look for these triggers, executives could have predicted the increased likelihood of a digital music future when these triggers would come to pass.

Having gone through scenario planning when confronted initially with Napster, industry executives would have seen the sign of change far earlier and could rapidly have gone into evaluating options to respond.

Strategy does not have to be monolithic. Microsoft does not have one strategy; it has a multiplicity of strategies. The ultimate goal of scenario planning is to create flexibility in the minds of everyone in the organization in responding to change. The ultimate goal is to create a learning environment. No company should bet its whole future on just one product or service. During times of rapid change, security is actually achieved through a diversity of strategies. For instance, Microsoft has the Net initiative, *Windows XP*, *Windows 2000*, *Windows ME*, Microsoft *Office*, single applications, Microsoft Network (MSN), *Encarta*, the X-Box game unit, and joint ventures such as MSNBC created with NBC. The company is constantly innovating and working to find new opportunities.

STRUCTURE

"As the number of people or businesses increases arithmetically, the number of interactions required to make things work increases geometrically," notes the McKinsey paper. "A company passing a certain size and complexity threshold must decentralize to cope."[6]

Once the executive team has decided on the strategies to employ, these must be communicated throughout the organization and structured to align with the strategy. So often organizations try to fit a new strategy into an existing structure, like trying to use a baseball bat to play tennis. The new game requires new equipment, new structures and new processes.

For this reason, in the past many companies have set up completely new structures to create new ideas. When IBM created the personal computer (PC) in 1980 to rival Apple's invention, its team was isolated in Florida, separate from IBM's mainframe operations. The PC unit decided to outsource the CPU to Intel and the operating system to Microsoft.

Author Geoffrey Moore cites the example of how Hewlett Packard shifted from laser printers to ink jet printers. It set up a completely parallel organization. He makes the point that it is not so much invention that has to be shielded from the dominant culture but the execution of the new strategy.

It is important to point out that for every case there is a counter case. Xerox Parc's Palo Alto facility was famous for creating all sorts of new inventions that the mother organization was not able to commercialize. (Steve Jobs saw the graphical user interface while touring the facility and created Apple as a result.) Similarly the research center for the Swiss Watch Institute created the quartz movement but Swiss watch-makers felt the invention was useless because it didn't fit their concept or paradigm of a watch. They let the researchers show their invention at the 1967 Swiss Watch Fair. The Japanese took one look and the rest is history.

While it may be necessary to create new products and services that cannibalize existing markets outside the company and build a sales and marketing organization outside the existing structures, that alone will not guarantee success. It may be *necessary* but it is *insufficient*. All of these 10S points are necessary, but in and of themselves, insufficient.

SYSTEMS

There is a "close inter-relationship between system, strategy, and structure. We could not make progress in one area without moving ahead in the others."

Dr W. Edwards Deming, the founder of the quality movement observed that upwards of 94 percent of all problems in organizations and their solutions are systemic.[7] The key then is not to blame people. Deming believed that people are inherently good and want to do a good job, but instead focus on misaligned systems, such as policies, processes practices and rules.

Similar to structure, systems are established and optimized based on the current (old) business model. These may threaten the new way of working. For instance, in the US 40 million (out of 200 million) workers now work from home. This will inherently change the systems and structures of organizations as they are realigned to enable telecommuting.

SUPERORDINATE GOALS

Superordinate is defined as a higher order. So superordinate goals are pre-eminent, or overriding above all others.

There is a great story about stonecutters. A management consultant asks the first stonecutter, "What are you doing?" His reply: "Cutting stone."

So the management consultant asks a second mason and receives a different reply: "Feeding my family."

A third mason replies, "Building a cathedral."

And a fourth, "Worshipping God."

All are performing the same work – cutting stone – but each has a different motivation. The first is purely functional, and focused on the task (physical). The second sees the job as a means to an end to feed his family (emotional, social). The third is focused on the overall project (mental). But the fourth has reached a deeper level of motivation (spiritual). While each mason has a superordinate goal the most powerfully motivating one is at the spiritual level.

In 1983, Steve Jobs enticed John Scully to become Apple's president with a challenge: "If you stay at Pepsi, five years from now all you'll have accomplished is selling a lot more sugar water to kids. If you come to Apple you can change the world."[8]

Jobs' superordinate goal was far larger than one individual or an individual task within an organization. In this case it was not to make computers, but to change the world.

In her book *Leadership and the New Science : Learning About Organization from an Orderly Universe*, Margaret Wheatley asks the reader to think about an atom and all its parts: the proton, neutrons, and electrons. She asks, "Which part is in charge?" The answer is none. So what governs the behavior of all the particles? Where does leadership come from at the atomic level? The laws of physics. In the same way, superordinate goals such as the mission and vision of an organization will be the organizing principles that should direct the behavior of individuals in the organization.

If the superordinate goal of an organization is to serve the customer in the best way possible – do you see how that frees up the individual and the organization to embrace new ways of working? If you truly wish to serve, that becomes the motivation and impetus to change.

Hank Berry, the former CEO of Napster and partner at Hummer Winblad, the venture capital firm that invested $15 million in Napster, talked about the attitude of recording industry executives towards new technology:[9]

> Their position is that they are in control and, that they don't have an obligation to make that work [music] available in any way, shape or form other than the way they want to. One executive said at a forum I was at, "Why do you keep talking about business models? We decide the business model and the consumer's job is to accept it."

STYLE

Style implies the personal operating style of an individual, such as the Myers–Briggs personality style regarding the primary way an individual processes or presents information. Style also implies the way an individual interacts with

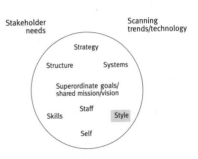

others. For instance, some individuals are shy or reserved and are nervous speaking in front of large groups. Some are unwilling to air their thoughts until they are fully thought through. Different cultures have different cultural styles. For instance, in Asian cultures, employees generally will not contradict their boss in a group setting.

The CEO's style will often permeate the whole organization. For example, Bill Gates' personal operating style has permeated all of Microsoft, because early on in the company history Gates was involved in hiring every programmer and team leader. He hired competitive, bright people who could solve problems quickly. In turn, the systems and structures that were created, such as hiring, promotion, and compensation, reinforced this approach until it became the persona of the company.

GEOFFREY MOORE

Interview with Geoffrey Moore, the author of numerous books, including *Crossing the Chasm*, who has some interesting insights:

Moore: The winners who have taken second mover advantage to a high art, actually solve the problem in a much simpler way – they turn out to be competition freaks. Meaning, they are not motivated by the customer, not motivated by the technology, they're almost not motivated by profit. What they are motivated by is absolute, hyper-paranoid response to competition.

Harris: Now, when you say that, Microsoft is the poster boy.

Moore: Microsoft and Oracle are the first ones that come to mind for me. What they do is, they don't understand the customer, they don't worry about understanding the customer. They see somebody spinning up with a lot of power, and they immediately attack them. It's almost a little like a retro-virus; they take the identity of their antagonist and beat them at their own identity. They may never understand that identity, but they out-execute. So all those things you described; those would take a thoughtful person a long time to work through. But, if you say, "I'm just going to beat the person who looks like the competitor," you don't have to go through any of those seven steps. All you have to do is, whatever that guy is doing, do it faster and better.

Harris: But what you have to do is be very hyper-vigilant to small signals in the marketplace.

Moore: Yes, I think this is like a version of Andy Grove's *Only the Paranoid Survive*.

Harris: At Microsoft, literally everyone uses competitive intelligence. It is a discipline. You don't make a presentation unless you know the strengths and weaknesses of every single competitor. It's not like a department where there's two guys who research competitors; it's hard-wired throughout the whole culture based on the personal operating style of Gates himself.

Moore: In *Living on the Fault Line*, there's a model of cultures that I borrowed from Bill Schneider. He talks about four different cultures and one of them is competition driven. He calls it "Competence Culture" and it's about defining yourself by your victories over your competitors. In a Competence Culture you would expect to see competitor driven presentations as the standard unit of thought. That's the best culture for making quick responses at scale and at speed. The second mover doesn't need creativity because they are letting the environment show them the change through the enemy.

Harris: In fact, that's part of Microsoft's strategy. I think they just kind of sit back, while they are always innovating themselves, they're scanning to see what is actually successful and see; do we buy it, like Hotmail, do we adopt it? Do we build it ourselves? Do we crush it? What do we do to *it*, whatever *it* is.

Moore: Exactly. Their first instinct is to crush it and that really is the test, because if they can crush it, they should crush it. If they can't crush it, then that gives them their second piece of information, which is should we buy it? Or what do we do now?

Harris: Do we build it ourselves?

Moore: Exactly. Do we clone it? Do we assimilate it? Just what do we do with it?

The next three Ss in the 10S model – skills, staff, and self – are going to be addressed in the following case study of Jack Welch's implementation of Six Sigma at General Electric. To briefly review these Ss:

SKILLS

Skills can be learned through experience and training and education. Communication, negotiation, delegation, and empathetic listening are all skills that can be learned.

STAFF

This is fairly self-explanatory although it may not be obvious that people are the key to everything else. As Stephen Covey notes, people are the programmers and everything else are programs.

SELF

Self is the one thing of all the 10Ss that I have control over. I have control over how I see problems. What skills should I develop to help me become more effective? Through his actions, Bill Gates has shown he is not afraid to change direction, implicitly admitting that the prior direction was wrong. A perfect example is the case of turning Microsoft around completely and embracing the Web as described in Chapter 2. To Gates it is more important to be competitive than to protect his ego and avoid having to say he was wrong.

NECESSARY BUT INSUFFICIENT

Each of the elements of the 10S model is important. It is the interaction of all the elements that makes an organization exceptional. Like baking, leaving one ingredient out changes the whole recipe.

Yet, one ingredient is not the answer. While I am a big advocate of training, training on its own is not the solution. Authors Baldwin and Ford claim that 90 per cent of US training expenditures result in no new skills transfer on the job.[10] US companies and governments spend over $100 billion a year on training and development. How can it be that 90 percent of it is failing? According to reports, three-quarters of North American quality initiatives fail. *Information Week* reported that two-thirds of re-engineering initiatives fail. According to Arthur D. Little Inc., only 16 percent of companies are satisfied with the results.[11]

Training is important. Quality is important. Re-engineering is a great strategy. But all of these are systems are single components of the 10S model. Any S within the model is necessary to bring about change, but insufficient on its own. Training employees on how to innovate, without empowering them to change systems and structures, without training managers to become coaches, without aligning compensation systems to reward the new behavior, is to waste money on training. What is required is a holistic understanding of organizations and creating alignment at all levels of the 10S model.

JACK WELCH AND SIX SIGMA

The Six Sigma program has been a huge success at General Electric. GE has received numerous accolades: *Fortune* Global Most Admired Company (1998, 1999, 2000); *The Financial Times* World's Most Respected Company (1998, 1999, 2000).

Jack Welch was appointed CEO of GE in 1981 and retired in 2001.[12] In January 1996 GE began rolling out its Six Sigma program. In the first full year the company trained 30,000 employees, spending $200 million and realizing $150 million in savings. The gains have grown significantly larger with each passing year (Figure 4.3).[13]

GE's operating margins increased from 14.8 percent in 1996 to 18.9 percent in 2000.[14] At the same time, top line revenues increased from $79.2 billion to $130 billion.

Larry Bossidy, a former Welch colleague who had become CEO of

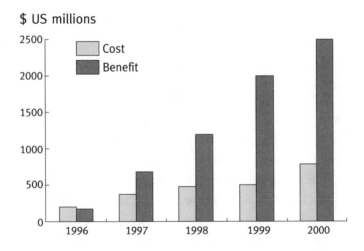

Figure 4.3 GE's Six Sigma.

AlliedSignal in June 1995, presented to the entire management team of GE how Six Sigma had made a significant impact on AlliedSignal.

Most US companies average 35,000 defects per million operations (3.8 sigma), but Six Sigma quality means there are fewer than 3.4 defects per million operations in a manufacturer or service process. That is 99.99966 percent correct, or near perfect. The table below shows sigma defects per million opportunities:

Sigma	No. of errors per million
2	308,537
3	66,807
4	6,210
5	233
6	3.4

Why is the goal for perfection so important? Because taking 3.8 sigma to be acceptable means it's okay to have 5,000 incorrect surgical operations per week, and 20,000 lost pieces of mail per hour. By contrast Six Sigma would only accept 1.7 incorrect surgical operations per week and seven lost articles of mail per hour.

The team left the 1995 retreat "psyched," in Welch's words, to make Six Sigma a big hit. "We told the business CEOs to make their best people Six Sigma leaders. That meant taking our people off their existing jobs and giving them two-year project assignments" to become black belts. The first key to the Six Sigma's success at GE was Welch's commitment to drive it through the organization, by aligning the goals with the reward system. As Jack Welch notes in *Jack: Straight from the Gut*:[15]

> As with every initiative, we backed it up with our rewards system. We changed our incentive compensation plan for the entire company so that 60 percent of the bonus was based on financials and 40 percent on Six Sigma results. In February, we focused our stock option grants on employees who were in Black Belt training. These were supposed to be our best.
>
> When the request for option recommendations went out in February, the phone calls started coming in. A typical phone call went something like this:
>
> "Jack, I don't have enough options. We didn't get enough for the business."

"What do you mean? You got enough options to make sure all the Black Belts were covered."

"Yeah, but we couldn't give options exclusively to our Black Belts. We had to take care of a lot of other people."

"Why? I thought the Black Belts were your best people. They're the ones who should be getting the options."

"Well . . . they aren't all our best," they'd say.

My reply was: "Get your best people in the Six Sigma program and give them the options. We don't have any more to give you."

Welch ensured the reward system was aligned to guarantee that by the second year the best people within GE would be leading the Six Sigma initiative. No head of a division wants to give up his or her best talent for two years, especially within a bottom-line driven culture like General Electric, where all Welch's direct reports had high targets. The heads of the division initially held back some of their best people to ensure they made their numbers. Having conflicting priorities is normal in corporations. Unless Welch had been consequent, the Six Sigma initiative would not have achieved the success it has. The role of the leader is to make it clear which is *the most important initiative*. And to create alignment – in this case through being consequent. Welch estimates that in the first year of the Six Sigma initiative, only a quarter to a half of the Black Belt candidates were the best and the brightest.

KEY LEARNINGS

There are a number of key lessons for me from GE's Six Sigma experience:

1. *Be consequent.* If there are no consequences for not following your direction, do not be surprised if your direct reports don't listen to what you say or act on it. Welch's action sent a clear message to the whole culture that the one thing that would be valued more than anything else would be a commitment to the Six Sigma initiative. Today no one can be considered for a promotion within GE unless they have Six Sigma training.

Example is the best and only way to teach. Leaders must model the behavior they wish to see throughout the organization. If you expect people to be consequent, you had better be consequent with them. The easiest way to create change is to have a commitment from the top of the organization.

I believe that Microsoft is such an intensely competitive organization because Bill Gates himself is so intensely competitive. Since the company was founded in 1975 he has hired other people who are also intensely competitive, and then these individuals have set up systems and structures within the organization that promote competitiveness – such as the hiring system that screens people for their mental agility, problem solving capabilities, and competitiveness.

2. *Consistency of communication.* In a large organization like GE, a CEO cannot communicate with the executive team or even to the executive team's direct reports and expect things to change. A leader has to communicate the key message or initiative over and over and over again to every individual within the organization, reinforcing it at every opportunity for years to actually bring about change. This requires patience, discipline and consistency. By the time every person in the organization has heard the message, the CEO has been saying the same thing for years. Communication is not only a skill in the 10S model, but also a style of being open and consistent.

3. *Every organization is perfectly aligned to get the results it gets.* This was the essence of W. Edwards Deming's work. The leader's role is to ensure alignment within the organization, systems and structures within the 10S model.

In our work we experience many competing forces: serve my customer, serve my boss, serve my direct reports, serve the mission of the organization, serve my family, serve my own needs, serve the new task force I have been assigned to. Amidst all these priorities, different individuals will put different priorities first. The organization must therefore send very strong signals continuously to individuals as to which goals, initiatives or strategies are superordinate and should come before all others. Welch's signals were strong, clear, and unyielding. Nothing matters more than Six Sigma. Again this ties back to the individual level (Self in the 10S model). The CEO has to have the courage and discipline to challenge individuals to create long-term organizational alignment. In other words, the CEO has to be willing to bear the disapproval of direct reports and to challenge them. The CEO has to care more about the long-term direction of the organization than peer approval.

4. *Most organizations suffer from what I call initiative fatigue.* It is not unusual for me to work with an organization that has 14 key strategic directions in a given year, each with a series of goals. By contrast, it is interesting to note that between 1981 and 2001, GE only really had five initiatives: globalization, services, work-outs,[16] Six Sigma and e-business. In 2001, GE was in its sixth year of Six Sigma and showed no signs of dropping the initiative. In fact, the company's commitment to the initiative becomes greater with each passing year and the benefits grow annually. Again this ties back to the individual level because the CEO has to have discipline and the consistency to stay with initiatives for the long term. The key role of leadership is deciding what strategy the organization is going to pursue for the long term and then working to align systems and structures. The hard work is deciding.

5. *GE's Six Sigma initiative gave everyone in the organization a common language.* From a management point of view there was synergy in that executives could transfer between divisions and still apply the same Six Sigma tools. Similarly, GE's prior initiative, work-outs and a discipline of continuous improvement gave people in every division a process by which to improve business performance. In the case of six sigma and work outs, the leadership of GE centrally made the decision about what process would be used to improve performance across all divisions, but the improvements were made by people within the divisions using the tools. By aligning systems and structures, Welch ensured the methods would be widely learned throughout the organization. In other words, the role of leadership is not improving performance, but in determining the absolute best tools to improve performance and then aligning systems and structures to guarantee that all the best people can learn and apply these tools. The role of leadership is determining which tools will best suit the organization, the industry and then, once decided, drive them through the whole organization.

I have used GE's commitment to Six Sigma as a way to highlight a number of aspects of the 10S model. Deciding on Six Sigma as a methodology began by scouting trends and by having Larry Bossidy present the case as to why Six Sigma had made a significant difference at Allied Signal. Once the senior exec-

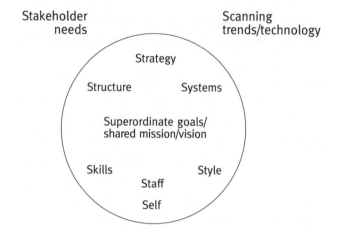

Stakeholder needs — Scanning trends/technology

Strategy

Structure — Systems

Superordinate goals/
shared mission/vision

Skills — Style

Staff

Self

utive team had decided on this strategy to achieve better performance, Welch began aligning systems and structures. The hardest challenge, and one of the stumbling blocks, was being consequent with direct reports. Here Welch had to develop internal fortitude at the personal level, the self. Because in dealing with staff we must, "Be the change you want to see in the world", as Mahatma Gandhi said. Welch's commitment to Six Sigma involved communication skills with direct reports.

A key learning from the 10S model is that each of the 10Ss is necessary but insufficient.

TRIM TAB FACTOR

R. Buckminster Fuller was a scientist, architect, mathematician, engineer, and innovator who coined the phrase "trim tab factor." To understand the concept, think about an ocean-going freighter more than two football fields in length, weighing hundreds of thousands of tons, steaming through the ocean.

To turn the ship to starboard (right) the rudder is turned to the right. The hydraulic force needed to turn the rudder against the force of the water streaming by it is immense. A 274-meter oil tanker that is 50 meters wide will have a rudder area of 60.8 square meters. To turn the rudder just one meter when the ship is traveling at 17 knots requires 190 tonnes of force.

As supertankers developed in the 1950s, marine designers created the trim tab, a tiny rudder within the larger rudder. To turn a supertanker to starboard (right) the trim tab is turned hard to the left and the force of water going by the trim tab counterbalances the force of water going by the large rudder and swings it to the right.

Six Sigma within GE has been a trim tab factor. Welch's insistence that the only people who would get stock options would be black belts was a trim tab. Leadership is all about looking for the small difference that will make a large difference.

The concept of a trim tab factor when applied within an organization is to look for the high leverage item(s) that will affect change within a whole system. I was working with a group of electrical contractors who were upset that unqualified contractors were increasingly encroaching on their work. All sorts of options are available to the association to counter this – lobbying government for legislation, public education campaigns, or even striking. But a trim tab might be working within the insurance industry to put a new clause in all home owner insurance policies that if electrical wiring of a house or repair or maintenance work is not done by a certified electrician and the house burns down, the home owner is not covered.

> *Why do you seek more knowledge when you pay no heed to what you know already?*
> **Dervish tale**

LARRY WILSON ON CAESAR, TRUST & THE NEW LEADERSHIP

Larry Wilson, the founder of both Wilson Learning and Pecos River, and the co-author of *The One Minute Sales Person* and *Play to Win: Choosing Growth over Fear in Work and Life*, does a fascinating exercise on leadership with senior leadership teams.

Imagine you're part of such a leadership team attending a seminar being conducted by Wilson. Wilson starts by challenging the team to do what he believes leaders should always be doing: working to create an organization that if it existed, would put theirs out of business.

Wilson asks, "What's it going to take to thrive in the next decade in a permanent white water world of change?"

"What part of your future success will depend on your employees behaving differently than they are today?" Most organizations proudly claim "People are our most important asset," but more often their policies and procedures and even their mindsets do not reflect that.

George Land, author of *Breakpoint and Beyond: Mastering the Future Today*, was vice-president of Advanced Research at Wilson Learning for more than 10 years. He called one of the models he brought to Wilson Learning, "the growth model." It defined growth in a unique way while showing how all things grow in the same way.

When Wilson starts his seminar, he will often use Land's model to help executives quickly identify what stage of growth they are in and what they are headed for. The model can apply to any change in life or nature. By studying the underlying and predictable processes of change, seeing how change changes over time, the leadership team can begin to develop strategies to be ready for it.

On a standard graph, Land would put increasingly complex connections on the vertical axis. Land describes growth as a process of increasingly complex connection. It affects all organisms and organizations, from a single cell dividing into two; a company growing its customer base; or a franchise expanding from 1,000 to 10,000 locations. Each organization will have to change to survive the growth.

The horizontal access is measuring time passing. Inside that frame, Land would then place the standard sigmoid or S curve (Figure 4.4).

According to Land's model, everything, including every business, goes

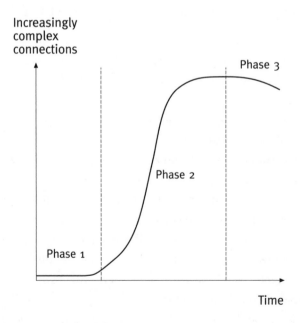

Figure 4.4 The growth model.

through all three stages. This is well explained in his book, *Breakpoint and Beyond*. Here we will just focus on the business side of the model.

Phase one is the entrepreneurial stage which is characterized by trial and error (learning) because everything is new. The culture is very informal and everyone is willing to do whatever it takes to make things happen. There are very few rules, procedures, or specialized functions and certainly very little turfdom exists. In this phase there is no need to talk about being close to the customer because the company is probably hanging onto the customer's leg waiting for the check.

Every day, people are figuring things out but usually not writing them down. Land calls this phase one. It is formative and the goal is to get out of it. In nature most life forms don't make it out of phase one (i.e. most tadpoles don't become frogs; most acorns don't become trees, and most new businesses fail in their first few years).

Organizations that grow beyond phase one have discovered and applied what George Land calls an RP, a replica process or pattern. In determining its RP, the entrepreneur, team or company have made two key decisions: "What we are going to be?" and "What are we not going to be?" In phase one, any idea or anything new was welcomed. In moving into phase two the welcomed ideas are only those that focus on improving the efficiency or effectiveness of the RP. Whereas in phase one you trust the entrepreneur, in phase two you start to trust the systems that are finally in place and running the business.

In phase two the organization focuses on improving the efficiency and effectiveness of its RPs (systems and structures). As the RPs become highly organized and systematized, the norm is for the organization to experience rapid growth and profitability.

The downside of phase two is that over time functional fiefdoms develop and silos get built. The organizational focus and energy often shifts from satisfying the customer to satisfying the boss. The focus moves from external to internal and the organization is less and less sensitive to the outside world. This organizational drift often misses emerging trends.

Inevitably there is feedback from the environment, representing early warning signals such as a slight fall in market share, lower than usual customer service ratings, dropping customer loyalty, and falling profits. The first response to these early warning signs is typically denial, but eventually there is a call to action. Unfortunately, the usual response is to go back to the basics (doing more of what we did in the past). More often, the goal becomes to rediscover the old RP.

While this flurry of activity may produce a short-term gain, it is usually a faithful predictor of a steeper slope to failure.

In phase two you no longer trust the entrepreneur; you now trust the system.

In nature, however, there is a phenomenon that occurs called a bifurcation (a new beginning). This can occur at any point in phase two, however, as a strategy, earlier is better. This flies in the face of the "if it ain't broke don't fix it" and "let's milk this cow till she runs dry" philosophies. This different strategy is a great example of trading the normal, short-term gain for the more enlightened long-term advantage that benefits all stakeholders.

The bifurcation represents a new beginning but it also represents the difficulty of letting go of things that produced successes in the past. Because the old RP was the dominant way of doing business, as the bifurcation is coming into being, there is often a tremendous tension between the "old line" (vested people, vested processes, vested products) and the "new line" (different, different, different) which requires superior leadership, terrific open communication, shared values and vision and a way to allow everyone to both compromise and win at the same time.

The old systems and structures are just not sufficient to deal with the magnitude of this change. What is required in this precarious situation is a new kind of leadership.

This means a leadership that understands, believes, and puts into practice policies, systems and structures that reflect the belief that people are the most important resources of any company.

At this point, Wilson helps each member of the leadership team understand the difficulty and personal challenge of this statement. He takes them through 10,000 years of control command leadership and shows how we have shifted to a new and more effective kind of leadership, which he calls "developmental leadership."

As more and more organizations are approaching phase three or are already confused by it, what is needed is not just change, but transformational change.

Unless organizations can embrace transformational change, stage three leads to death, sometimes slowly, but usually quickly. While organizations can re-create themselves, facing this change requires a fundamental shift in leaders' mindsets. If executives are willing to go through this personal challenge, the organization can launch the beginning of a new S-curve.

In phase three you have to trust people. That's a big shock for most leaders because their experience has been phase two-command and control. Trouble is, a phase two style won't work in phase three. Leaders need to empower people, helping them to assume more authority and responsibility. To grow as a business in phase three you have to trust the people and allow them to grow, in order for the organization to also grow.

It's in phase three that purpose (mission), vision and values become essential reference points. People who are going to be asked and expected to take on more responsibility will have to learn and apply new ways of choosing direction. Otherwise, how can you give people power? Leadership must be dispersed in phase three. Ideally you want to reach a point where every person in the organization thinks, feels and acts as a leader.

What does this mean practically for organizations today? Leaders are going to have to be the first to change. Traditionally they will have to move from a fear-based, command and control philosophy to a trust-based developmental one. Leaders will have to be the fastest learners, and demand that the organization follows their lead. Leaders will have to deeply understand that leadership is, "someone following someone else, because they want to, not because they have to." In short, leaders will have to lead.

The world is rapidly moving into the third phase of change. Yet, most institutions and few organizations are at phase two. Most have to make that difficult move from command and control (pleasing the boss), to developmental leadership (pleasing the employee) who will in turn please the customer.

The difficulty is that we are dealing with a 10,000-year-old norm. We need to change at the speed of light. Today companies are trying to cope with discontinuous change.

In a seminar, Wilson draws a ladder and asks participants, "What's this?" Answers typically include: "a ladder" and "a hierarchy."

"Right, a hierarchy" says Wilson. "Where did they come from?"

"The church and the military."

"Right," well, we're *not* going to get into a religious discussion here – so let's go with the military."

Then Wilson draws an image of Roman leader Caesar at the top of the ladder and a lowly private at the bottom. This hierarchy doesn't represent just the military but all our institutions: schools, governments, and businesses.

"Now this structure didn't appear magically," says Wilson, "there had to be certain values in place that would encourage this structure to become and remain dominant for so long in our cultures and in society."

"The first value, was that 'I, Caesar, have all the answers. Your job, private, is *to do* the answer. Yours is not to reason why, yours is but to do and die'." [17]

"The second value is that 'I, Caesar, *do not trust* that you, private, will do what you are told.' (The private is going to be asked to do some pretty unpleasant things. Charge this army; take that hill. I, Caesar, know I wouldn't be excited to do many of these things, and neither will the privates. Therefore I, Caesar, am going to have to control you, private, to do what you don't want to do.)"

So, the third value was Control. Caesar had to ensure control – in other words, ensure the private did what he was ordered to do. Hence, hierarchy developed. The primary function of hierarchy is control. Information was given only on a need to know basis. And severe punishments were instituted for not doing what you were told.

Wilson points out that today this whole model is quickly breaking down. First, Caesar no longer has all the answers, and even he knows that. The world is just too complex, and changing too fast; there are too many emerging contradictory trends for any one individual to have all the answers. Though reluctantly, Caesar now has to turn to the private and say, "Do what is right."

That is a huge shift for both Caesar and the private. It means that Caesar must now trust the private, which means trusting that the private has a brain, and is willing and able to use it. In most situations the private is closer to the action, and therefore more in tune than Caesar about what is happening.

In some ways it's like revisiting phase one. We are in a new environment, one we have never seen before, but it's more difficult than phase one because we are carrying our past on our backs. In phase one we didn't have a past to slow us down. Nor did we have to deal with the fact that what got us here may not take us where we want to go.

The private is being asked to take the risk of making choices, something he never had to do in the past. The implicit old employment contract was do what you're told, work hard, don't question authority and in return you will get job security. That was the *quid pro quo*: hard work and loyalty for a gold watch after 40 years.

We all know the old contract is dead.

Today, companies *have* to trust employees. Trusting implies accepting mistakes as learning. But this is very hard for Caesar, who we all know is a control freak. No longer can Caesar say, "Do it right the first time," especially if its never been done before. Reality is if it's worth doing, it is worth doing wrong, at least the first time. Caesar has to realize that, and trust people are going to make some mistakes.

Wilson then says something that confuses executives and gets their attention. It's okay to make mistakes as long as people meet *all three* of the following conditions:

First, the mistakes are on purpose. People are taken aback by this statement – and often ask, "What do you mean, on purpose?"

Wilson clarifies: mistakes are all right as long as they are made in an effort to carry out the organizational purpose (i.e. the purpose of total customer satisfaction).

Secondly, it's okay to make mistakes as long as people learn from them.

And thirdly, it's okay to make mistakes as long as people share their mistake with everyone else in the organization. This third requisite is founded on a belief that anyone can learn vicariously from everyone else's mistakes and thus not have to repeat them.

Wilson next asks the question, "Typically, what do people in your company do with their mistakes?"

Participants answer, "Bury them." "Hide them." Or "Blame others for them."

Wilson then points out that the organization is being robbed of its intellectual capital. He asks executives to imagine an organization where, when someone makes a mistake, they ring a big bell and yell, "Gather around. I made a doozy of a mistake that I want to tell you all about!"

Can you imagine that ever happening in your company? Most people say, "Never in a million years!"

Then it's here that your worst nightmare will occur. You wake up some morning and find out that your toughest competitor has learned to ring that bell, gather people round and share their mistakes. The fact is, they would become the fastest learner in the valley. They would be the fastest to change, and the toughest to compete against.

Wilson points out that it was British philosopher Herbert Spencer, not Charles Darwin, who coined the phrase "survival of the fittest." Darwin used the term in his work but said, "It is not the strongest species that survive, nor the most intelligent, but the ones most responsive to change."

Land's growth model and Wilson's *I Caesar* are powerful teaching tools to help executives disengage themselves from the day-to-day muck of phase two micro-managing and get to the higher altitude of true leadership. As Wilson says, "It's only when we get above the day-to-day problems that we can see the bigger picture, especially the patterns, trends, challenges and opportunities. It's from there that leaders can start to lead people who are ready, willing and able to follow a developmental leader, because they want to, not because they have to."

SEPARATE ACTION FROM OUTCOME

I need to separate *action* from *outcome*. To put it another way, I have to separate the *process* or *discipline* from the *outcome*. By guaranteeing the process or discipline is followed, I trust the outcome will follow. Here's an example . . .

I returned to Canada in 1988 after traveling around the world for four years and I swore I would have a job, any job, within a week of my arrival. I got one as a telemarketer. During breaks and days off, I called companies to find out more about positions, and on evenings and weekends sent out applications for more than 300 jobs. Some were in response to advertised positions; others were unsolicited and aimed at companies I thought I would enjoy working for. I probably called 1200 companies to find the 300 jobs, which led to 12 interviews. From those I was offered six positions. Of the six, I was really only interested in four, and I chose the best one. This was working as a researcher on a new edition of *The 100 Best Companies to Work for in Canada*, a book published by the *Financial Post*, Canada's national financial newspaper.

After a year of work, I was made a co-author of the book, which became a Canadian national bestseller. Some people tell me, "You are so lucky." In one sense they are right. The more important lesson here, however, is the replicatable process. The systems and structures that enable me to be lucky.

What is important is the ratio of inquiries to applications to interviews to offers to interesting offers to the final job I accepted, which was 1200:300:12:6:4:1.

Had I only applied for 100 jobs I would have only had four interviews and only one offer I was interested in, which is what I would have had to take, which may or may not have led to as interesting an outcome. Had I only applied to 50 positions I may have only been invited to two interviews and not received any offers. It's a numbers game.

Many job hunters take rejections personally. The rejection ratio in my case was 288 out of 300 applications. The point is to not take the rejections personally and to understand the dynamic from the hiring company's perspective. In the late 1980s, a company advertising a position might receive 50 applications. Therefore my chance of getting the position was only 1/50 or 2 percent. To base my emotional life on such long odds is to set myself up for failure. I need to understand the system.

This was the essence of W. Edwards Deming's teaching and that of systems dynamic thinkers, such as Peter Senge, author of *The Fifth Discipline*. It is the systems and structures that govern behavior. I need to think beyond my own involvement and understand the system dynamics in play.

The same law applies to organizing political rallies. The success or failure of a rally has nothing to do with the number of people who turn out and everything to do with the size of the room. If 150 people turn out to a political rally in a hall that holds 1,000, the media will report that the candidate has no supporters in that area. However, if 150 people turn out to a rally and the room only holds 100, the media will report: "In a standing-room only event tonight, Candidate X said . . ." TV cameras at the event will show people squeezed together, shoulder to shoulder, straining to hear the candidate. The perceived success or failure has nothing to do with the turn out and everything to do with the size of the room. Good political candidates don't take events with a poor turn out personally because they know the organizer selected too large a room.

So how does this philosophy apply to organizations? If a company needs to fill a position and they hire the first person that comes along, no one should be surprised if the candidate is not ideal. Microsoft hires only 2–3 percent of all job applicants. Microsoft's success has nothing to do with the excellent quality of people it hires. It has to do with the systems and structures, the discipline of interviewing 100 candidates to select only two or three.

In programming circles there is a concept known as the super programmer. A super programmer is someone who is much more productive than an average programmer. It is not just quantity, but the quality of the code. According to Michael Cusumano, a super programmer is 10 times better than the worst programmer in the organization and two to three times better than the average programmer.

The average Microsoft programmer therefore will be better than programmers hired by the competition.[18] Microsoft has developed a system for hiring only the best programmers. Company recruiters are famous for asking job applicants questions that test their problem solving and reasoning abilities. A typical question used to be, "How many gas stations are there in North America?"

One approach might be to begin estimating the US population at 300 million people. Assuming that people live in families of three (the average family is four but some people live on their own), that would make 100 million households. Not everyone has a car, though. Assuming that only 77 percent of people have a car, that would mean 77 million cars. Assume that it takes on average 1,000 cars to support one gas station. That would mean that there were 77,000 gas stations in North America.

Whether the answer is correct (in fact, there were 126,889 gas stations in North America in 1997[19]) is not as important as giving the interviewers insight into how creative, and intuitive an individual is at quickly seeing and solving problems.

The key to Microsoft's hiring approach is to develop a replicable process. It is an interviewing system that guarantees that the company will hire the best employees. The key is to understand the underlying system dynamics, and then create systems and structures that will always work.

Thomas Jefferson said "I'm a great believer in luck, and I find that the harder I work, the more I have of it." I disagree with this statement. Hard work doesn't have as much to do with understanding the underlying system and then optimizing my behavior based on that underlying system.

Consultant Robyn Allan, asks the question, "What was Thomas Edison's greatest contribution?" People will often answer the light bulb or phonograph. "No," she will reply, "the discipline of invention," i.e. the process, the systems and structures necessary to guarantee invention. It is said that Edison's greatest strength as an inventor was his ability to keep trying different things until he found one that would work. It took Edison two years to develop the light bulb. The problem was finding a "filament" that would not burn up or explode when an electrical current was passed through it. Edison sent people as far away as the Amazon and Japan to look for vegetable fibers that would work. Edison tested 6,000 different fibers, none of which worked.

Finally Edison hit upon the idea of using a carbon thread as a filament. He took some of his wife's sewing thread, coated it with carbon and baked it in a U-shaped mold to create a semi-circle of carbon. The filament was put in a vacuum-sealed glass bulb. The carbon filament lit up the instant Edison passed an electric current through it, and burned steadily for 44 hours.

The genius of Edison was his ability to not get discouraged when attempt after attempt failed. In 1910, he developed an alkaline battery. After 8,000 trials Edison remarked, "Well, at least we know 8,000 things that don't work."

This same philosophy can apply to anything else. Character traits of patience, courage, and faith are the key. In other words, I need to engage in the action to understand the system, and in time be confident that the outcome will follow. Separate *action* from *outcome*.

THE GARDENER

Many people think of gardening as a passive activity. In fact, it is very active. Do nothing and see what happens to your garden. Within a period of weeks it will be overrun with weeds. Where there is no gardener, there is no garden.

A gardener has to weed, prepare the soil, plant the seeds, ensure there is enough water and fertilize. But in another sense the gardener does nothing. The plants grow themselves. It's like a Zen paradox. The gardener isn't completely responsible for the outcome, but without the gardener nothing will happen. It is the same with leadership.

A leader has to create systems and structures within an organization to weed, plant, water, and fertilize on an ongoing basis.

In an organization, weeding involves identifying and removing bad management habits. What 360-degree tools are in place to ensure that bad managers are identified. What systems are in place to help correct their behaviors? Does the company use employee attitude surveys? Does the company have appeal mechanisms in place so managers do not make arbitrary decisions that affect the livelihoods of people? What does the company do to weed out fear? Do executives model the behavior of being open to challenge themselves? Is an individual's 360-degree feedback taken into account before he/she receives a promotion?

FedEx uses a survey action feedback (see p. 176 of *The Learning Paradox*) to proactively survey all employees every year. High-tech companies such as Sun Microsystems is using online tools that can survey everyone in a department as they log onto their workstations. This can allow the organization to react faster than traditional paper-based surveying techniques.

When bad management or employee behaviors are identified, what corrective action does the organization take, such as intervention from the human resource department and training programs?

If a company does not put in place systems and structures that identify and remove bad management habits among leaders, the weeds will grow faster than the flowers or fruit-bearing trees.

In this analogy, planting would equate to hiring the best people, with the highest potential possible. What is the company's hiring strategy? Is it designed to win the best and brightest employees? Consider Microsoft's hiring strategy discussed above.

Watering. Without frequent water, most plants will die. Is the company meeting all the basic needs of its employees in growing and achieving maximum productivity?

In *Flow: The Psychology of Optimal Experience*, Mihaly Csikszentmihalyi describes the conditions required to achieve optimal performance. In simple terms: if I have a competence equal to 100 and you give me a job that only requires a skill level of 80, I will be bored because I know how to do it. On the other hand, give me a job that requires a skill level of 200 and I will be paralyzed with fear. But give me a challenge that is at a 120 level and I will be excited and challenged. A sign that we are in flow is when we lose a sense of time and it speeds by.

Does the company have in place systems and structures that continually challenge people? Microsoft doesn't have very many formal training programs for programmers because you can't teach creativity. Instead, the company moves people onto different projects, and has a mentoring program.

Most organizations dramatically under-challenge their people. I believe we also often dramatically under challenge ourselves. We often don't know what we are capable of achieving.

In organizations, fertilizing would correspond to strategies that would accelerate individual and organizational growth: training programs, mentoring programs, and new tools such as eLearning that allows employees to learn anywhere, any time.

Someone I know went on holidays for six weeks. Before she left she weeded her garden. She only had enough time to plant half the garden with her favorite flowers. When she came back from holidays, the half of the garden that had been weeded but had no flowers planted was again overrun with weeds. By contrast, the other half had weeds but they were very small because they had to compete with the flowers she had planted.

This provides an interesting insight. It is not enough to weed out bad practices in an organization. They must be replaced with good practices. It also highlights that weeding is not a one-time, but an ongoing process.

This metaphor of gardening as leadership applies not only to leading other people but leading myself. If I leave my mind on its own, it will be overrun by weeds, thoughts of anger, resentment, hatred, envy, and jealousy. However, if I want to live a happy, joyous life it requires active work. I have to actively plant good thoughts. And I have to have a system, a discipline of weeding. I can't just say, "I don't feel like weeding so I won't." I have to engage in the activity of weeding.

BENCHMARKING ARCHITECTURAL FEES

The average architectural fee is between 5.5 and 7 percent of the total construction budget of a large building. A celebrity architect will charge 6–8 percent. The design (design, construction drawings, and engineering studies) of a project account for 70–75 percent of an architect's fee or 3.85–6 percent of a building's cost).

What's the cost of designing an organization? While the blueprints for a building are static, those of an organization are continually evolving. It's like trying to build an airplane while flying it. Using the architectural fee analogy, organizations should be spending between 3.85 and 6 percent of their cost structure on determining direction, strategy and ensuring alignment.

If you have to choose between doubling your speed or heading in the right direction, which should you choose? How much time and effort do senior executives spend scanning, and ascertaining stakeholder needs, ensuring alignment, and ensuring systems and structures are designed to support the strategy?

CONCLUSIONS

The 10S Model presents a way to fully understand organizations and suggests ways to bring about change. My hope is that the 10S model will be used to help leaders see their organizations more clearly, create more effective change management programs, and help executive teams, individuals and organizations significantly reduce the risk of being blindsided.

REFLECTIONS

- On which of the Ss does your organization require the most focus?
- Theoretically can you create an organization to put your competitors out of business? To do so, what will haved to change within your organization?
- What are the trim tab factors for you
  - Personally?
  - Departmentally?
  - Organizationally?
- Identify all of the organization's stakeholders. What would repesent added value for each stakeholder group?
- What techniques do you use to scan for new trends and plan for possible future developments?
  - Personally?
  - Departmentally?
  - Organizationally?
- Which of these strategies – risk management, disaster planning, and scenario planning – are currently in place in your organization? And what would have to change to begin using one or all of these strategies?
- Is the organization's mission and vision clear to all employees?
- What are the personal, departmental, and/or organizational superordinate goals? How are they communicated and how are people articulating their use?

- Identify all of the organization's stakeholders? What could the organization do to add value for each stakeholder group?
- How does your organization encourage all employees to act like leaders? List more ways you could.
- How would using 360-degree feedback better align personal behavior with organizational goals?
- What incentives does your organization provide that encourage employees to share honestly their feelings about their work environment? (For example, GE's policy of giving stock options only to Six Sigma Black Belts.)
- What multiple strategies is the organization employing to ensure it doesn't get blindsided?

PART II

How do you future proof your organization? How can a company avoid being blindsided? The following chapters will explore strategies, tools, and tactics that the best organizations are using to increase their speed in recognizing and responding to change. All of these approaches are tools, but tools are not the only answer. They are necessary *but* insufficient. *For instance, even though Cisco has the virtual close, it was blindsided by the telco meltdown.*

The new tools and techniques presented in the remainder of the book raise the question, "Who's in charge now?" The rate of change is so fast and the volume of information so overwhelming that no one individual or small group can have all the knowledge or answers. In order to recognize and respond faster to change leaders have to give up the notion of centralized control. The role of the leader is to put in place systems and structures that create alignment.

CHAPTER 5

The Real-Time Enterprise

If you had to select only one strategy to avoid being blindsided, what would it be? How can companies blindside their competition? How are old-economy companies or industries embracing a real-time philosophy to increase profit and blindside their competition?

REAL-TIME ERA

We are entering the real-time era, where all the organizational systems and structures are moving to become real-time systems.

My body works in real-time, which means if I stick my finger in ice water I know immediately that it's cold, allowing me to react instantly. Very few organizations work in real-time. Most companies have quarterly financial reports, annual employee reviews, and production delays that range from weeks to months.

Imagine my body worked the way most organizations do, receiving biofeedback only once a quarter! Would I thrive? Survive? I could walk into the kitchen, stick my hand on a red-hot burner and not even know I had a problem until 89 days later.

The drive to become a real-time organization is affecting every aspect of companies. This effort goes under a lot of different names: just-in-time (JIT) inventory, cycle time management and kanban – the Japanese concept of flexible manufacturing.

> *Our age of anxiety is, in great part, the result of trying to do today's jobs with yesterday's tools.*
> **Marshall McLuhan**

CISCO INFORMATION ON VIRTUAL CLOSE

Cisco has worked to have all its systems operate in real-time. As of October 2001, Cisco sold $1.5 billion of product a month over the Web, more than 90 percent of orders, with less than a 1 percent order error rate, saving the company $57 million annually. More than 83 percent of Cisco's customer inquiries are serviced over the Web.

Some 90 percent of Cisco's customer support is now done over the Internet. Customers prefer to use the automated system than talk to a $250,000-a-year engineer, which saves the company $600 million a year and generates higher customer satisfaction. The company saves $86 million a year with electronic downloads and $107 million with online configuration and documentation, yielding 25 percent higher customer satisfaction.

Cisco works to do everything electronically, from employee expense reporting to training.

By using networked applications over the Internet and its own internal network, Cisco is seeing financial benefits of nearly $1.4 billion a year, while improving customer/partner satisfaction and gaining a competitive advantage in areas such as customer support, product ordering and delivery times.

CISCO'S VIRTUAL CLOSE

Since becoming a public company in 1990, Cisco has seen its annual revenue grow from $69 million to $18.9 billion in fiscal 2000, a compounded annual growth rate of more than 66 percent! Cisco acquired 23 companies in 2000 – one every 16 days. The challenge of rapid growth, compounded by the pace of acquisition, meant that producing financial statements was a problem.

CFO Larry Carter joined Cisco in 1995 from Motorola, where he had experience with the Six Sigma quality improvement program, which Motorola had applied not just to manufacturing, but also to functional areas within the company.

In 1995, Cisco took 14 days to close its financial books at the end of every month. Carter assumed the task of restructuring the company's financial systems. "I was concerned about the timeliness and integrity of our overall financial information," said Carter, noting that with a 14-day close in a company with rapid growth, "you can spin out of control."

"Anyone in manufacturing can tell you if you can reduce the cycle time to manufacture a product, good things happen. Costs go down, inventory goes down, productivity improves and quality goes up," notes Carter. The same is true of finance.

With this in mind, Carter set to work to reengineer the financial processes at Cisco and compress cycle times. Wherever possible, he used the Web to automate transactions.

A close is "the transfer and recording of expense accounts." Cisco's virtual close is "the continuous monitoring and analysis of critical information necessary to effectively run the business." It has allowed the company to close the financial books within an hour's notice, all within an electronic infrastructure that almost instantly shares all information. Or, as Carter puts it, "the ability to run your global plants as though they were one."

He viewed the challenge as how to scale the company while maximizing shareholder growth amidst rapid expansion, technological change, acquisitions, and a shortage of experts. The results have seen Cisco grow 10-fold since 1995, while reducing finance expenses by more than $75 million.

The virtual close enables Cisco to analyze and instantly react to market changes, whether caused by a single customer, or by an entire continent.

Wherever possible, the finance team reengineered the financial processes using the Web to automate transactions, a huge step in bringing the company closer to Carter's goal of virtual close.

"Because of the nature of the Web, transactions were being downloaded to our ledger virtually every day," he recalls. "Suddenly, it dawned on me that by having this information, selecting the right metrics, and making sure they were in the management reporting system, we could change the way we ran the company."

The company hasn't had to make any next-day adjusted entries since 1998. In 1999, the company achieved its goal of the virtual close.

Ironically, Cisco sees great value in how the process actually "opens up" a world of real-time company information for use throughout the workforce. The same system that feeds the ledger also provides executives with the data they need to react to the rapid-fire changes in the Internet world. Totals on everything from bookings, discounts, revenues and margins are all available on a daily basis.

Now, more than 90 percent of orders arrive at Cisco via the Internet and half are never touched by a Cisco employee.[1] The company has orders automatically farmed out to subcontractors, who ship finished products directly to customers.

Cisco has implemented dozens of applications, which assist in achieving the virtual close and the real-time consolidation of the company's financial information. Three of these applications are Metro, Ariba, and EIS.

Metro is an expense reporting system. Expense reports, travel info, and corporate credit card charges are tracked and updated in real-time. The reports enhance employee productivity by providing managers with better tools to manage their expense costs, while improving reimbursement turnaround times. Company charges on Amex are now posted within 72 hours and the individual can allocate them online. Amex is then paid within 48 hours. Cisco processes 15,000 expense claims a month with two auditors. To do this manually would require eight auditors. The cost of processing an expense report has fallen from $50 to $8 and is saving the company $6 million a year.

Ariba streamlines Cisco's administrative expense activities by connecting the company to its suppliers over the Internet. Internal costs of Cisco's purchase order process have been cut in half. An online catalog listing computer equipment, copiers, fax, furniture, and office equipment and supplies allows employees to place orders that must be in line with corporate financial guidelines before any dollars are committed. For example, an employee places an order online for $15,000 of computer equipment, but the budget only allows for $12,000. The system will immediately recognize the deviation from budget and will reject the request before the supplier ever receives the order.

EIS is the executive information system. It provides fiscal reports on a daily, monthly, quarterly, or annual basis. Andrew Cailes, Cisco's director of business planning worldwide sales, says that previous attempts to report through *Excel* were not going to scale. The Web-based management reporting system (available daily at 8 a.m. local time in San José, London, and Sydney) allows sales managers to view how their team is performing against actual and forecast. In 2001, the status of orders was available to sales reps on an hourly basis so that sales teams and managers around the world could check where they were at any point in time.

Though only a few companies have moved to a virtual close, there is a general move to automate financial systems. Carter predicts that by 2005 the virtual close will be the norm for most large companies. Companies that don't switch over in the next decade will be at a competitive disadvantage. The Office Depot implemented virtual finance in 2000 with the installation of broadband communications for all its stores, and GE has created a new position, eFinance Leader.

The ability to get data on key elements of the business very quickly has a powerful effect on decision-making. For a fast growing company, shortening cycle time for financial information is important. And while it is a challenge to implement, sooner is better, because it doesn't get any easier when you wait.

WHY?

In many organizations finance staff wasted their time begging every global unit for sales figures and then keying in the data. By automating the recording of financial history, the virtual close frees up finance professionals to become more proactive, focusing on adding value through analysis, coaching frontline managers on how to improve financial performance, and forecasting.

Cisco's finance team eliminated practices that yielded little financial gain for the required effort, such as capitalizing assets valued at less than $5,000. The goal was to reduce the number of transactions that the systems and employees had to monitor. For the employee expense reimbursement system, expenses are electronically submitted to the manager. If the manager does nothing, the employee is paid in 72 hours. No positive approval is necessary.

By eliminating non-valued-added functions, finance professionals can focus on higher value-added functions such as tax planning. Between 1996 and 1998, Cisco's finance group was able to reduce the company's effective tax rate from 37.5 percent to 33 percent.

Cisco paid no federal income taxes in 1999 because stock options exercised by employees wiped out profits for tax purposes.[2]

The ability to monitor its performance in real-time has given Cisco a clear advantage over competitors, many of which were forced to wait until the end of the quarter before gauging their overall performance.[3]

HIGH GROWTH × CONSISTENCY = HIGH PREMIUM

Companies with the highest market capitalization and price earnings (P/E) ratios achieve high growth, rarely, if ever, disappoint, and marginally over-perform analysts' expectations. The virtual close has allowed Cisco to track and fine-tune its performance throughout a quarter so it can consistently meet or exceed analysts' expectations. As a result, the market has placed a huge premium on Cisco's valuation and P/E ratio over those of its competitors, adding billions to Cisco's value and briefly propelling the company to become the world's most valued company at $579.2 billion on March 24, 2000.

Cisco's earnings consistency led some analysts to chide the company for "managing earnings." One analyst complained in the *Wall Street Journal* that, for the eighth straight quarter, Cisco had topped Wall Street's expectations by precisely 1¢ per share and suggested that accounting games were being played. CFO Carter took it as a compliment.

CISCO BLINDSIDED

In August 2000, CEO John Chambers told investors: "The second Industrial Revolution is just beginning." But the revolution seemed to stall on February 6, 2001, when for the first time in six years Cisco failed to meet or beat earnings estimates when it reported its second quarter earnings. Cisco's inventory had more than doubled to $2.5 billion from $1.2 billion six months earlier. Then three months later it reported a third quarter loss of $2.69 billion, most of it in excess inventory write-offs. Cisco's virtual close was supposed to prevent surprises like this.

At the end of the third quarter in 2001, Cisco had more than 88 days of inventory, a 19 percent increase over the previous year.

CEO John Chambers said, "The first four months of 2001 were extremely challenging as we went from year-over-year bookings in excess of 70 percent in November, to 30 percent negative growth within a span of several months. This may be the fastest deceleration any company of our size has ever experienced." In other words, Cisco knew about the slow down in December, January, and February.

Part of the problem was that Cisco was getting growing amounts of revenue from dot-coms and upstart telecom companies. These upstarts didn't have the same ability to correctly forecast demand as do more traditional customers. Cisco was relying on these fast growing new companies to warn them of a change.

Many analysts had forecast that the mobile phone operators who paid huge sums for third-generation operating licenses in the UK and Germany would have less to spend on new networking equipment.

CAUSES

What caused Cisco's falter? Some analysts speculate that the virtual close gave Cisco a false sense of security. The virtual close accounts for past performance, but it is not predictive. Cisco not only misjudged customer demand, it also over-estimated its ability to react quickly to such a sharp and sudden drop in sales.

SUPPLY CHAIN BUILD UP

Cisco executives say that the inventory problem was, in part, caused by the need to maintain good relations with its suppliers, notably semiconductor manufacturers, by honoring long-term commitments. Dell's agreements with suppliers, by contrast, are based on actual market demand not on forecasting.

Having a virtual close is necessary but insufficient in coping with rapid change. Dell has consistently worked to get suppliers to embrace JIT manufacturing. If one party in the supply chain is working in real-time but all its suppliers are not, and it is tied into long-term agreements, then the chain is only as strong as its weakest link.

There is also a suspicion that management chose to ignore early signs that demand was on the wane, even though they had access to excellent market intelligence.

EARLY WARNING SIGNALS IGNORED

Cisco took a sales adjustment charge of $1.1 billion, or 15 percent of revenue, on October 28, 2000. Bill Parish, a financial analyst with Parish & Co., noted that this adjustment was for loans and leases made to customers, many of whom had trouble paying Cisco back once they lost the ability to raise money on Wall Street or from venture capitalists. This should have been an early warning signal.[4]

LEADING INDICATORS

Could Cisco have anticipated the downturn? What leading indicators could have sent off alarm signals?

- Time to close sales – seeing the sales cycle is lengthening.
- Seeing that the receivables are lengthening – customers not paying as fast.

- Increase in vendor financing – customers unable to pay for or finance capital costs.

"The slowdown happened at Internet speed," says Carter. Chambers compared the pace of the downturn to a "100-year flood" and said in spring 2001 that the company was "in a valley much deeper than any of us anticipated." He referred to the uncertainty in the market as "low visibility" – the "fog" in the driving metaphor.

REACTION

Companies plagued by a lack of visibility traditionally react by cutting jobs. (See telco meltdown in Chapter 1.) Motorola cut 30,000 jobs in 2001. Cisco certainly fared better than Nortel and Lucent Technologies, who both cut over 50 percent of their workforce in 2001. Companies also traditionally slash discretionary spending such as travel, expenses, and hospitality. Cisco reduced operating expenses by $1 billion in the six months after March 2001. Companies also typically work to reduce inventories.

I have been giving Cisco a hard time here because I feel that the early warning signs the virtual close provided were either overlooked, ignored, or executives were working to wish them away. While Cisco's stock has fallen from a high of more than $80 a share in March 2000 to a low of $11.04 in September 2001, its market cap is still more than double to that of its next seven competitors combined![5]

Despite its own layoffs that cut 17 percent of its workforce, Cisco's management remains confident and won kudos for navigating the slowdown. While the company will likely see its revenue shrink in 2002, it still has $19 billion in cash and investments, and no debt.

The market capitalization comparison before and after the high-tech stock market meltdown is an interesting picture. While Cisco's value has fallen – its relative value compared to its competitors has increased (see Figure 5.1). This, I believe is because it is the leading company in becoming a real-time enterprise.

A more constructive response to uncertainty is for companies to become more agile and create supply-chain relationships that can react swiftly to sudden changes in demand or customer preferences. To become more agile,

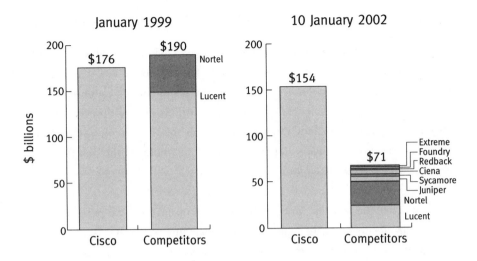

Figure 5.1 Market capitalization comparison.

suppliers have moved from a push to pull concept in the demand chain to JIT delivery of inventory, and from a manufacturing perspective to kanban, the Japanese philosophy of flexible manufacturing.

Rather than having six months of inventory to guarantee supply, manufacturers need to look at speed and flexibility as the solution to variable demand.

KANBAN

The philosophy of kanban works to simplify product lines, standardizing on core components, and differentiating products late in the production phase. This reduces inventory and increases flexibility. Instead of long production runs, kanban allows for short production runs, so that products are made to order. This allows manufacturers to increase or scale back production in response to market conditions. (For a full kanban case study, see *The Learning Paradox*, p. 263.)

Nokia has benefited from having a simpler product line than its rivals. Because its components are more standardized, suppliers find it easier to crank up or cut back on production and deliveries.

CONTRARIAN VIEW

It is important to have the discipline and willingness to be a contrarian. A powerful example was provided by Vishwa Marwah, the founder of Tattoo, a boutique branding agency in San Francisco, whose clients included Campbell Soup, Monsanto, Nabisco, and Sears. The company attracts clients through referral: Molson Breweries helped land Purina, and Martha Stewart was referred by *Time*.

"As you probably have watched, the khaki has replaced the denim jean in the last 15-year clothing cycle," notes Marwah:

> But one of the consequences of that is, all of us have several pairs of khakis in our closet, far more than we could wear in a week. It's like the white shirt. We have exhausted the potential number of khaki pants we'll purchase.
>
> If the past was a predictor of the future, and you looked at the business of a clothing store that focused on khakis, you would say that between 1990 and 2001, khaki sales grew by XYZ percent, and conclude that *"make more khakis"* should be our mantra.

Tattoo went out and asked core customers of a clothing retailer, "What do you have less of in your wardrobe than five years ago?" One of the answers was jeans. Similarly researchers asked, "What do you least need another pair of?" Customers answered, "I wouldn't mind another fresh pair of khakis but I don't really need them."

These counter-indicator clues only come through dialogue. Whereas most marketers would look at the sales of a brand that has been growing steadily and step up production, Tattoo went back to the client and found, "Khakis have grown really well, but for the future, try and think about the wardrobe as a receptacle. There's just not room for the eleventh khaki."

"Our work has advised them to make more jeans, on the simple notion that the wardrobe of khakis is exhausted," said Marwah:

> There might be a cycle that comes back again in 10 years, but for now the predictors indicate that it's time for denim again because that's what's not there in the wardrobe.
>
> Khakis don't die; by the way. They're hard to kill. So what we really have

to do is shift the focus. You will see starting in Fall 2001, actually the campaign is just kicking in as we speak. It's all denim.

A contrarian view would have helped Cisco. "We perhaps would dig into the basis of some of our customer's forecasts, especially those in emerging markets, and understand the basis for their growth," said Carl Redfield, Cisco's senior vice-president for worldwide manufacturing and logistics.

"In a great number of cases, we had customers whose business models were shallow, and those were part of our forecasts," said Redfield.

REAL-TIME PRECISION FARMING

Some people might think that the real-time era will only affect high-tech companies. Nothing could be farther from the truth. Even farming is beginning to work in real-time. Real-time precision farming applies the newest technology to one of the oldest professions.

A farmer creates a computer model of his farm consisting of the legal boundary, soil composition, topology, drainage works, and crop yield data, as well as previous crop histories and inputs (fertilizer, lime, and pesticides or herbicides).

While seeding, the farmer's seeder measures a number of soil conditions in real-time and ties this data to location by using a global positioning system (GPS) which relays this information by radio to a computer.

Nitrates are essential to achieving maximum yields. Yet they are one of the most expensive farming inputs. In the past, farmers applied one amount of fertilizer everywhere. The philosophy was "the more, the better," because excess nitrates won't hurt plant growth. So farmers tended to err on the side of excess. This inevitably led to nitrate build up in many areas while in others there may not have been enough. Nitrates, if applied excessively, however, are an environmental hazard that contaminates ground water. Rain washes excess nitrates into streams and rivers, and contaminates local water tables.

Precision farming measures the soil for nitrates in real-time and applies only what is needed, exactly where it is needed. The cost savings for this input alone can pay for the equipment and set up. Until 2001, farmers did not have the tools to create the perfect balance between maximizing plant growth and minimizing damage to the environment. Real-time precision farming is the answer.

The acidity of the soil also affects crops, so achieving an optimal pH level improves yields. Therefore lime can be applied in varying amounts, to bring the soil to the optimum pH level.

A third variable is herbicide and/or pesticide application. New farm equipment has small cameras on the front that monitor the soil. When weeds are spotted they are sprayed locally at the back end of the planter. So rather than take a shotgun approach and spray the whole field, new systems spray only the areas that need it, saving the farmer input costs and the environment from excessive impact.

A final variable is the water retention of the soil. At the top of a hill the land is arid so the planter will sow a seed variety that thrives with little moisture. At the bottom of the hill where water collects, the planter will sow a seed variety that thrives on lots of moisture.

The data from all these inputs is captured, tied to the GPS data, and uploaded by radio to computer. At harvest time the yield per acre is also tied to position and farmers can then measure the effectiveness of inputs and make adjustments to the inputs to increase the yield the following year.

These data help the farmer increase crop yields by varying crop type, seeds, and inputs. A farmer with 16,000 acres of land, investing $90,000 in hardware and software, could save several dollars per acre. Thus the equipment can pay for itself in a year or two, raising crop yields and lowering input prices while reducing negative environmental impact.

FASHION – A WHIM IN TRANSITION

Vishwa Marwah highlights how the Internet and, by implication, real-time efforts, have the ability to amplify and kill trends. "It cuts both ways," he notes,

> The second part never got much attention. The Internet can explode something to the point where the avant-garde rejects it, particularly in fashion. You haven't seen much innovation in fashion in the last five years. Some people think it's because it socializes so quickly. It used to be that the cutting edge designers showed their stuff and a year later the sort of front edge retailers carried it and it showed up at the mass market, Sears, in year

three. That's no longer happening. One of the key reasons is the Internet. It's because those ideas get transmitted instantly and they're available within a three weeks. Zara, for example, turns over their merchandise every 11 days.

Some people might think that only companies in the high-tech industries are at risk of being blindsided. Nothing could be further from the truth. The rag trade is one of the oldest professions. By working in real-time, Zara has become the fastest growing retailer worldwide and threatens to blindside its competition.

ZARA

Zara is a Spanish retailer that is the envy of the fashion business. According to Vishwa Marwah,

> The reason is that they cycle their apparel products so fast that they are almost never off-trend, which is killer in the industry. The fact that you spent $2,000 on a Versace suit is not satisfying because the amount of time that you will enjoy the outfit as being special and unique is dead. It used to be you'd have a good year's wear out of it. The fashion business really was set up as this sort of food chain with the designers on top and the discount merchants on the bottom. But that's all been flattened out. One of the things that's killing that business is it is no longer important to go scout out what's going on in Milan or Paris or Tokyo, because it's going to be on the Internet within moments of people walking down the cat walk. It is a critical factor in the re-trenching that you're seeing in the fashion business right now because the fashion part of the business is just frightening. The hierarchy is gone.

Zara is an incredible success story. The company is able to get fashion into stores in just two weeks, from design concept to stock in stores, while other retailers take six to nine months! The company has established a brand identity and loyal customers without any advertising.

In 1975, Amancio Ortega, a clothier, and José Maria Castellano, a visionary IT professional, recognized the difficulty of predicting fashion trends and matching supply with demand. Together they developed and implemented a revolutionary business model to resolve the problem. Zara, the apparel manufacturer and retailer that they formed, is now the largest member of the Inditex Group, based in La Coruña, Spain. In 2000, sales reached $2.3 billion, of which Zara accounted for about 80 percent. Ortega believed that, in the future, clothing would be looked upon as a perishable commodity. Castellano believed that information flow was key to an industry that revolved around rapidly changing customer desires. Together they created a network of real-time information flowing between the customers, retailers, suppliers, manufacturers, distributors, and head office. Production was not triggered by forecasting and guesswork but by actual customer demand. This enabled Zara to respond quickly and accurately to changes in customer preferences.

Fashion retailers have long procurement lead times with buyers placing orders based on their predictions of what will be in fashion six to nine months in advance. To drive costs down, retailers outsource manufacturing offshore to Asia and Latin America where labor is cheap. Disparate manufacturers in distant locations complicate logistics and increase the time-to-market. The end result is an inability to react quickly to emerging trends.

The "pre-season" is six to nine months before a collection rollout, when clothing is designed, material procured, and production begun. The "in-season" phase is characterized by sales at premium prices through high-end boutiques. As the season draws to a close, stock begins its discount journey from the boutique's sales racks to leading mass retailers like Sears and J.C. Penney and finally, after the season, to discounters like Wal-Mart and Target.

Fashion is a whim in transition. What is *in fashion* today may be *out of fashion* tomorrow. The fatal flaw of traditional supply chains is that they are driven by forecasts. *As no one can forecast the future accurately, this guarantees that inventories will build up at every stage within the supply chain and that retailers will only provide a crude approximation of the product mix that customers want.*

Zara's simple premise is that, "People want what they want the moment they want it."[6] The key then becomes to find out what it is that they want. While the competition suffers from slow, unreliable information flows that seldom bring the customer into the loop, Zara designers and store personnel go straight to the source, their primary target audience, wherever they "hang out": in the plazas, discos, rave halls, and schools. Designers focus on what "it" or "happening" people are wearing.

Zara designers also attend the ready-to-wear shows in Paris, New York, London, and Milan, doing quick sketches of runway models and snapping digital photos, which are e-mailed back to Spain.

It's important to recognize that fashion trends are set by blockbuster films or Madonna's latest video. In this fickle, unpredictable world, speed is of the essence. Zara is the fastest fashion retailer worldwide.

Zara manufactures all of its clothing onshore, in and around the company headquarters in northwestern Spain because, as Castellano puts it, "proximity is vital to rapid reflexes." Everything, including more than 1,160 retail stores in 34 countries, is linked to head office by information technology. In fact, all factory output is controlled by the daily sales in stores.

Having real-time sales information is not unusual today. But many retailers do not share this information with their suppliers. This in turn prevents suppliers from being able to quickly react to emerging trends.

Zara relies on its customers to define what is "hot," but they also rely on them to tell Zara when it is not. Capitalizing on a high-tech communication network, Zara stores place daily orders to their manufacturers using the Internet. Each store uses point-of-sale computers to keep close track of stock movement. Daily sales determine what is still in demand and therefore what needs to be manufactured. In other words, customer's priorities and choices are what set in motion the wheels of procurement, manufacturing, and delivery. Information pertaining to customer demands and preferences is immediately transmitted to the Zara design team so that they can quickly assess shifts in fashion trends and adjust the size and styles of the orders.

Because they control production, Zara can quickly discontinue undesirable fashions and replace them almost overnight. This constant communication greatly reduces the need to make risky fashion bets. Zara designers are in contact with the stores daily. The feedback, from customers via sales reps on styles and colors allows the company to continually fine-tune production.

Production is done in small batches and if an item does not sell, production of that item is stopped immediately. The strategy minimizes the risk of inventory buildup and it maximizes prices because very little gets remaindered. It also means that Zara can be profitable selling at prices far below those of the competition and can capture the market segment that is unwilling to pay high prices but still wants the latest fashions.

A look at the industry numbers paints a very clear picture. While traditional retailers commit an average of 60 percent of their inventory six months in advance, Zara commits only 20 percent. The following table compares the industry average stock commitments to those of Zara:

	Stock commitment (percent)			
	6 months pre-season	Start of season	In season	Sold in clearance
Industry average	60	90	10	40
Zara	20	50	50	20

Source: UBS Warburg.

Six months before the season, a normal clothing retailer will commit to buying merchandise for a larger proportion of the season than Zara will. Zara waits until close to the beginning of the season to see directions for colors and fabrics. That flexibility is key, and is why the quantity of stock Zara has to dispose of in sales is almost half that of many competitors. The promise of fast cycles and last-minute changes is clear: increased sales and fewer markdowns.

Zara's IT and logistics network enables it to keep stores supplied with fresh, trendy stock. Twice a week, a fleet of trucks leaves Zara's headquarters in La Coruña for its stores in 34 countries around the world, with small shipments for each store. (By comparison Zara's competitors send large shipments as little as once every 12 weeks.) The rigs depart, loaded with apparel, from a state-of-the-art logistics center the size of 90 football fields. Optical readers sort and distribute more than 60,000 items an hour. Because time is of the utmost importance, Zara pays to fly its shipments to all non-European destinations. This high-speed approach enables the company to deliver new shipments to stores in any country, twice a week. This deviates drastically from the traditional timetable of spring, summer, fall, and winter fashion lines. Most importantly, a constant supply of new stock entices customers to visit Zara regularly.

Creating a climate of scarcity has been one of the keys to Zara's success. Luis Blanc, an Inditex director, explains: "We want our customers to understand that if they like something, they must buy it now, because it won't be in the shops the following week." While Spanish customers have discovered this sense of urgency, Zara has found it more challenging initially to create it for UK and North American consumers. According to Castellano, when Zara opened its first UK store, shoppers would come in to browse and then leave. "They would tell our assistants that they would come back when the sales started, and we would have to explain that what they liked would not be on sale because the stock changes every week. It took a while for shoppers to understand." However, UK customers did catch on, so much so that devout clientele now form long lines at Zara stores on designated delivery days, a phenomenon known as "Zaramania." Shop assistants complain that they rarely have time to put the newly received merchandise on the racks because customers dive right into the boxes as soon as they hit the floor. Amazingly, this popularity has been achieved with minimal advertising. Zara spends about 0.3 percent of sales[7] on marketing compared with an industry average of 4–5 percent. Instead, they rely on word of mouth and prime store locations.

Because Zara has its finger on the pulse when it comes to changes in trends, the retail stores attract a trend-conscious crowd. A survey by *Vogue* revealed that it is the favourite store of Parisian mesdemoiselles. According to an article in *The Times*, "Fashionistas swear by it [Zara]."[8] Dylan Bierk who works with Ford Models in New York, and appears on a popular US TV show, points out "I just bought a coat and there were only 10 of them so that you know that not everyone else is going to be wearing what you are wearing. Not like a Gap or Banana Republic." Like the Beanie Baby phenomenon in the US, Zara will create unique styles and limit production so as to guarantee its clientele feel unique and special in wearing Zara fashion.

The Times has ranked Zara at the very top of its list of the 25 most dynamic forces shaping fashion worldwide. Susie Forbes, the deputy editor of British *Vogue*, calls herself a "disciple."

Inditex's profit margins are the best in the industry. While Zara spends 15 percent more to produce garments in Europe as opposed to Asia or Latin America, the company spends nothing on advertising, has little to no inventory costs, and has to discount half as much inventory as competitors. Zara's business model has proven that real-time manufacturing, flexibility and JIT inventory is more important than cheap labor.

Zara's success is reflected in its numbers. The following table compares figures from the financial statements of Inditex (Zara accounts for 80 percent of its revenues) and its two most comparable competitors: the Gap, one of North America's leading clothing store chains, and Hennes & Mauritz (H&M), one of Europe's leading clothing store chains:

	Inditex 2000	Gap 2000	H&M 2000
Inventory turnover ratio	6.0	5.1	3.7
Days' sales in inventory	61	71	98
Gross profit margin (%)	51	37	51
Operating profit margin (%)	10	7	8

Inditex's operating profit is 25 percent higher than H&M's and 42 percent higher than the Gap's. Because Zara can provide its customers with what they want, when they want it, Zara achieves faster inventory turns, can operate with less inventory, sell it at lower prices, and yet achieve a higher operating profit margin. According to Inditex income statements, consolidated post-tax income increased by 35 percent between January 31, 1999 and January 31, 2000, and by 27 percent between January 31, 2000 and January 31, 2001. This latter figure is impressive given the global economic downturn of late 2000 and 2001.

Inditex is now the world's third largest clothing retailer. Within the first few minutes of its initial public offering (IPO) in 2000, Inditex shares shot up 26 percent, despite the dismal climate for IPOs everywhere. Amancio Ortega Gaon's 60 percent share of the company was worth $6 billion, making him the richest man in Spain and the second richest man in fashion (after Bernard Arnault of LVMH, the French fashion giant).

With its proven business model, Zara has been expanding around the globe. In 1989, the company opened its first US store in New York. As of September 2001, Zara had five stores in New York, one in New Jersey and four in Canada (two in Vancouver and one each in Toronto and Montreal). Plans for expansion are ongoing at a time when many competitors have been forced to close stores. In 2001, German clothier C&A (Clemens and August) pulled out of the British market following disastrous losses, and Britain's Marks & Spencer closed all its stores in mainland Europe. In July 2001, the Gap cut 10 percent of its US workforce.

In any situation where one competitor has a delay in its ordering system and the other is working in real-time I can guarantee, over time, which one will win? It doesn't matter how much you care about your customer or how good you are at predicting the future or how much you care about your employees – the delay is killer. The success of Zara's business model has forced competitors to re-evaluate their ways of doing business.

While many retailers focus their sights on playing catch up, Zara continues to reap the benefits of having the foresight to build its organization around meeting two key objectives: creating fashion ideas that cater to its customers' fast-changing tastes, and to get those ideas from the design room to the stores in record time. As Zara continues to grow profitably it is taking market share from its rivals who are not working in real-time.

BROADBAND PREDICTIONS

Broadband access is one of the key enablers of the digital economy. The backbone of the Internet is run on fibre-optic networks. Today one strand of fibre can carry close to one terabit of data per second (1 terabit = 1,000,000,000,000 bits). Data traffic has grown exponentially and by 2001 exceeded voice traffic across telecom networks. A report by J.P. Morgan predicts that IP (Internet proto-

DVD Movie Download (7.81 Gbytes)

	Minutes	Hours	Days
Modem 56 Kbps	18,595.2	309.9	12.9
ISDN 128 Kbps	8,135.4	135.6	5.6
Cable modem 1.5 Mbps	694.4	11.6	0.5
DS-1 1.54 Mbps	674.4	11.2	0.5
FedEx	600.0	10.0	0.4
DSL 8.5 Mbps	122.5	2.0	0.1
OC-3 155 Mbps	6.7	0.1	0.0
OC-12 622 Mbps	1.7	0.0	0.0

to move it from New York to London

Figure 5.2 Time taken to transfer a DVD movie. Source: Worldwide Packets.

col) traffic will grow to 82 percent of all network traffic by 2005.[9] In Canada, the IP market is predicted to grow by 40–60 percent annually from 2000 to 2003, according to a report by NBI/Michael Sone.[10]

What is driving growth is the streaming and downloading of video and audio files. Figure 5.2 shows how bandwidth affects downloading times of a 7.81 gigabyte file

File-sharing programs such as Morpheus radically increased bandwidth demand as users share not just songs but video clips and whole movies. In fact, Napster was banned from use on many college and university campuses because the bandwidth demands it placed on the networks were so high.

In August 2000, a Gartner study of 50 wired US campuses showed that 40 percent had banned Napster. Universities' networks were created for academic purposes, and in some cases Napster was siphoning off 75 percent of the bandwidth.[11]

Individuals and organizations seem to have an infinite appetite for bandwidth. In August 2001, a one megabyte cable connection was considered fast for a home user, but with new applications like streaming video, video on demand, and VoIP (voice over IP), the projections are that by 2005, 30.7 percent of North American households will have a high-speed Internet connection, according to

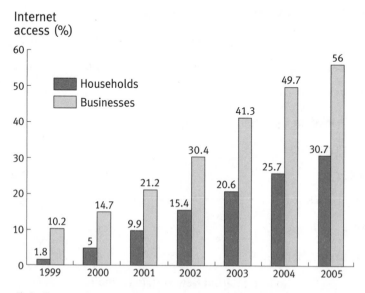

Figure 5.3 Percentage of US households and businesses with broadband Internet access. Source: Jupiter Media Matrix, August 2001.

Jupiter Media Metrix. Figure 5.3 shows the predicted growth of broadband Internet in the US. Bandwidth demand will continue to grow exponentially as more businesses and home users sign up for high-speed services.

THE LAST MILE PROBLEM

There is a roadblock to the exponential growth of bandwidth. There is an excess supply of fiber *between* North American cities but a lack *within* cities. As of August 2001, more than 90 percent of buildings in North America are not yet equipped with fiber optics. In the industry this is known as the "last mile" problem.

The roadblock to building this last mile onramp to the digital highway is asphalt. The traditional way to lay fiber is to rip up the road with a backhoe, lay cable, and fill in the trench. The result is ongoing construction, traffic congestion, noise pollution, disruptions to storefront businesses, and higher road maintenance costs.

The City of Vancouver estimates that road life is shortened by 30 percent when roads are dug up and that it spends $500,000 a year in extra time and cost to work around telecom cables when repairing sewers and water services.[12]

With telecom deregulation in Canada, a large number of service providers are competing to provide access to customers, and this is causing problems for municipalities because each service provider wants to lay its own fiber network.

With so many different companies wanting to lay fiber, all at different times and in different locations, some municipalities have responded by putting moratoriums on tearing up roads. In Toronto, after a road has been resurfaced the moratorium is generally three years, and five years on roads that have been reconstructed.

Other municipalities are forcing what is known as "joint builds." When one telco or utility wants to tear up a street, it must contact and coordinate with every other service provider so they can all take advantage of the opportunity. This in turn adds complexity and slows the process of laying fiber within cities, meaning customers experience lengthy delays in getting service.

For carriers, joint builds are not advantageous as all parties involved must build on the same route, at the same time, even if additional fiber is not required at that time. Joint builds force carriers to make potentially unnecessary capital outlays in the hope that future customer demand will justify the up-front expenditures.

Because of these challenges, and because municipal governments are not known for moving quickly, it takes an average of three months to get a permit.

The response from many telecom providers has been to spend more time asserting their rights by taking municipalities and regulatory bodies to court to force them to grant permission faster.

REINVENTING THE RULES

One US company has been able to reduce the time it takes to lay fiber optic cable by almost 90 per cent, by reinventing the rules. The Dublin, Ohio-based Ca-botics lays fiber-optic cable using robots in the sewer system, which eliminates lengthy construction, road damage, traffic disruption and high cost. While typical open trench construction lays only 100–150 meters of cable a day, a robot can lay up to 800 meters a day, up to eight times faster. In addition, Ca-botics only requires a crew of three to run the robot while the traditional approach requires a crew of six or more.

The cable-laying robot is about 1.8 meters long and is equipped with five video cameras to monitor operations and is fed into the sewer system through manholes. It can operate in pipes ranging from 200 millimeters to 1200 millimeters (8–47 inches) in diameter and is operated from a control vehicle via a 200-metre long cable. Once cable has been fed into the sewer system, the robot, using a diamond bit, drills holes in the pipe ceiling and fixes the cable to the roof at three-foot intervals using tie-bolts. The robot can access drainage systems directly into buildings, allowing the company to make connections to buildings without tearing up sidewalks.

The robotic technology is attractive to municipalities because it allows them to build high-speed data communications – which attracts business – without tearing up streets and disrupting businesses and residents.

And getting a permit is a lot faster. Instead of applying for a permit for each job separately, Ca-botics negotiates a master sewer access agreement with a municipality. A robot can complete a project in days, compared to weeks with conventional excavation methods. The result of this innovative approach is that the company can respond to a customer faster, taking as little as 23 hours from finalization of the request to completion of installation. Compare this to traditional telcos, which take on average 30 days, and in worst-case scenarios have been known to take three to six months.

Customers of traditional telcos are often frustrated with lengthy delays in dealing to get high-speed access. The robotic technology offered a strategic advantage – a reliable way to lay fiber that is less intrusive, and would motivate municipalities to work with cabling companies as opposed to viewing them as the enemy.

Ca-botics licenses the technology from Robotics Cabling GmbH Kabel-verlegung (RCC) in Germany. RCC is a joint venture between Berlinger Wasserbetriebe (BWB, Berliner Water Authority), Marubeni Corp (Japan), Marubeni Germany and Nippon Hume Corp. (Japan). The technology was first developed in Japan in the 1990s to build a fiber optic network for the G7 summit.

MORE THAN ONE APPROACH

There is always more than on approach. Intelligent fiber companies are now buying bandwidth during national radio frequency auctions, allowing them to immediately provide customers with broadband access where fiber is temporarily unavailable. High bandwidth wireless radio can serve as a long-term solution, or a temporary one while before fiber is laid. A radio dish is installed on the top of the client's building and pointed directly at a receiving dish. With a very narrow and focused beam the signal is only given enough power to reach the receiver, which means a single frequency can be used by hundreds of clients in the same city and can be used in cities all across the country.

MEASURE OF SPEED

Return on Invested Capital
Return on invested capital (ROIC) is a critical measure of speed and is more important than other financial measures. To understand in a general way what ROIC measures, think about McDonald's restaurants.

The first McDonald's restaurant, built by the McDonald brothers in 1940, was only open for lunch and dinner. Ray Kroc opened the first McDonald's franchise in 1954, then bought the rights to McDonald's in 1961 from the brothers.

In 1973, the company introduced the Egg McMuffin, its first breakfast menu item. Opening for breakfast increased McDonald's revenue with little or no additional capital investment. The only additional costs were some operating costs and variable costs. In this way, the operation was made more efficient. Opening for breakfast increased the chain's ROIC.

In 1975, McDonald's opened its first "drive-thru" in Sierra Vista, Arizona. This increased the location's ROIC, because for slight incremental costs to modify the existing building, the restaurant could increase the sales for the particular location.

In 2001, more than 60 percent of McDonald's US sales were through drive-thrus, meaning that McDonald's has more than doubled its sales without having to double the size of its parking lots, the square footage of eating areas, or even expand washrooms, because when customers drive through, they provide their own seating and use washrooms elsewhere.

Increasing speed of transactions increases ROIC. McDonald's has reduced the average length of a drive-thru transaction from 170 seconds to 130 seconds in 2001. The company is now testing ways to make drive-thrus cash-free. At four McDonald's drive-thrus near the Orange County tollway, in California, McDonald's customers' orders are automatically charged to their FasTrak highway toll transponder pass. Not digging around for money shaves at least 10 seconds off every drive-thru customer with a pass. That adds up for a restaurant where 70 percent of the business is drive-thru and more than half of the customers have FasTraks. The program has been so successful that by 2004 the company will expand to 50 stores in the western Unites States. Two McDonald's drive-thrus on Long Island are letting customers use their tollway E-ZPasses to pay for food, and nine stores in Chicago are letting customers use their Mobil Speedpasses. In 2001, the company announced plans to expand the program to more than 400 restaurants in the Chicago area.

McDonald's Express is another strategy aimed at increasing ROIC. It is a trimmed-down version of a traditional restaurant that are typically placed in high traffic pedestrian locations such as bus and train stations. McDonald's Express typically offers a limited seated area and menu. Again this strategy offers a way to increase volume sales with limited capital investment.

Finally, being open 24 hours a day is another strategy to increase ROIC.

ROIC

In uncertain times, strengthening the ability to generate cash is key. ROIC shows exactly how much profit is generated by each dollar of capital. ROIC helps explain why companies with similar profitability and growth rates merit different premiums. Imagine two companies with identical earnings ($10 million/year) and growth rate (10 percent/year) but Company A needs only $5 million in capital while company B needs $20 million. Company A generates $2 of profit for every $1 of capital employed, whereas B generates only 50 cents for every $1 of capital.

ROIC doesn't receive the same attention as earnings per share (EPS), return on equity (ROE), the price-to-earnings ratio (P/E) or earnings before interest, taxes, depreciation and amortization (EBITDA). One reason: you cannot obtain ROIC straight out of financial statements.

ROIC is an unbiased measure of how much value a company creates. It measures the profitability of their core operations, unlike EPS or earnings which includes investment income.

$$\text{ROIC} = \text{Net operating profits after taxes}[13]/\text{invested capital}[14]$$

Net operating profits after taxes (NOPAT), the numerator, is perhaps the best metric to measure the cash generated by operating activities. It is better than net income because it excludes items such as investment income, goodwill amortization, and interest expense, which are non-operating in nature.

ROIC encourages a company to minimize its invested, or tied-up, capital by keeping inventory and accounts receivable as low as possible and accounts payable as high as possible. Focusing on ROIC has prompted Dell to collect its accounts receivable faster and shrink inventories, reducing the risk of obsolete products.

Economic value added (EVA) measures the difference between the ROIC and the cost of capital. A positive EVA indicates that value has been created for shareholders, while a negative EVA signifies that value has been lost. EVA is a more reliable measure of performance than earnings per share (EPS) because EPS says nothing about the cost of generating those profits.

There's a direct statistical correlation between ROIC and market capitalization. A study by Credit Suisse First Boston analysts shows that a high ROIC leads to high rates of stock-market appreciation. The study focused on media companies. "A television company's market valuation has a 71 percent likelihood of rising at a rate comparable to its estimated ROIC. In radio, the correlation is an even higher 76 percent. EBITDA, on the other hand, was predictive of nothing statistically."

EBITDA gives a better measure of a company's growth potential than looking at net earnings. EBITDA, another name for operating cash flow, measures how much cash a company generates before factoring in debt costs. It also comes before such non-cash charges as depreciation of equipment and amortization of intangible assets like goodwill.

WHY ROIC IS CRITICAL TO DELL

For the fiscal year 2001, which ended February 2, 2001, Dell's ROIC was a staggering 355 percent. Which means that for every dollar of capital investment, the company generated $3.55 of profit. Returns like that are unheard of in the computer industry. Dell's ROIC in 1997 was 85 percent; in 1998, 186 percent; in 1999, 195 percent, and in 2000 it was 243 percent.

Dell's ROIC is higher than any other computer maker because it can turn its inventory faster than any competitor. It explains why Dell has done so well even as PC prices drop rapidly.

In 1992, Tom Meredith became CFO of Dell and immediately refocused the company from "growth for growth's sake" to growth, profitability, and liquidity. The metric he used was ROIC.

The company focused on what Dell calls the cash conversion cycle, which consists of inventory, payables, receivables, and cash flow from operations. The compensation packages of the company's top 500 managers were based on ROIC as well as growth. Training videos and newsletters spread the message throughout the company, stressing the importance of ROIC.

Dell's direct model is well suited to maximizing the cash conversion cycle. Because Dell sells direct to customers, it carries little or no finished-goods inventory. Because it buys components on a just-in-time basis, there is very little parts inventory, and because customers often pay Dell faster than it pays suppliers, cash flow is positive. With little inventory, reductions in component costs can be passed on immediately to customers, improving Dell's competitive position. This is particularly important in an industry where component prices on average fall by one percent a week.

In 2001, Dell had only five days of inventory on hand. Dell's build-to-order philosophy has a number of advantages. By selling direct, Dell eliminates middlemen in the value chain, eliminating mark ups at every point, and wasteful duplication.

"Inventory and accounts receivable are risks; if you don't have any, you don't have any risk," notes Michael Dell.

In 1998, Dell was paid, on average, eight days before it had to pay its suppliers. That's a cash conversion cycle of –8 days. Compare that to Compaq's 15 days or Micron's 14. The industry average is 10 days – a full 18 days off Dell's breakneck pace. It's riskless growth because Dell uses customer capital to finance its growth.

The problem for Dell's competitors is their reliance on the traditional supply chain. While Dell has only five days of inventory on hand, its competitors have up to 80 days when you consider parts, unfinished and finished goods at manufacturing, and the inventory at distributors, wholesalers, department store warehouses, and on the sales floor of retailers.

Given that PC component prices fall on average by one percent a week, if competitors have a total of 12 weeks of inventory in the supply chain, this puts them at a 12 percent disadvantage to Dell. It also means the customer doesn't get the latest technology.

Every time a traditional PC maker wants to lower prices, it has to price-protect product in the supply chain. PC makers compensate dealers for reductions in suggested selling price. This freezes PC makers from lowering prices more frequently because it creates a financial penalty.

By contrast, Dell advertises new configurations the moment they become available, thus reinforcing the perception that it has the latest technology. Dell can change pricing daily, instantly passing on falling component prices to consumers. When trying to understand the importance of ROIC it helps to think of your products as fresh fish – unless you sell it quickly it spoils. Dell has only five days of inventory on hand. Focusing on ROIC forces a company to increase inventory turns, decrease inventory, and apply JIT delivery and manufacturing philosophies.

Dell's direct sales model gives the company an intimacy and understanding of the customer that indirect competitors don't have. In the late 1990s, Dell noticed a sudden increase in customers ordering two-gigabyte hard drives instead of one-gig drives. Dell immediately called its supplier and shifted its order to two-gig drives. No problem, said the supplier, which then called a Dell competitor and offered a big discount on one-gig drives. That competitor grabbed the offer. When the one-gig PCs hit the channel 12 weeks later, the market for them was dead. The competitor lost market share and took a huge write-off.[15]

This example highlights why when two companies are competing — the one working in real-time always has the advantage, while the other continually risks being blindsided.

Dell focuses on attracting experienced computer buyers because first-time buyers place a heavier demand on support.

Online ordering improves order accuracy, reduces lead-time, and allows Dell employees to engage in richer, more valuable activities. The Web even has an impact on telephone sales. A Dell customer who prices a system online is 1.5 times more likely to buy a computer than if he or she only dealt with a telephone sales rep.

Because of Dell's cost advantage, when PC sales began slumping in early 2001, Dell was able to declare a price war in February 2001. While this may appear counter-intuitive, having a lower cost structure gives the company flexibility in strategy. By launching a price war, Dell has been able to steal market share from its competitors in 2001. As a result of the price war, most PC makers have been losing money in 2001, but Dell has remained profitable, although its margins have been hurt.

SOUTHWEST AIRLINES

Southwest Airlines' market capitalization of more than $13 billion in November 2001 is greater than that of any airline in the world *and almost double* that of the four biggest US carriers – United, American, Delta, and Northwest – combined![16]

Why? Southwest has the highest ROIC of any US airline.

Southwest squeezes more flying time out of an average day and therefore more revenue out of each aircraft. Jets are on the ground 20 minutes between flights versus an hour for the typical hub operation used by competitors. If Southwest averaged one hour to turn around every flight it would need another 124 planes to fly the same number of flights a day. Southwest flies only one type of aircraft and has the world's largest fleet of 737s. Using only one airplane type considerably simplifies maintenance, spare parts, crew training, and operations. Southwest studiously avoids the complexities of the multi-aircraft fleets that often sharply increase costs at other carriers. As a result, Southwest's costs are about 40 percent lower than competitors.

To increase speed, Southwest also foregoes meals and reserved seating.

Southwest began in 1971 with three planes serving three Texas cities. In 2001 Southwest had more than 350 airplanes, serving 57 cities with more than 2,700 daily flights. The company was profitable in its second year and has been the only major airline to be profitable every year since.

Southwest was the first airline to establish a home page on the Internet. With more than 2.7 million subscribers to its weekly Click-N-Save e-mails, 30 percent of Southwest's 2000 revenue ($1.7 billion) was generated by online bookings. Southwest accounts for 14 percent of online ticket purchases, more than any other travel site except Travelocity.com.

By ensuring the company has the highest ROIC of any major US airline, Southwest remained profitable in the wake of the events on September 11, 2001. Southwest's advantage became even more apparent as security measures exponentially increased the likelihood of delays for spoke and hub carriers.

Spoke-and-hub carriers center their operations in one or more airports – called hubs – and offer connecting flights to other locations, called spokes. In most cases, customers will not be able to get a direct flight between two cities with a hub and spoke carrier (unless they live in a hub city). Instead they must first fly to a hub and take a connecting flight to their final destination.

Back to W. Edwards Deming's point that the systems and structures dictate performance. Southwest will continue to grow, gain market share and dominate other carriers in terms of market capitalization because its ROIC dictates only operating point-to-point routes.

ROIC: A MEASURE OF SYNERGY

Danny Murphy is a businessman living in PEI, Canada's smallest province (0.1 percent of Canada's land mass) with a population of only 139,000 people. Murphy owns the franchises for Tim Hortons and Wendy's for the island.

Tim Hortons is a coffee and donut shop chain with more than 1,900 stores in Canada and 120 locations in key US markets as of 2001. Wendy's is the third largest hamburger chain in the world with sales of $7.7 billion in 2000 and nearly 5,800 restaurants in the US, Canada, and international markets.

PEI is a province of small communities. In 1989, Murphy bought a piece of land on spec in Montague, a town of only 3,000 people. He began asking Tim Hortons executives for permission to open a store in the town. Until then the company had only opened franchises in towns of more than 10,000 people, but preferred a population of 12,000–15,000 to support a franchise. Executives laughed at Murphy's request, but Murphy persisted for three years until the corporation allowed him to proceed.

Normally franchise chains buy the land, construct the building, and rent it to the franchise owner, who buys the franchise license and equipment package. Because Tim Hortons felt the location would fail, it required Murphy to buy the land and build the store.

Because he had to take all the risk, Murphy began asking how he could make the location more successful in such a small town. He began to think about creating a combination store that would house both a Wendy's and Tim Hortons. In this way the franchises would share common facilities, such as the parking lot, building, washroom, and dining area. Amortizing these fixed costs against two franchises would double the store's chance of success.

In the early 1990s, Wendy's was eager to expand and was aggressively opening new locations. Wendy's quickly approved Murphy's unusual request to build a 4,000 square foot combo facility. Tim Hortons agreed because Murphy was taking all the risk and because they probably thought, according to Murphy, "Who is going to see it anyway? It's in Montague, PEI after all."

Murphy recalls that Tim Hortons co-founder Ron Joyce said at the time, "I have been in this industry a long time. What you are doing goes against every rule in the restaurant business. You're wasting your money. It won't work."

The restaurant opened in March 1992 and the grand opening in June 1992 was attended by the CEOs of both companies, Ron Joyce of Tim Hortons and Dave Thomas of Wendy's.

Surprising Synergy

Once the store opened, Murphy saw the synergy. Tim Hortons does 65 percent of its business between 6:00 a.m. and 11:00 a.m., whereas Wendy's doesn't even open its doors until 10:30 a.m. Wendy's peak periods are lunch and dinner and Tim Hortons clientele fill in the slow periods in between.

A combo store shares staff. For instance, the Tim Hortons baker who starts at 8:00 a.m. baking donuts, at 11:30 puts on a Wendy's uniform and becomes a grill man cooking hamburgers for the two-hour lunch rush period, and then goes back to his Tim Hortons responsibilities. A Wendy's franchise requires 15 employees to work the lunchtime rush but by 2:00 p.m. needs only seven people. Combo stores can hire employees more easily in a tight labor market because they can offer employees more eight-hour shifts than stand-alone stores. Stand-alone stores have to have a number of part-time employees to staff up for rush periods.

Word of the combo format success began to spread among Tim Hortons franchisees in Eastern Canada and other Tim Hortons/Wendy's combos began opening in Moncton, New Brunswick, and then New Glasgow, Nova Scotia. It was a fantastic vehicle for Wendy's to grow and these combos started popping up all over. Finally, one opened in Toronto.

What the combo strategy did in big cities was incredible. A prime piece of real estate in a city may cost $800,000. Tim Hortons couldn't afford to buy it. Wendy's couldn't afford to buy it. Even McDonald's couldn't afford to buy it. But two franchises together could afford it. So using the combo strategy, Tim Hortons and Wendy's worked together to beat McDonald's because they could afford very expensive real estate in prime locations by sharing the cost. It gave them an advantage in development. It is interesting to note that this benefit only became apparent to both companies once they tried combos in a big city.

Ron Joyce was thinking of succession and was spending more time with the Wendy's head office in Ohio because there were so many combos. One day he planted the idea of Wendy's buying Tim Hortons and in 1995, Wendy's did just that in a deal worth $425 million.[17] At the time, Tim Hortons had 1,197 stores and Wendy's had 4,667.

By selling to Wendy's, Joyce ensured the future of the Tim Hortons chain because Wendy's has begun expanding the Tim Hortons concept aggressively in the United States. Tim Hortons now accounts for about a third of Wendy's pre-tax income.[18]

Combo locations increase Wendy's and Tim Hortons security and reduce the company's chance of being blindsided. By drawing on two distinct clientele, combo locations increase the company's diversity of clientele thereby increasing security. A recession may adversely affect hamburger chains, but not coffee shops. Similarly a ban on importing any beef into North America would affect all hamburger chains but not affect coffee shops.

Secondly by being able to afford real estate that even McDonald's, the largest restaurant chain in the world, can't afford, Wendy's and Tim Hortons combos can blindside their competition.

RETOOLING AND RETRAINING IN REAL-TIME

With so much change occurring so quickly, how can individuals and organizations keep up with the speed and volume of change? In this fast-changing world, high-tech employees need 12 days of training every year just to stay current. That is predicted to grow to 32 days a year by 2010.[19] Companies like Cisco and Nortel Networks introduce new products every 45 days – and these products have a lifecycle of only nine months before they are substantially changed or relaunched. A traditional training program takes a year to develop, pilot, test, refine, and roll out to thousands of people across the organization in hundreds of different locations. eLearning shortens that cycle to weeks, and can train 100,000 on the same day.

If you learn something but don't use it within 48 hours it is likely that you will forget it. Given this 48-hour use it or lose it principle, why do universities engage in four-year degree programs? Instead of just-in-case training and development, corporations are embracing just-in-time learning, and embracing eLearning as a way to shorten the time-to-competence. Companies provide just the information that is needed, *when* it is needed, *where* it is needed to *whoever* needs it. John Coné, vice-president of Dell Learning, notes, "More and more of what we know today is disposable. So don't fill up your short-term or long-term memory with stuff that doesn't matter. Just know how to get it when you need it." Companies employing eLearning are able to more quickly adapt to this fast-changing environment.

COMPETITION FOR TALENT

In 2000 there was a shortage of more than 720,000 IT workers in North America – and this shortage is growing by 25 percent a year. Globally, the shortage exceeds one million IT workers. How can companies compete in the war for talent? eLearning will grow in part because time-to-competence has become a bottleneck for most organizations. How can companies accelerate learning?

A staggering 70 percent of *Fortune 1000* CEOs say that finding and keeping qualified people was the number one barrier to sustaining growth, according to a PriceWaterhouse-Coopers study![20] Never before has human capital been so important. Finding, developing, and keeping knowledgeable workers will be the key to success and growth. Any strategies that will shorten the time-to-competence, the amount of time required to get up to speed in hot skill areas, will be rapidly embraced. While the recession in 2001 created higher unemployment than at any other time since the early 1990s, and job shortages in hot skill areas are not so severe, the underlying drivers of eLearning remain. How can organizations accelerate learning?

For a full discussion of eLearning, read Chapter 9 of *The Learning Paradox*.

eLEARNING BENEFITS

- *Lowers costs.* Up to 70 percent of the cost of traditional training are travel and accommodation expenses.
- *Faster learning.* eLearning takes up to 70 percent less time to convey the same amount of information because pre-course testing eliminates all material the student has already mastered.
- *Scales.* Can train thousands of people in a single day online. In-class doesn't scale.
- *Triple the return on investment (ROI).* Training developed for external customers can be used for employees and supply chain partners. Cisco sells $500 million of online learning to customers each year. Typically the courses focus on the company's products, services, markets, and Cisco product certification. The company achieves three times the ROI of traditional training investments, because it offers the same eLearning courses to employees and channel partners. As eLearning course costs are overwhelmingly in the up-front development, each incremental user has only a small marginal cost. Cisco not only recoups course development costs with customers, but eLearning is a profit center. Cisco then gets to use the same courses, essentially for free, for employee and partner training. This means the company gets triple the ROI on traditional in-class courses, because in-class course don't scale at minimal cost.
- *Employee communication.* In 2000, Cisco acquired a company, on average, every 16 days. In buying these companies, Cisco was really buying intellectual capital. Integrating people is essential or there will be high turnover.
- *Managing distributed intellectual capital.* eLearning is essential to Cisco because of the pace and complexity of the industry and because of a distributed knowledge-base, all knowledge is no longer kept in any one building. How can organizations manage and leverage the distributed human capital across multiple organizations? eLearning is the answer.

- *Real-time response.* When Cisco CEO John Chambers has an important message, everyone in the company has a link that takes them to a served video, audio, or a slide show. The message is unfiltered, and can't be changed by personal agenda. All 40,000 people get the same message.

CONCLUSION

Technology now allows every individual in every part of an organization to access information in real-time. The impact will be to improve quality, reduce cycle time, reduce inventory, and increase profitability. This reduces the chance of an organization being blindsided as individuals and teams can recognize and respond to challenges and opportunities in the market faster.

The real-time era applies to all organizations in all industries. The Zara and precision farming examples highlight how even companies most associated with the old economy are benefiting from real-time focus.

The days of making decisions based on quarterly results are over. Companies that fail to adopt real-time systems increase the chance of being blindsided, while those that become real-time enterprises are more likely to blindside their competitors. Working in real-time will increasingly differentiate the corporate leaders from the losers.

REFLECTIONS

- What can you identify as early warning signals (leading indicators) that would indicate a shift within the dominant business paradigm within your
  - Industry?
  - Company?
  - Department?
  - What external non–traditional benchmarks could you seek?
- How would applying ROIC as a key metric for success change operations
  - In your organization?
  - In your industry?
- How welcome is contrarian thinking within your organization?
- What beliefs or attitudes could hold you back from being a contrarian within your organization?

CHAPTER 6

Customer Relationship Management

Why is CRM so important? How can CRM increase profitability? Reduce the chance of being blindsided? And increase the chance your organization will blindside your competitors? What are the best CRM practices? What are the trends, technology and market strategies that are driving CRM? How is CRM best implemented? What are some of the dangers of implementation?

Customer relationship management (CRM) is *the* hot new buzzword. CRM is the implementation (software, training and systems) to support the theory of one-to-one marketing. Here's why:

- Lexus sales are 2 percent of Toyota's sales but 33 percent of the company's profit.[1]
- In the UK, the top 6 percent of cola drinkers drink 60 percent of all cola sold there.[2]
- Business travelers account for only 8–10 percent of air passengers but produce over 40 percent of airline revenue.[3]
- It costs five times more to attract a new customer than to retain an existing one.[4]

Don Peppers and Martha Rogers,[5] authors of *The One to One Future*, use a great example. Imagine that a car rental company hosts a customer appreciation event at a 40,000-seat baseball stadium. Every customer invited turns up, filling the stadium. The company's best customers, those who rented 25 percent of all vehicle rentals, would represent 0.02 percent of attendees or just 80 people!

In other words, the 80 best customers do one-third of the business of the remaining 39,920 added together!

Most companies can't even name their customers, let alone identify their most important ones. So to communicate with their best customers, most companies in this situation would take a mass marketing approach, talking to all customers at the same time. So within the stadium they would advertise on the stadium monitor and make public announcements.

If the company was using CRM, it would identify the 80 most important customers, and it likely would not hold the event. Instead it would spend more money providing value-added services to those 80 customers. In this way, the company could ensure it retained its most profitable customers and prevent a competitor from luring them away.

Because most companies can't identify their most important customers, they have to put on customer appreciation events for all customers. So, in holding a baseball customer appreciation event, it is unlikely the company would have a CRM system and be able to name its most important customers. A sharp competitor, however, hearing about the event, could work to identify the customers of its competitor that would likely be the most valuable and send in 80 sales reps to sit beside these frequent renters during the game, buy them a beer and a hot dog, and find out what it would take to win their business. At the end of the game, the competitor could walk out with 25 percent of the company's business and the non-CRM company would not even know what had happened.

The car rental company would be left to service 39,920 customers but with 25 percent less revenue.

WHY CRM IS SO IMPORTANT

Imagine that I forget my mother-in-law's birthday until the actual day arrives. In a panic, I call a Custom Florist and have some flowers sent. Next year, three weeks before my mother-in-law's birthday, I receive an e-mail from Custom Florist reminding me of the date and proposing three different floral options with three different prices. What florist am I most likely to buy from?

If the florist was highly proactive, sales staff would have posed as a market survey firm doing a survey on favorite flowers, called my mother-in-law and found out what her favorite flowers were and why. The florist would then e-mail me three options, in the order of my mother-in-law's preference with associated costs. The e-mail would finish with "send us back which option you'd like and we'll bill your credit card." Is this adding value?

A highly proactive florist would call me to find out who my family, friends, business partners, and staff were and their birthdays, anniversaries, and other important dates. If I was unable to provide this information the florist would research it for me, at the same time finding out their favorite flowers, wines, chocolates, etc. The florist would then send me reminders of the dates and appropriate gift suggestions.

The majority of fresh cut flowers in North America are imported from Latin America. Imagine that due to some disease, the federal government bans the import of all flowers for six months. During this time, thousands of florists go bankrupt because most retailers don't even know the names of their customers, let alone the key dates in their lives. Custom Florists would immediately begin selling chocolates, bottles of champagne, and jewelry. During the six-month ban on floral imports, Custom Florists would thrive.

This highlights a key insight into CRM: rather than having a product and trying to find customers, Custom Florists has a relationship with customers and is working to find products and services that meet their needs.

CRM is not new. One hundred and fifty years ago, the local general merchant knew customers by name. He also knew their preferences, and stocked his store accordingly. We moved into an era of mass marketing where merchants did not even know the names or preferences of their customers. In the 21st century, technology is allowing organizations to customize the products and services they provide to customers the way the local general merchant once did.

IS $50 WORTH $7,000?

I bought a $300 inkjet printer from an electronics superstore. You know the kind. One that offers low, low prices and at the check out has a sign in big, bold letters: "Returns only accepted within 30 days of purchase. You must have all packaging and a copy of the original receipt." Because I travel so much, by the time I installed and tested the printer, and discovered that I didn't like it; it was 35 days after the purchase. I prepared myself for a fight. I was ready to be rejected by the clerk, and then appeal to the manager of the computer section, then the manager of the store, followed by the president of the company. Then I was prepared to launch a campaign with the consumer affairs reporter with the city newspaper to campaign for fairness in retailing.

I arrived at the store, looked at the 18-year-old clerk and stated my position. She asked for my phone number and after keying it into her terminal said, "Mr Harris, we will be happy to give you a refund." I was actually disappointed. I had been prepared for the fight.

By keying in my phone number, the system pulled up my customer history. She could see that I had bought $7,000 of goods from the store in the past year, and $14,000 from the chain over the last two years. She decided to give me a full refund on the spot. She knew that the $50 profit on a $300 inkjet printer wasn't worth upsetting a $7,000-a-year customer.

Now I am sure this 18-year-old had never been to Harvard and studied the complex methods of modeling the net present value of a customer over his or her lifetime. She just used common sense.

But most retailers don't know the names of their customers let alone their value to the organization. This company, however, had systems that allowed frontline staff to make important decisions in what Jan Carlson, the former president of SAS airlines, calls a "moment of truth,"[6] the 15-second window in which a service rep can either deliver or deny service to a customer.

The example highlights to me why the centralization/decentralization debate is futile. The organization had centralized information technology (IT) infrastructure decisions so that all parts of the business had a common IT platform and software so that information could be shared throughout the organization in real time. However, decisions were made decentrally.

SEAMLESS SERVICE

Customer relationship management is a philosophy, software, and process that integrates all customer information and makes it available to any employee dealing with customers. From a customer's perspective, it means there is "no wrong door," in that any employee, from any department, can help them.

Today most organizations keep information in many different silos; different departments have separate databases: accounting, call center, sales department, marketing, store locations, and the Web. Customers, however, look at a company as a single entity, and not as separate departments. Customers expect to be able to deal with anyone in the organization as though they represent the whole organization. Which means that any employee dealing with customers should be able to access a customer's up-to-date history, at any time.

COMPETING WITH WAL-MART

In 1981, Chris Zane opened his bicycle store in Brantford, a mid-sized Connecticut town, and sold $56,000 of bikes the first year. By 2001, Zane's Cycles' sales had grown to more than $5.3 million a year, despite the fact that Wal-Mart, the world's largest seller of bicycles, came to town in 1997.

Competing against Wal-Mart is a major problem for most retailers. Of the top 100 US retail discounters in business in 1976, fewer than 20 remain in existence today.

In 1983, Wal-Mart's 641 stores had sales of $4.8 billion. By 2002, Wal-Mart had grown to 4,150 stores with collective sales of more than $220 billion. Studies show that when Wal-Mart opens a store in a new town, sales for other retailers can decline significantly. Losses in hardware, jewelry, shoes, and a variety of other categories can run as high as 30 percent. How can retailers compete with Wal-Mart? Chris Zane knows how – by creating one-to-one relationships.

Years ago at a conference, Zane learned a key fact about consumers: 30 percent of customers buy based on service, 30 percent buy based on price, and the remaining 40 percent are a swing group who will fall into the group that they perceive offers the most value (see Figure 6.1).

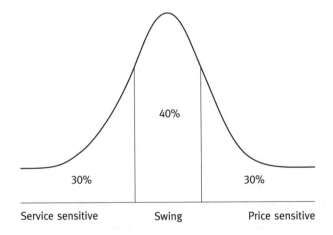

Figure 6.1

Using this philosophy, Zane knew he could beat Wal-Mart in service. By offering unparalleled service, Zane knew he would win the 30 percent of the customers who want exceptional service. He also knew the 30 percent of customers who are only price sensitive would be buying from Wal-Mart. Zane did not want these customers anyway.

"So that left the 40 percent in the middle that sways from price to service. If you can prove to those customers that service is a better deal than price, then you capture those sales. So when Wal-Mart came into the marketplace, I only focused on 40 percent swing customers."

While bikes and accessories are Zane's product, he has always known that relationship selling is his business. That's why Zane did not see Wal-Mart as a threat. Customer relationship selling, and deep customer loyalty have been critical factors in Zane's success from the beginning.

> Our lifetime, free service policy was truly to take care of the customer so that they would maintain a relationship with us. They would continue to come in, bring their bike in and get it serviced, see new products, buy accessories, look at new bikes, and eventually we'd continue to sell to them. We never look at our customers as a one-time transaction, we look at them as a lifetime commitment.

With a promise of free lifetime service, Zane collected names, addresses, and other information from 27,000 customers, and began the process of deepening relationships with each customer. For example, every year the company runs through its database identifying every customer who bought baby bike seats two years prior, and sends them a postcard promoting their line of kids' bikes.

While most direct mail campaign marketers are excited to get a one percent response rate, Zane's efforts typically result in more than 50 percent of customers who receive the post-card coming back to the shop to buy their child's first bike.

Zane once got a call from a supplier wanting to quickly sell off large-sized cycling shorts at a 50 percent discount. Zane found 150 customers in the database who recently bought large-sized clothing, offered them 30 percent off the regular price and instantly sold 60 pairs of shorts. *CRM allowed Zane to help a supplier, offer his customers a 30 percent saving while at the same time raising his margin!* This highlights how CRM enables a retailer to mine for information. Next time the supplier wants to sell some excess inventory off quickly, who is he going to call?

"It's better to build a long-term relationship," says Zane, "than try to make money on every sale."

There is one segment of customer that Zane has virtually eliminated from his business: the bike enthusiast. Intuitively you'd think this was the most profitable customer. Wrong.

Part of the problem is they're very educated in terms of how to get the best price. They're very knowledgeable in how to service their own product. They like to hang out in a store, they like to talk bikes, talk tech, and talk about the weight of a derailer and the material that a spoke is made out of. We affectionately refer to them as "spoke sniffers" because they're so involved in every little nut and bolt on the bike.

But when it comes time to make a purchase, they get on the Internet, or they go to a mail order catalogue, or they play one retailer against another to get the absolute lowest price. They tie up my staff, and they're really a drain on a company, because they come into a bike shop and they hang out, and they take your employees away from customers that want to buy product. They're very opinionated, and they'll interfere with sales transactions with customers on the floor.

Some retailers think that spoke sniffers are valuable customers, because they will buy a $3,000 bike. In order to win the sale, however, the retailer may have to lower his margin to 25 percent, and if the cost of running the store is 26 percent of sales the retailer is in fact losing money on the transaction. Zane points out that most retailers don't pay attention to this important margin issue. A CRM focus helps organizations identify their most profitable customers but also their most unprofitable ones.

Wal-Mart focuses on low prices. Chris Zane focuses on building customer lifetime loyalty because he knows his customers, can anticipate their needs, respond to unique marketing opportunities, and offer each one lifetime service because he is focused on life time value.

MAXIMIZING BENEFIT

Human nature seeks to maximize opportunity for benefit, not to maximize benefit itself. What does that mean? Well, if I am a sales rep and I have a choice between spending a day deepening my relationship with my best client, or sending out 1,000 pieces of direct mail to people I don't know, I will chose to send out the letters because 1,000 is greater than one. But in fact deepening my relationships with my best customers will yield more.

The Sufi wisdom "Why do you seek more knowledge, when you don't apply what you already know?" is powerful. The same can apply to companies and customers: "Why do you seek new customers, when you don't serve existing customers well?" If you have a leaky bathtub there are two things you can do. Increase the rate of new water into the tub so that it will fill faster, or plug the leak. It's more effective to plug the leak. The key to growth is customer retention and not just any customers, but your most profitable ones.

THE LOYALTY EFFECT

One of the most accurate descriptions of why customer loyalty is so important is in *The Loyalty Effect* by Fred Reichheld. In it, Reicheld notes, that "on average US corporations now lose half their customers in five years, half their employees in four and half their investors in less than one."[7]

"Loyalty is the absence of a better value alternative," notes Dave Nichol, who revolutionized supermarket retailing in Canada through the introduction of high-end private label products. I find this a powerful way to look at loyalty – I remain loyal to organizations that consistently provide me with the most value.

"As a customer's relationship with a company lengthens, profits rise," note Reichheld and co-author Earl Sasser.[8] "Companies can boost profits by almost 100 percent by retaining just 5 percent more of their customers."

In *The Loyalty Effect*, Reichheld uses the example of a credit card company (see Figure 6.2).[9] The cost to acquire a customer is $80 and in the first year the credit card company will only make $40. Therefore, the company suffers a net loss of $40 in the first year on newly acquired customers. Credit card companies only become profitable if newly acquired customers stay well into the second year. Acquisition costs are determined by taking the total sales and marketing expenses and dividing by the number of newly acquired customers.

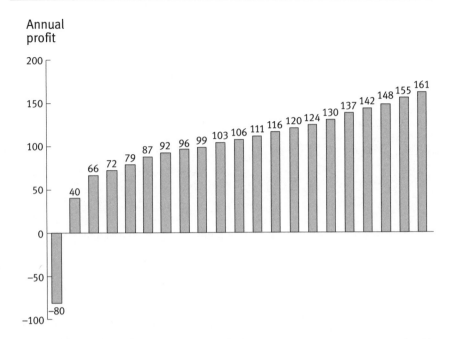

Figure 6.2 Annual profit from a credit card customer. Source: *The Loyalty Effect.*

Customers become more profitable over time because they place less burden on the organization's support (new customers place the heaviest demand on a company as they get to know how the product or service, support and invoicing work). Their net worth increases over time. Companies need to study the economics of loyalty. Segmenting their customers, and even segmenting their customer acquisition sources to determine which are profitable and which are not.

PARETO

Pareto, an Italian mathematician, coined the 80/20 rule, which states that 80 percent of a company's profit will come from 20 percent of the customers. It is important to note that not all customers are equal. But most organizations don't even know who their best customers are, and therefore have no ability to treat them differently.

If an organization treats all customers the same, the company will treat its best customers like its worst, ensuring that the organization is most vulnerable

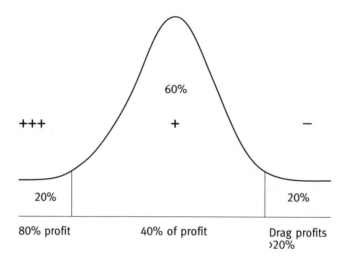

Figure 6.3 The 20/60/20 rule.

to having its most profitable customers enticed away by a competitor. Similarly, by treating its worst customers like its best, the organization guarantees it will retain all the customers it is just breaking even on, or worse yet, losing money on. In other words, treating all customers the same is a recipe for lower profitability, customer churn and ultimately bankruptcy. CRM helps organizations differentiate its customer base and treat customers differently.

I have modified the 80/20 rule to create the 20/60/20 rule, illustrated in Figure 6.3.

Twenty percent of a company's customers will generate 80 percent of the profit. The next 60 percent will generate 40 percent of the profit and the remaining 20 percent of customers will generate a loss of 20 percent.

Each of these three segments requires a different strategy: for the most profitable customers the goal is to increase intimacy by (1) deepening the relationship; (2) adding value at every step; (3) creating barriers to exit; and (4) allowing the customer to build equity with the product, service or company.

With the 60 percent of customers that represent 40 percent of the profit, the strategy should be to get a larger share of the wallet of the customer by cross selling and up selling.

For the final 20 percent of customers who are unprofitable, the goal is to reduce the cost of service and to make them profitable through automation and self-serve. We'll look at each group in turn.

MOST PROFITABLE

The most profitable 20 percent of customers generate 80 percent of a typical organization's profit. The obvious question then is: are sales reps spending 80 percent of their time with these customers? The goal here is customer intimacy. Are reps spending one-on-one quality time with your most important customers? Does the organization understand the most important points of customer service and product differentiation for these customers? It is not about getting on the golf course with them, but working to deeply understand their current and future needs. (See the section on unarticulated needs in Chapter 8.)

A key with this group is to create barriers to exit. The airlines achieve this through frequent flier programs. The more frequently you fly with an airline, the greater the benefits you receive. American Airlines' frequent flier status is based on miles. Gold or Elite status requires 25,000 miles, Platinum 50,000 miles, and Executive Platinum 100,000. The higher the status, the greater the benefits. Frequent fliers fly on their primary airline in order to re-qualify every year and receive benefits.

Another way to create a barrier to exit is to allow customers to build equity with you. I like to use Microsoft *Word*'s autocorrect feature. This feature has allowed me to create my own shorthand that has radically increased my typing speed. For instance, whenever I type "org" it automatically types "organization," or "wrt" becomes "with respect to." I can define a few characters to represent a standard letter closing. Having figured out this usage on my own, and built up a library of definitions over the years, the likelihood that I will switch to another word processing program is very low, unless the new program offers the same feature and allows me to port my preferences. *Word* allowed me to build equity with it and as a result, I get better performance as an end user and I am less likely to switch.

Air Miles is a loyalty program that rewards customers for shopping with partner businesses. Over 56 percent of Air Miles collectors say they will drive by other restaurants to get to an Air Miles restaurant. Similarly they will drive twice as far to get to a hardware sponsor than a regular store.

ADDING VALUE, BUILDING EQUITY & CREATING EXIT BARRIERS

Peppers and Rogers use a case study to highlight what I call building equity and simultaneously creating a barrier to exit. Organizations that have a large number of cellphones will typically receive a consolidated monthly bill sent to the accounting department. Centralized billing is convenient for the cellular company because it doesn't have to mail hundreds of individual bills, and it meets the account department's need for control.

Someone in accounting identifies which invoices are for the sales department, which belongs to marketing, IT and engineering, and then makes copies and sends each department its invoices. In turn, someone in each department assigns bills to individual employees to categorize calls and assign costs to different accounts, typically using spreadsheets like Microsoft *Excel*. This entire process can take hundreds of hours and isn't really adding value, but it has to be done.

Vodac, a South African cellular company, has developed a unique way to allow customers to build equity. Vodac asks its clients to send back the spreadsheets and the following month Vodac supplies the invoices electronically using the client's template. By providing billing information just the way the client wants it, Vodac saves its clients thousands of hours of non-value-added work per year. This adds significant value for customers and locks them into the relationship. Another cellular company could offer a cent less a minute for airtime but the savings would be miniscule by comparison to the cost of going back to the old accounting method.

The switching costs would be prohibitive. It is interesting to note that at the same time, Vodac has lowered the cost of serving the customer, as electronic transactions cost a fraction of paper based ones.

Credit card companies should pay heed. They have all the data of my credit card purchases in digital format, but every month they produce a paper statement and mail it to me. I then have to pay a bookkeeper to turn it back into a digital format and categorize it. This is a wasteful process, which forces organizations to spend millions of dollars annually on unnecessary bookkeeping.

This is one example where companies can add tremendous value, while at the same time lowering the cost of service.

BULK OF CUSTOMERS

Sixty percent of a company's customers will generate 40 percent of the organization's profit. The key for this group is to cross-sell and up-sell products, to increase the organization's share of the wallet. A fascinating study by the First Union Bank in Charlotte, North Carolina, cited in *The One to One Manager* by Peppers and Rogers, showed that customer attrition within the first year varies significantly by the number of products a customer has with the institution. The more products, the lesser the likelihood of defecting:[10]

> . . . at a typical US bank nearly half of the customers with only a single checking account and no other product line will leave within a year. A third of the bank's customers who have only a time deposit product, such as a CD (certificate of deposit), will leave within a year. But only 10 percent of the customers who have both a checking account and a time deposit account will leave within a year. For customers with checking, time deposit and mortgage products, annual attrition drops to just two percent, and for customers with checking, time deposit and mortgage and credit card products, the attrition rate is less than one percent.

In summary:

Products and number of products	First year churn (%)
Checking account (1)	~50
Time deposit product (1)	33
Checking and time deposit (2)	10
Checking, time deposit and mortgage (3)	2
Checking, time deposit, mortgage and credit card (4)	>1

The more products you have with a customer, the lesser the likelihood that they will defect to a competitor.

I ask seminar participants, "Is $10,000 a significant sum of money?" People invariable agree it is. Then I ask, imagine you found a house just as beautiful as your own, in the same neighborhood, but for $10,000 less than yours is worth, would you move? Most people would not. Why not? The hassle of selling your house, the commission paid on selling yours and buying the other one, the cost and hassle of moving, and setting up house in your new home would cost more than the $10,000 saving. These costs are called *switching costs*. The more products and services that a customer has with your company, the greater the switching costs, and the less likely they are to move. Switching costs are a barrier to exit.

UNPROFITABLE CUSTOMERS

Twenty percent of a company's customers will be unprofitable. The key to this group is to automate transactions, to lower the cost of doing business with this group and return customers in this category to profitable relationships. This group is likely the price-conscious group. Companies can employ three different approaches to bring this group back to profitability:

- Automate transactions to lower cost of serving these customers.
- Raise prices to make these customers profitable.
- If all else fails, get a stack of your most fearsome competitor's business cards and refer customers in this segment to them (there are exclusions to this rule discussed below).

The contrarian view to the philosophy of dumping unprofitable customers, is having systems in place that identify customers who are currently unprofitable, but have a high likelihood of being your most profitable customers in the future. Organizations should have methods for predicting which currently unprofitable customers have high lifetime value potential – these could include, for instance, the children of parents who have high net worth, which they will eventually inherit, or students who are studying in fields that generate high incomes such as medicine, law, or business. Companies that studied this would eventually develop other predictors – such as national athletes or scholarship recipients that may eventually have high net worth. The point being to not just automatically reject all unprofitable customers – but to keep those that have the highest net worth potential.

A study by Booz, Allen & Hamilton shows the cost of serving customers through different channels.[11] It costs $1.07 to do a face-to-face transaction at a teller; 52 cents by phone; 27 cents at the ATM, but less than one cent using the Web (see Figure 6.4). Here is the principle at work – water runs down hill. Over time, I can tell you which way the market will move based on the cost structure.

During presentations, a participant will often say, "But Jim, the vision you are presenting of banking in the future, there's no valuable human interaction."

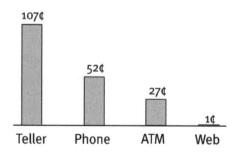

Figure 6.4 Banking transaction costs (¢). Source: Booz, Allen and Hamilton.

That's an interesting comment, because I never defined standing in a bank line-up for 30 minutes over my lunch hour to be *valuable human interaction*. We as consumers will automate those transactions we don't feel add value.

And it's not an "either/or" – it's an "and." In our company we use electronic banking wherever possible, but we still use a teller for complex transactions. It's not about restricting customers' choice; it's about increasing it. Customers will choose to automate routine and simple transactions to save themselves time and money, at the same time significantly reducing operating costs for the bank.

Banking is necessary.
Banks are not.
Richard Kovacevich
Wells Fargo[13]

Failing to embrace the Web as a channel for servicing the customer will restrict the organization's ability to lower the cost of transactions for unprofitable customers, increase margin with all customers, and ultimately hinder the company's flexibility.

FEDEX

FedEx empowers customers by giving them access to real-time information. More than 2.6 million FedEx customers use shipping software provided by FedEx, allowing them to order pick-ups online, track billing information, and transfer payments to FedEx, either by electronic funds transfer or credit card.[12] FedEx allows customers who don't have the software to log on to its Web site, key in their waybill number, and track packages in real time. As a result of these initiatives, more than 700,000 package tracking inquiries a day are answered online by customers, more than twice as many as are answered by FedEx's call center agents.

Because customers print waybills off their own laser printers to attach to packages, FedEx does not have to pay to print, sort, and file more than two billion forms a year![14] Because of deflected queries to the Website, and the fact that customers are inputting waybill information into FedEx systems, the company has not had to hire an additional 20,000 staff as package volumes have grown. In fact, customers answer two-thirds of all queries online. In essence they have outsourced the data entry function to customers, who are thankful because it gives them access to their information 24 by 365.

CALL DEFLECTION

"Call deflection" is when a company diverts a customer inquiry that would have gone to a call center to the Web. Each deflected call has a tremendous financial impact. An average call center interaction will cost a company $32.74. To resolve the issue by e-mail costs $9.99, while if the customer can self-serve and solve the problem over the Web it will cost $1.17. Known as eCRM, the field offers incredible opportunities for organizations.[15]

This explains why companies such as Dell and Cisco have invested so heavily to make their Websites easy to use. Customers will solve their own problems. Dell has built its success using the Web: 50 percent of its sales and 70 percent of support is done over the Web. For Cisco, the figures are even higher: more than 90 percent of orders and 90 percent of support is done over the Web.

Southwest Airlines has also embraced the Internet:[16]

It now books 35 percent of passenger revenue online, through a simple Website that gives customers lots of information and control. Building on its lead, the company has added an online tool that lets corporate travel managers track employees' business travel on Southwest, stimulating that source of revenue. By avoiding travel agents and the company's own phone agents, online booking will save Southwest more than $100 million in 2001. The airline's cost per booking online is about $1, vs. about $10 through a travel agent. That's a huge advantage; no other airline books anywhere near as large a proportion of business online.

Amazon.com is using eCRM to tremendous advantage. The company encourages customers to do everything over the Web. Amazon.com uses e-mail to stay in touch with its customers throughout the entire ordering process – to confirm the receipt of order, to confirm the availability of the books, and to confirm the shipment of each part of their order. Broadbase Software surveyed leading online retailers, including Amazon.com, and found that each one sent its customers an average 3.4 e-mails every 90 days.[17] So, if each of Amazon.com's 29 million customers received 3.4 e-mails every 3 months, it means Amazon is sending approximately 394 million e-mail messages each year! It is important to note that this is not spam – but entirely customized to the interests and preferences of each customer.

SELF-SERVICE MODEL

"The self-service model has two primary benefits to an organization," notes Greg Gianforte, president of RightNow Technologies, which has 1,200 customers, including Cisco, Intel, Motorola, Black & Decker, and the US Air Force.

"First is that companies are unprepared for spikes that occur in service enquiries that occur because of seasonality, market issues and new product introduction. In January 2001, Pitney Bowes was getting 500 customer enquiries a day on its Website. And then the US postal service raised postal rates. The daily enquiries exploded to 86,000 a day for about a two-week period, then fell back to 500 again. So how does the company prepare for, or deal with, a situation something like that?"

Background: Pitney Bowes also experiences peak demands whenever there is the threat of a strike or service shutdown at the post office or FedEx or UPS, or threats of a rate hike by the post office or either courier. With such unpredictability, the company is guaranteed to be blindsided and overwhelmed by spikes in customers demanding information. Based upon the company's experience with the 1999 US post office rate hike, Pitney Bowes' technical team populated the Website with information likely to be asked, and deflected an estimated 50,000 phone calls to the Web. This was a reduction of 50 percent over 1999 call volumes, just after the post office announced the rate hike. By serving customers over the Web, as opposed to through call centers, Pitney Bowes estimates it will save $1.3 million in 2001 – paying for its eCRM application in just two weeks.

Traditionally, companies have delivered customer service through call centers, with individual CSRs (Customer Service Representatives) answering calls as they come in. "Well the difficulty with that, is the model is very linear," notes Gianforte. "There is a one to one correspondence between the enquiries and the responder. It's very difficult to scale up or down. Basically they have to add people or get rid of people. In the situation when a company experiences these spikes, the time periods are so short. There is no way to add people and get them trained. So the result is your current service load is either above your capacity or below your capacity at any given time. Either you are providing poor service or spending too much money.

"So, what self-service provides is an opportunity to fundamentally change the way the service is delivered by allowing companies to scale their service capacity to meet demand.

"The second benefit is its fundamental change to the cost structure. According to Forrester; a telephone call costs $33 on average to answer; an e-mail costs $10; and a self-service model about a dollar.[18] As a company shifts customer enquiries from expensive channels to less expensive channels, you get huge efficiency gains.

When we ask customers "What is the primary benefit you are getting from self-service?" The number one thing they say is increased service quality.

A properly configured e-service system learns from every customer interaction. Thereby continually improving service.

Insight: This helps individuals and organizations see through the fog of uncertainty that shrouds the future. Pitney Bowes can't predict *when* the post office will raise rates, but by installing an eCRM system the company can ensure it will deal with call volume spikes whenever it does happens.

Harris: How does your software learn from every interaction?

Gianforte: We use implicit and explicit methods to learn from customer interactions. Every time we present a piece of information, there is a little one-click survey at the bottom of the page that asks, "How helpful was this?" If you say it was very helpful the information shows up higher next time.

If someone says that the information wasn't useful at all; a little red flag goes up and an error gets reported and sent to someone in the company saying " You may have incorrect information on your Website." That's an explicit feedback.

The second method we use is "Adaptive Bayesian Network" to actually analyze the click stream data when everyone comes to the Website. This is an implicit method. The Social Security Administration is one of our customers. If you go to the Social Security site and you type a query like "when can I retire?" Let's say some subset of the people who ask that question also, during the same session search on how to change their address; because when you retire; you are going to move and you want your check to go some place else. The system learns that these pieces of information are related.

An Adaptive Bayesian Network (ABN) is a form of neural network, that learns from interactions. The next time somebody comes and searches for "when can I retire?" the system is also going to tell them how to change their address. If that information proves useful, that link would get strengthened. If it proves to not be useful; the link would be broken.

The third step in the process is a knowledge aging process, because no business is static. If I am an e-retailer; I want information on gift-wrapping and overnight shipping to be visible in December; I want information on how to return products to be very visible in January and February. Our system learns that automatically. Useful information ages; we call it knowledge half-life. Information that is being used more recently has higher visibility than stuff used some time ago.

When you have a system that learns from every customer interaction, it's very easy to identify key issues, what customers are really concerned about, and this can help to clear some of the fog.

Insight: Because the amount of data to sift through is so massive, unless a company has an automated system to identify subtle shifts in the information customers are seeking, and identify correlations with other information, and as a result continually make small adjustments to the Web site, the organization will not be able to continually maximize the value of the self-service experience for customers.

Gianforte: When using a self-learning knowledge base to serve customers, accuracy can be so high that you can achieve, on average, an 86 percent self-service rate, according to a study by Doculabs, entitled *Self-Service Index Report*.[19] The study documents how 200 companies in 22 industries saved over $100 million in a 90-day period using self-learning, self-service systems. The report's conclusion is that self-service is the ROI sweet spot of CRM because it delivers very tangible results.

Background: Certain products are seasonal, for instance, toy companies sell between 60 and 80 percent of their annual sales in the eight-week lead up to Christmas. For toy companies the window of opportunity to sell products is very tight. Communication with customers can play a key role in increasing sales and decreasing returns. Once children have opened presents at Christmas toy companies have a narrow window of opportunity to help children and parents reduce frustration if they can't get the item to work. In December 2000, one of RightNow Technologies' large consumer products customers launched a new product. Everyone bought them for Christmas and put them under the tree. On Christmas morning, the gifts were opened and everyone wanted to figure out how to use them. So the week between Christmas and the New Year when most of the support staff was on vacation, the company experienced a 16-fold increase in customer service calls. The company was able to deflect 90 percent of those to self-service. It was a critical point in time where people are making a decision, "Do I or don't I like this new product?" It has to do with first impressions. Without deflecting calls to self-service, the standard call center would not have been able to cope with the spike in demand.

Gianforte: Even though you're automating, automating, automating, you have to keep in mind that, in fact, you are still dealing with people, and people have feelings. There are specific things you can do to incorporate their feelings into the quality of service that you provide. We have a capability that we call Smart Sense. It automatically identifies customers or prospects that are angry or dissatisfied.

Harris: Now how does it do that?

Gianforte: It's technology that includes a vocabulary of words that have an emotional impact and a set of rules so it actually can do a natural language parsing of a customer inquiry, and then you can define actions that can occur if certain criteria are met.

Let's say you're getting e-mails from clients. If somebody is angry or dissatisfied, you may want to respond to him or her quickly. Your standard level of service may be – "We'll get back to you in 24 hours, thanks for your inquiry." Well if you get an e-mail that is angry or dissatisfied you may want to immediately assign it to a supervisor, send an apology and tell them you will call them within two hours. You can create business rules that allow you to route inquiries based on the emotional content of the e-mail. This allows you to incorporate your clients' feelings into a highly automated system; the result being personalized service, from an automated system.

Harris: The company might want to query the database to determine the value of the customer? So if it's a very important customer, the customer service group might want to call the customer back in five minutes...

Gianforte: Right. You can create business rules to do this. So you could say, if the customer is a platinum customer, apply this different service level, independent of emotion. Or you can combine them – if they're platinum and they're pissed off...then, put somebody on a plane, or however you want to respond.

Our systems monitor customer satisfaction with surveys. So that if you have a service relationship with a firm, the firm will follow that up with a very brief e-mail saying, "Jim, thanks for coming by yesterday, we enjoyed helping you with this installation issue. Could you please take a minute to answer the following three questions?" Typically these are single-click surveys, with three questions: "Were you satisfied with the outcome of the inquiry?" "Were we prompt in responding to you?" and "Please rank the ability of the customer service representative." We get a 40–50 percent response rate.

Harris: That's high.

Gianforte: It's a company being proactive to see how they did, and it follows up the day after they had the service interaction. So response rates tend to be high. Now also, anybody with a problem tends to respond, which is an extremely valuable thing. We have them rank on a scale of 1–5, where 1 being Very Dissatisfied, 5 being Very Satisfied. So if anyone says they are Very Dissatisfied or Dissatisfied, either a 1 or a 2, we have a customer rule that immediately forwards that survey and the customer information directly to our VP of Customer Service. You're probably familiar with the studies that have shown, if a customer has a problem and you work and satisfactorily resolve it, that customer is actually more loyal than a customer who never had a problem. So this is a powerful tool in quickly identifying those people who you may not be providing the kind of service they need. In addition, you get the tabulated results of how you're doing. And you can slice it by customer service representative, by product line, by month, so you can look at your customer satisfaction ratings over time. You can also identify quickly those customer service staff members who had the highest satisfaction rating according to the customer. Some pretty powerful things. These are all ways to bring the human element into a highly automated system.

Harris: What are other applications where your technology is particularly appropriate?

Gianforte: A product might be recalled, on order of a judge, it goes on the news and the first thing everybody does is pick up the phone and call. And some of our clients have millions of products out in the field. Again, you are at a point where the customer is forming their opinion as to whether to continue to do business with you. They may be able to forgive the fact that you shipped a malfunctioning product, but your ability to handle those inquiries promptly and properly will determine whether they will buy future products from you. What you have to avoid is a situation, particularly on the service side where you do something that mortally wounds your ability to get business from that customer.

Harris: The Ford Motor Company and Firestone tire recall comes to mind. Or toy companies and Christmas seasonality. When consumers get that toy out of the package at Christmas, the decision to keep or return it could mean the difference between profit and ruin for that company. The critical point is when the customer is deciding, do I want to keep or return this product?

Gianforte: Organizations have to be aware of the context around them because fundamental shifts occur in efficiencies, cost structures and technology. The technology that we are introducing is a disruptive technology in that, if companies don't implement e-service but their competitors do, they'll be out of business in five years. Because we are fundamentally changing the cost structure of how service is delivered. And for many of our clients, adopting this e-service capability is the difference between being profitable or not. Here's why: according to Forrester, a telephone call costs, on average, over $33. An e-mail costs on average, $10. A self-service session on average, costs about $1. Take a cellular phone business company. If I'm a cellphone customer, with a $39 a month plan, but I call the company twice a month because I have issues with my bill. Is there any way that cellphone company can make money on me? Not if it costs $33 a phone call. Yet, if I'm able to shift my customer interactions from these high-cost channels; e-mail and telephone over to Web-based service; that extra money all goes to the bottom line. So for companies where the cost of service is a large component of the total transaction value; e-service has the opportunity to totally change the landscape.

Harris: Even if it's not a large portion. Even if your service costs are only 5 percent of your top line revenue, right? And a company can deflect 80 percent of its calls from the call center to self-service over the Web, it would reduce service costs by almost 80 percent. Meaning that would all drop to the bottom line.

Gianforte: And if you put that back into lower prices, you've now got a structural and strategic advantage over everyone else in your market.

And we've seen this – like in the shoe business, to pick one: we signed up Nike; then we got Reebok, Dexter and Rockport. We signed up Air Canada ; then we got Lufthansa, British Airways, Swissair, Ansett, Air New Zealand, and Hawaiian Airlines. We have 15 airlines. We signed up NCR, WorldCom, AT&T, Nortel, then we got Seimen's, British Telecom and now we have 65 telecoms around the world. So what we found is that when one vendor in a market adopts this, others adopt it quickly.

Harris: So really e-mail isn't the answer.

Gianforte: No, here's why. If you go to the Web, you've had this experience, how many companies have you sent an e-mail to, and you've never had a response from?

Harris: It's terrible.

Gianforte: Right. So you have people coming to your Website – e-mail is the support method of last resort. The only time you send the e-mail is when you can't find the answer on the Website. So in essence, every e-mail that a company receives is an indication that something's missing on their Website. And yet most companies are throwing bodies at trying to answer all these e-mails. The fundamental problem is you've got poor content on the Website. So they're sticking a band-aid on the symptom when the core disease is left untreated.

SELF-SERVICE APPLIES TO ALL CUSTOMER SEGMENTS

It would be incorrect to think that this philosophy of automating non-value added transactions should only apply to unprofitable customers. It should be a focus for all organizations, for every customer segment. In August 2001, Dell Computer's sold more than $50 million of computers a day over the Web – more than 50 percent of its sales. In an interview Michael Dell said, "The only thing that would be cheaper would be mental telepathy." That's where you just think you want a Dell, and two weeks later it arrives.

DELL'S PREMIER PAGES

Of Dell's $50 million of daily online sales ($18.25 billion/year) two-thirds of these orders flow through Premier Pages. Dell creates Premier Pages on a customer's Intranet, behind their corporate firewall. This allows employees to buy computers from a selection of configurations, pre-approved by the company's IT department, and priced according to agreements with the purchasing department. The tool efficiently manages the purchasing, asset management, and product support of computers, lowering the total cost of ownership.

The creation of new Premier Pages is automated, and Dell staff can manage the Web pages remotely. In 2001, there were more than 46,000 customers using the service – each with unique pre-approved configurations and pricing.

Premier Pages has been a great success. Orders flow directly to Dell, and go into production 19 minutes after receipt. A Premier Page order costs Dell $8 less than one placed over the phone. Annual savings run in the tens of millions of dollars.

Similarly, more than 70 percent of Dell's support is done over the Web. My computer is a Dell Inspiron 5000 notebook. Each Dell system has a service tag, a unique alphanumeric code. When I log onto Dell's Website and go to Support, I key in my service tag and the site brings up a customized page that lists all the updated drivers that I can download for my notebook. If ATI has an updated driver for my video card, or Dell has released new software specific for my notebook, these are listed on the page.

Technical support costs companies more because call center staff are highly paid technical specialists. While technical support may be free to customers, each call to a support center costs the vendor $35–50, according to Dataquest. If a customer spends an hour on the phone with a senior support technician, the call can cost as much $400.[20]

Another problem for call centers is that if the work is boring for technical support, it results in high staff turn over. Therefore it is essential to eliminate the need for simple support solutions that customers can solve themselves.

DATA MINING

Database marketing, or database mining, is a powerful tool that works in conjunction with CRM. For instance, frequent fliers tend to be high net worth individuals. CIBC Aerogold Visa in Canada is the number one premium credit card in Canada with 500,000 members. City Bank American Airlines Visa card in the US has more than 2.6 million members. Both have taken the highest net worth individuals away from other credit cards by appealing to a trait in this group. Airline cardholders are significantly more affluent, with average household incomes of more than $70,000 a year as opposed to $47,000 for average classic-card households. In 2000, airline cardholders charged an average of $25,000 to 30,000 a year to their cards while the average classic cardholder charged just over $6,300 a year. Airline credit cards make up 45 percent of the total credit card market.[21] By launching these credit cards, CIBC and City Bank literally stole the entire high-end segment of the credit card market.

In 2000 there were 42.7 million credit cards in Canada, which had $US86 billion charged to them. Of these CIBC had 4.19 million cards – about 10 percent of the cards, but $23.4 billion of the charges – over 27 percent of the amount![22] These figures include CIBC's non-Aerogold cards. Aerogold only figures would be even more impressive.

Every other credit card company lost market share because they (1) did not work to deeply understand their most important customers; (2) did not work to understand their deep unarticulated motivators ; and (3) did not implement customer loyalty programs that would ensure their retention. Not doing these things is like letting your competition walk into the stadium during your customer appreciation event with your 40,000 customers, sit beside your 80 best customers and ask what it would take to win their business. If you can't identify who your best customers are, there is little that you can do to avoid a competitor stealing them.

KEEPING CUSTOMERS COSTS LESS THAN ATTRACTING NEW ONES

It is widely cited that it's five times more expensive to attract a new customer than to keep an existing one.[23] The reasons for this are why CRM implementers experience higher profitability:

- New customers place the greatest demand on your company as they familiarize themselves with your product, service and how to interact with your organization (how to reconcile errors).
- You have no mass marketing costs in dealing with existing customers.

- You have already developed a relationship with existing customers. You have built up some level of trust. It is therefore easier to cross sell them other products and services.
- Through this relationship you can gain insight into what they like and don't like.

Think about how often you get sales solicitations. I get them every day – by fax, mail, phone, and person-to-person solicitations in airports. But how often do I hear from companies that I already do business with? Usually only when there is a bill to pay. In other words, organizations are very pro-active in winning business, but very poor at growing the business.

eLERT

I like a local high-end men's store I'll call Designer Suits for Men. But I miss the semi-annual sales because I travel so much and therefore don't see the sales ads in the local newspaper. Imagine if instead of investing in mass marketing such as newspaper, radio, and billboard ads, the store chose to implement CRM. What would the impact be?

Imagine a business called eLert. You'd go to eLert's Website, identify the city you live in, and select retailers or categories of goods and services that you are interested in, and then set certain criteria. In my case, I would select Designer Suits for Men as the store I wanted to be eLerted about, and then identify what I was interested in (i.e. designer label suits such as Armani or Hugo Boss, or a cashmere winter coat). I'd then be able to select other criteria, such as a percentage discount or advance notice of a sale. Finally, I would select the method of contact (e-mail, fax, phone call) and frequency of contact (no more than once a quarter).

Three weeks before Designer Suits for Men's semi-annual sale I would receive an e-mail: "We want to give you advance notice that we will be closing the store, on February 22–26 and are inviting you to a special advance sale. As one of our most important customers, this ensures that you will have the best selection of clothing, while shopping in a relaxed atmosphere."

The retailer has to begin by collecting information about its current customers and use it strategically. If Designer Suits for Men sent out an invitation to all existing customers for a private pre-sale event, the sales from the pre-sale would far exceed any publicly advertised sale, and no expensive, mass market advertising would be required. This exclusive, private sale would communicate to existing customers, "You are special. You have the inside edge and we treat you preferentially to the rest of the public."

> *I know half the money I spend on advertising is wasted, but I can never find out which half.*
> **John Wanamaker**

EFFECTIVENESS AND EFFICIENCY ELERT

I love Aretha Franklin's music, but I never get to hear her in concert for the same reason I never get to buy suits on sale from Designer Suits for Men. I travel so much that I never see the ads promoting the concert. By the time I do hear about it, the concert is either sold out or only really bad seats are available.

Each year concert promoters in North America spend tens of millions of dollars advertising concert tours. When you consider there are event promoters for sports events, theatre, art exhibitions, museums, zoos, and special events, that figure could easily double or triple. With eLert, customers would go to a Website, select the events they would attend if they were to be held and request special advance notice. In return for this information, they have the opportunity to buy tickets before the rest of the public.

This would allow concert promoters to determine the viability of events *before* deciding to proceed. In other words, it would take a lot of risk out of the business.

It would also increase the profitability of the business by reducing advertising costs and in some cases, all the seats to a concert could be sold out without ever paying for any advertising and promotion costs.

I did buy tickets to see Aretha Franklin a couple of years ago and she cancelled the concert. The concert promoter had to call each of the 2,000 ticket holders, propose an alternative date or offer a refund. A system like eLert would have eliminated the majority of the cost of this by automating the rescheduling of the concert and refunding of the tickets.

In North America, the largest demographic group is known as the baby boomers (born 1947–1966). They are at the peak of their earning potential in their careers but they have very little free time. On average, this group is working longer hours than at any other time in their lives. They have aging parents to look after, and in some cases, young children. And they feel they deserve the good life, but because they don't have time, you will never see them camping out overnight in ticket line-ups to get seats for a concert. In other words, they feel they deserve to have the best seats in the house but don't have the time to get them. They are angry because promoters require them to do things (such as stand in line, or holding on the telephone) that are waste-ful of their time. This is what allows what is known as scalping or touting to thrive. Scalpers buy tickets to a con-cert and on the night of the event resell them for as much as 10 times their face value. The fact that scalping exists

Imagination is more important than knowledge
Albert Einstein

proves that there is a need that concert promoters are currently not meeting. A segment of the population would be willing to pay a premium for a service such as eLert. I would gladly pay a premium to get the best seats in the house and advance notice.

eLert would be similar to American Express' very successful Front of the Line service for card members. This allows Amex card members to buy tickets to events (concerts, plays and art shows) before the general public thereby receiving the best seats. But eLert would expand on this concept, giving those who registered preferential seating at *potential* events. It would allow event organizers to sell out an event – guaranteeing a profit – before making any financial commitments (to the artist or venue). For instance, if 6,000 people reg-istered to see Aretha Franklin at a concert hall that held 2,000 – the event is guaranteed to sell out before the promoter has contracted with Aretha or the hall. Registrants for the service would receive preferential seating in return for their early show of interest.

mCOMMERCE

Much like the concert promoters, clothing stores and other retailers spend a great deal of money on advertising. Why not identify key customers and have a one-to-one method of notifying them of advance sales?

Imagine having a personal agent who knew all your tastes in concerts, spe-cial events, and clothing sales and would have notified you in advance! As well, this agent would notify you when certain stocks you track advanced or declined by a certain amount or traded a certain percentage over their volume.

The new third generation (3G) cellphones will have GPS (global position-ing systems), which will allow the position of the cellphone to be determined.

Imagine that as I walk down the street in Seattle my cellphone goes off, and on the screen is a text message: "The cashmere coat you wanted from Designer Suits for Men is on sale at our Seattle store just two blocks away from you. Come on in and get it." This is the promise of one to one marketing tied in with GPS 3G wireless.

RETAILERS

In the digital age, retailers are going to have to do something to add value for customers. The eLert service is one way of adding value without having to cut costs. In the Aretha Franklin example, many people would pay more for concert tickets if they could get the best seats. If retailers don't add more value for customers, the danger is that price will become a more important factor. In the Internet age where there are comparison engines that compare the sale price of a product from different retailers, more and more customers will move to the best price.

PRICE

We all think that price is so important. But price is just one dimension of value. If you knew you were going to have a heart attack in three weeks, unless you had a triple bypass, would you look for the cheapest surgeon or for the most experienced?

WHY CRM WON'T WORK

CRM is not an end in itself. CRM is only a tool. It is ultimately how an organization implements it that will create success and higher profitability. Successful implementation of CRM requires technology, people and processes. Ultimately, CRM is all about relationships. And relationship implies listening and being willing to change. If corporations implement CRM, but are unwilling to change policies, procedures or practices that anger customers or create dissatisfaction then CRM will not yield high returns. In other words, the technology is *necessary* but *insufficient*.

A great example of this is the airline industry, which was an early adopter of segmenting their customers and creating loyalty programs to reward their most frequent fliers.

Because of the nature of our work, my wife and I spend a lot of time flying and amass quite a few frequent flier points. My wife decided to fly to Australia on points. She was able to book a seat in business class from Toronto to Sydney, but on the date she wanted to return only economy was available.

A return economy ticket costs 75,000 points, while a business class is 150,000. Air Canada's policy is that if you fly business class one way and economy the other you are charged for business class both ways.

My wife argued, why not deduct 75,000 points for business class one way and 37,500 for economy class one way? The reply from the Air Canada was, "Because that is not our policy."

Air Canada's policy is *guaranteed* to create customer dissatisfaction regardless of the customer's actions. If the customer flies business class one way and economy return, he/she feels the airline is unfairly overcharging 37,500 points. If the customer flies economy both ways,

Loyalty is the absence of a better value alternative.
Dave Nichol

he/she is angry at the airline because the Toronto to Sydney flight is almost 24 hours long and business class would have been more comfortable. A policy that is guaranteed to anger customers regardless of what they chose to do is a bad policy.

It is useless to implement CRM, segment your customer base, or reward your best customers, if you are unwilling or unable to alter policies when they are unfair and create customer dissatisfaction.

CRM is not just about technology. It is about a philosophy and it implies a willingness to change. The R in CRM is relationship. What defines a good relationship? Think about your own experience.

VIRAL MARKETING

Viral marketing is a powerful concept. Four friends, average age in their 20s, decided to duplicate Amazon.com – the only difference was Bigwords.com sold textbooks to college and university students. The site typically advertised books for up to 40 percent less than campus bookstores. Once you bought your books you were given a unique customer ID, such as TZ2003. If anyone else came to the site, bought books and keyed in your code, you got a 5 percent referral fee on their initial order. College kids who are short on cash and long on time were plastering their campuses with posters at their own expense advertising:

Go to www.bigwords.com
Save up to 40 percent off campus bookstore prices
By keying in code TZ2003

Known as "Tell a Friend," the program was a huge success. On the Big Words Website, there was a "Tell a Friend" area where customers could fill out the e-mail addresses of their friends and the system would send them e-mail. A second part of the "Tell a Friend" program was that, upon receiving the order; the customer also received bookmarks and flyers. The flyers had a spot where the "Tell a Friend" ID number could be filled in. These flyers were handed out to friends. This concept of viral marketing is particularly brilliant for a number of reasons:

- The referral credit is only on new customer's initial purchases not their lifetime purchases – so if their initial order is $100 but the following week they order another $300 of books, the referral credit is only $5.
- The incentive is credit not cash – meaning it is a deferred liability; the referring customers have likely already bought their books for the year and are not going to exercise the credit until next year, improving Big Words' cash flow. Not all credits are exercised because students drop out of school or the company can go out of business.
- By rewarding customers with credit, Big Words guaranteed customers would remain loyal and keep coming back to exercise their credits.
- The credit is in the form of product that has a margin on so it didn't even cost Big Words the full 5 percent.

One way to measure the effectiveness of a marketing campaign is to calculate the cost of acquisition (total marketing and sales costs, divided by the number of customers acquired) for the "Tell a Friend" program from January to September of 2000:

- 99,630 people participated in the "Tell a Friend" program, sending e-mails to friends
- 131,381 e-mails were sent
- 11,269 orders were received through the program
- $1,070,390 of "Tell a Friend" sales

- Average "Tell a Friend" initial order was $95
- Average cost per acquisition of $4.75
- Average cost to acquire customers through traditional sales and marketing efforts: $20–30 depending on the program;
- "Tell a Friend" accounted for about 10 percent of all sales.

While banner ads on the Internet typically have click-through rates of less than 1 percent, Big Word's e-mail campaign had a click-through rate of about 75 percent! That means 75 percent of students who received notices from friends extolling the virtues of Big Words clicked on a link in the e-mail and visited the Big Words site. As Jeff Sherwood, co-founder of Big Words notes, "Nothing is more powerful than receiving an e-mail from a friend!"

Viral marketing turns customers into sales reps. W. Edwards Deming said that performance in organizations is due to systems and structures. In this case the, 20-year-olds created a structural incentive for customers to refer their friends, acquaintances, and peer group to become customers.

The brilliance of viral marketing is highlighted in the economics. While the cost of acquisition per customer was $20–30 through normal channels, the cost to acquire customers virally was only $4.75 on average. Here is an exercise: add up the total marketing and sales budgets (salaries, benefits, capital costs, advertising campaigns, etc.) and divide by the number of new customers in a year and you will get a cost of acquisition per customer. You will find that the average cost is huge by comparison. This also highlights that the acquisition cost per customer needs to be broken down and analyzed by each marketing method, as opposed to being aggregated across all customers (i.e. lumping all acquisition methods together).

Jeff Sherwood was the Chief Information Architect of Big Words. To his knowledge, "Nobody else was using monetary compensation or store credit, to get customers to tell other customers."

Opened in August 1998, Big Words grew to more than 100,000 customers in its' first year of operation and had achieved a run rate of $14.9 million a year in sales before the company closed in October 2000.

Viral marketing made perfect sense in the $5.5 billion US college textbook industry because members of generation Y (those born between 1979 and 2000)[24] are highly computer literate. Big Words sold both new and used textbooks and offered free shipping. The company had "Tell a Friend" members at more than 1,500 US colleges and universities. The company had established direct relationships with more than 700 North American textbook publishers and distributors and had venture capital funding from Geocapital Partners and 21st Century Internet Venture Partners.

Big Words closed because, like many start ups, the company expanded quickly on the urging of its venture capitalist partners. When the NASDAQ composite index crashed, the company was not able to raise enough capital to sustain its corporate overhead.

HOTMAIL

Hotmail is another powerful example of viral marketing. Hotmail was launched on July 4, 1996. Founders Jack Smith and Sabeer Bhatia dreamed up the idea while working at Apple. They wanted to e-mail each other ideas, but they were worried someone in the office might read their e-mails. Web based e-mail was the answer.

By December 1997, when MSN acquired the company for $400 million, Hotmail had grown to nine million users.[25] The acquisition helped make Microsoft's MSN, the largest online service worldwide. In May 2001, MSN Hotmail had grown to 100 million users worldwide.

At the bottom of every outbound e-mail is an advertising message: "Get your free e-mail at Hotmail." The message was a subtle endorsement by the sender, encouraging friends to get a Hotmail account. Therefore each Hotmail user was a company salesperson, and the message spread like wildfire.

CONCLUSION

The Internet and other new technologies enable companies to deepen their relationship with customers and add value in new ways. How much do you know about your customers, beyond basic demographic information? If you don't have detailed information about your customers and their needs, you increase the likelihood of your organization being blindsided. CRM enables companies to customize products and services while lowering costs by eliminating non-value added processes through self-service.

REFLECTIONS

- What criteria do you use to define a good relationship? What creates loyalty? Think about your experience in both your business and your personal life.
- How does your company determine who its most important customers are?
- Do you treat your most important customers differently than your average customers? Does your organization have the political will to create preferential treatment for its most profitable customers? Are your most important customers synonymous with your most profitable?
- Do you know the value of customers? The best ones? The worst ones? How much would it cost, in terms of time and money, to keep your best customers, compared to acquiring new ones? How much could you save by eliminating your least profitable customers? Are your least profitable customers ever your most important customers? If so, how can address this anomaly?
- How could your organization enable customers to serve themselves?
- Have you taken advantage of every opportunity to use the Web as a channel for customer service?
- How does customer information inform your product and service development?
- How could your organization use viral marketing?
- What barriers to exit have you created for your best customers? How can you create opportunities for your customers to build equity with your organization?
- How do you take maximum advantage of the Internet for
  - Competitive intelligence?
  - Marketing?
  - Service?
- How could customers be treated better by your company, so they would be less likely to migrate to a competitor? How will you determine what the new value is that you will add?

CHAPTER 7

Break the Rules!

How can individuals and organizations challenge existing paradigms? How can the open source philosophy significantly benefit an organization's competitive position, lower costs, and increase market value? Can the open source philosophy apply to companies outside of software development? How can creativity be developed?

BLIND SPOTS

While we may think we see well, we all have blind spots. In the back of the eye where the optic nerve inserts into the retina, there is an area with no rods or cones for detecting light, known as the "blind spot." Our blind spots go unnoticed, because the images in the blind spot of each eye are filled in by the visual field of the other eye. However, cover one eye and you'll swear any objects appearing in the blind spot of your seeing eye are simply not there. But our brains abhor a visual vacuum, so instead of seeing a hole or a black spot, they fill in the blind spot.

Research reported in *New Scientist* magazine on blindness and attention is revealing. Picture the following:

You're walking across a college campus when a stranger asks you for directions. While you're talking to him, two men pass between you carrying a wooden door. You feel a moment's irritation, but they move on and you carry on describing the route. When you've finished, the stranger informs you that you've just taken part in a psychology experiment. "Did you notice anything change after the two men passed with the door?" he asks. "No," you reply uneasily. He then explains that the man who initially approached you walked off behind the door, leaving him in his place. The first man now comes up to join you. Looking at them standing side by side, you notice that the two are of different height and build, are dressed differently, have different haircuts and different voices.

It sounds impossible, but when Daniel Simons, a psychologist at Harvard University, and his colleague Daniel Levin of Kent State University in Ohio actually did this experiment, they found that fully 50 percent of those who took part failed to notice the substitution.[1]

We see far less than we think. The article goes on to point out that of all the myriad visual details of any scene that you could record, you take only what is relevant to you at the time. This leads to a phenomenon called inattentional blindness: if you are not paying attention to some feature of a scene, you won't see it. In a 1999 experiment, Simons and Harvard colleague, Christopher Chabris notes:

[We] showed people a videotape of a basketball game and asked them to count the passes made by one or the other team. After about 45 seconds, a man dressed in a gorilla suit walked slowly across the scene, passing between the players. Although he was visible for five seconds, 40 percent of the viewers failed to notice him. When the tape was played again, and they were asked simply to watch it, they saw him easily. Not surprisingly, some found it hard to believe it was the same tape.[2]

Organizations have blind spots too. Typically, they are called paradigms.

WHAT IS A PARADIGM?

"Paradigm" is very much a buzzword these days. Whenever I see a buzzword appear in a Dilbert cartoon I get very wary of using it. However, a paradigm is a very powerful and useful concept. I once saw Stephen Covey do the following exercise with an audience to drive home the point.

> *Insanity is doing the same thing over and over again and expecting different results.*
> **Alcoholics Anonymous**

What was the "paradigm," or medical theory, in the 1500s as to why people fell ill? What did people at that time believe to be the cause of illness? *Bad humours, or evil spirits in the blood.*

Now let's pretend that it's the 1500s and we really *believe* that this is an accurate paradigm, or representation of reality. We really believe that this is true and we all work in a hospital. Someone comes into the hospital and is sick. What would we do? *Bleed the patient with leeches.*

Now let's say the individual didn't get better. What would we do then? *Bleed him some more.* Yes. After all, we care about him.

What are some of the management buzz words you have heard in the last few years that are put forward as panaceas to all our problems in organizations? Let's apply them to our 15th-century hospital:

- *Reengineering.* What we need to do is look at the value chain and eliminate unnecessary steps. We study the process from the moment the leeches arrive on the shipping dock until they are applied to the patient's arm and eliminate unnecessary steps. If we are really ambitious, we will reengineer the whole value chain and go out to our suppliers and our suppliers' suppliers and make sure the whole value chain is efficient.

- *Just-in-time (JIT).* We will cut costs by reducing inventory levels, so that we only receive the exact number of leeches that we need for today's leeching. Again, we may insist on our suppliers demanding the same of their suppliers to compress the inventory levels in the whole value chain so that our whole value chain only has 10 days of inventory in it while our competitor's has 90 days, giving us 10 times more turns a year.

- *Quality.* That's what we need around here. If we only had ISO 9000 leeches then all our problems would be solved.

- *Customer focus.* We would ask patients, "When we are leeching you, do you like the brown leeches or the black leeches more?" Whatever they answer, we will provide. Or we might ask, "While being leeched, do you like listening to Brahms or Beethoven?" After all, we care about your experience.

> *We can't use the same level of thinking as we did when we created the problem in the first place.*
> **Albert Einstein**

- *Empowerment.* Great. "You are all empowered to leech anyway you want. When one team discovers a new way of leeching we'll have a group meeting to ensure the best practices are transferred between groups."

- *Benchmarking.* We would benchmark against other fine leeching organizations to discover how they leech. We might even create a database of the best leeching practices. One of the keys in increasing your consulting rate is to coin a new buzzword or a new acronym. So we would create one: TQL (total quality leeching). And then the imperative generated consulting would kick in: if you're not doing TQL by 1560 you may not be in business.

- *Trust.* We might send all the executives away to the mountains to do a ropes course to increase trust, so that when the team gets back to the hospital it operates more effectively, making faster decisions about leeching.

- *Hiring criteria.* What would the hiring criteria be? People often answer "experience in working with leeches." Or individuals who come with their own hip waders to find leeches.

- *Research and development.* How would this organization spend its research and development budget? *Focusing on breeding bigger, faster, blood-sucking leeches.*

I am not against any of these strategies – each is necessary – but alone each is insufficient. All of these are management strategies that operate within the existing paradigm. Leadership questions and changes the paradigm. This is the difference between leadership and management. Management works within existing paradigms while leadership moves between them.

It is easy to laugh at how little the medical professional knew in the 1500s, and hard to imagine that such a situation could occur today. But paradigms are so powerful that even highly educated medical professionals will dismiss evidence that contradicts their current worldview.

STOMACH ULCERS

In 1983, Barry Marshall, then a medical intern in Perth, Australia, discovered a truth about stomach ulcers that should have changed the medical world instantaneously, but for some reason didn't.

Stomach ulceration is a chronic, debilitating condition that affects about 10 percent of US adults. An ulcer is a raw wound inside in the stomach – and the stomach is awash with acid strong enough to corrode metal. The burning, stabbing pain of an ulcer usually begins a few hours after eating. Left untreated, an ulcer can eat into stomach arteries, trigger internal bleeding, or even burn a hole through the stomach and spread infection throughout the body. Ultimately, an ulcer can be fatal.

Until the 1970s, the only treatment for ulcers was weeks of bed rest, lots of milk, and years spent eating a bland diet of porridge, boiled eggs, and weak tea. In serious cases, surgery was necessary to remove the ulcerous parts of the stomach and intestines in order to stop the spread of infection and save the patient's life.

In 1976, scientists at Smith Kline Beecham[3] discovered that the stomach secretes acid in response to several stimuli, including a histamine called H2. They found a way to block that response with a drug called Tagamet. The drug was wildly successful. Within days of taking the drug, ulcer patients experienced relief from their pain and the ulcers seemed to heal. Ulcer surgeries declined by one-third a year after the drug's introduction. Tagamet's annual sales reached nearly $600 million by 1980 and Smith Kline's earnings rose by 266 percent from 1976 to 1980.

In 1981, Glaxo introduced a similar acid-blocking drug called Zantac that had fewer side effects, and was aggressively marketed. It began outselling Tagamet in 1988 and, until its patent expired in 1997, it was the biggest selling drug on the market. In 1995, sales of Zantac reached $3.5 billion.

The only problem was that these drugs didn't cure ulcers. The drugs reduced the level of acid long enough for the ulcers to heal, but within a year of stopping the medication, the ulcers returned in 70 percent of patients.

Pharmaceutical companies made billions selling antacid drugs, which were treating ulcer symptoms instead of curing the cause. Anti-ulcer drugs generated $17.4 billion in sales in 2000 and represented 5.5 percent of all pharmaceutical drug sales worldwide.[4]

In 1983, Dr Barry Marshall began wondering if there wasn't another explanation for ulcers. He discovered that the bacterium *Helicobacter pylori* (*H. pylori*) was present in all of the ulcer patients he examined. Animal experiments with the bacterium failed to generate ulcers, so in desperation Marshall used himself as a guinea-pig. He drank a beaker of water laced with *H. pylori*. A week later he began suffering headaches, stomach pains, nausea, and vomiting. An examination of his stomach lining revealed that he had gastritis, the precursor to ulcers. Marshall was thrilled.

Marshall had discovered that *H. pylori* causes most stomach ulcers. Further study revealed that more than 80 percent of people who had ulcers have *H. pylori* present in their digestive tracts.[5]

These findings went against conventional wisdom that peptic ulcers were caused by excessive amounts of stomach acid, stress, and spicy foods. Marshall's discovery launched him on a campaign that put him in conflict with other medical researchers and the major pharmaceutical companies: if bacteria caused ulcers, then simple antibiotics could, in theory, cure them.

Marshall began traveling to gastroenterology conferences to promote his findings, but his discovery fell on deaf ears. Most scientists thought Marshall's decision to infect himself with *H. pylori* was highly unscientific.

Marshall's luck began to change when he described his finding in *Lancet*, the highly respected British medical magazine. The report was ignored in medical circles and the general media, but the *National Enquirer*, the supermarket tabloid that reports on alien abductions, ran a story in November 1984. Soon after, the *Cincinnati Enquirer* ran a story about Marshall's findings, which was seen by a Procter & Gamble research scientist who called Marshall.

P&G became a major supporter of Marshall by funding his research, holding *H. pylori* conventions, and underwriting Marshall's move to the University of Virginia in 1986. P&G had recently purchased the company that produced Pepto-Bismol and had launched a pharmaceuticals division.

Despite Marshall's findings, it still took a number of years to find an effective treatment for eradicating *H. pylori* in ulcer patients. Marshall had some success with bismuth, but it only eradicated the infection in 20 percent of cases. With P&G's backing, Marshall began experiments that combined PG's product, Pepto-Bismol, and antibiotics. The combination of Pepto-Bismol and the antibiotic Metronidazole cleared up *H. pylori* infections in 70 percent of cases.

Eventually, the antibiotic Biaxin and the antacid Prilosec emerged as the standard treatment for ulcers. Prilosec is a new breed of antacid called a proton pump inhibitor that stops acid production entirely, unlike Zantac and Tagamet that stop acid in response to the histamine H2. The antacid medication stops stomach acid from breaking down the antibiotic, allowing it to do its job.

In 1996, 13 years after Marshall infected himself with *H. pylori*, the US Food and Drug Administration recommended that antibiotics be used to treat ulcers.

In the long run, Marshall's discovery of *H. pylori* may prove to be even more important in the treatment of cancer. Outside of developed countries,

H. pylori infection is a leading cause of cancer. It spreads in crowded or unsanitary conditions, so in parts of Africa and South America rates of *H. pylori* infection are extremely high.

The medical establishment finally recognized Marshall's achievement in 1995 when he was given the Lasker Award, an honor that is usually seen as a precursor to the Nobel Prize for Medicine.

BREAKING PARADIGMS

The brain is a network consisting of billions of interconnected neurons. Our brains work in such a way that patterns are reinforced. Think about a sand bank. Whenever it rains, the run off water wears channels in the sand. The next time it rains the water uses these same paths. The greater the use, the deeper the channels become. Our brains work in the same way. The more we think a certain way, the stronger the associations become. Over time we get into a "rut" in terms of our thinking. Individuals and organizations need to use tools to actively "break" their paradigms.

Edward de Bono, one of the world's leading thinkers on creativity, suggests a number of techniques for thinking laterally. One technique is to associate unrelated words with what you are thinking about. So you might take a whole bunch of random words and put them in a hat. One person draws a word out of a hat and the group begins associating the word "blue" with running a bar. Blue might connote water and water might be associated with a beach, so one idea would be to have sand in the bar and have people playing volleyball.

The real power to change markets and increase profitability is by breaking the rules of the dominant industry players. The open source movement is an excellent example.

OPEN SOURCE

The open source movement is a radical, new approach that is revolutionizing computer programming. *Linux*, an operating system for computers like *Windows*, is an example of an open source program. Companies that develop *Linux* publish the source code so that customers and even competitors can understand how the system works. Customers can alter the code if it suits their needs. It's like

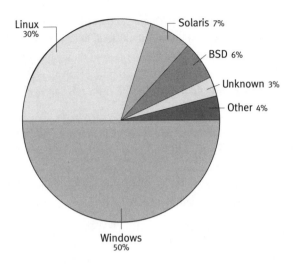

Figure 7.1 Public Web servers worldwide. Source: www.netcraft.com/survey/.

Coca-Cola publishing its secret formula and allowing Pepsi or anyone else to look at it and make improvements.

Bob Young is the founder and Chairman of Red Hat, the leading *Linux* supplier with 72 percent of the open source Internet solutions market.[6] The open source movement has become a force to be reckoned with. In 2001, 30 percent of Web servers were running *Linux*, stealing market share from Microsoft (Figure 7.1).

The open source movement came up under the radar (Young's book is titled *Under the Radar*), and is challenging the traditional software development paradigm.

If Red Hat gives away the operating system, how can the company make money? Young humorously replies, "Microsoft charges for the operating system and gives away hats and T-shirts at trade shows. We gave away the operating system and charged for hats and T-shirts at trade shows." The real answer is by charging for service. At least 50 percent of people who are using Red Hat *Linux* in a serious way buy a product or a service from Red Hat on a regular basis.

BOB YOUNG

Young: When we [Red Hat] deliver control over the technology to the customer it frees the customer to do what he needs to do with that technology. We have no way of knowing in advance what that customer needs to do with that technology because we happen to have over a million customers, all of whom need something slightly different, some of whom need something radically different than what we would otherwise deliver. That's why free markets work so well compared to the hierarchical production model that the Soviets had adopted, which in the short run can work very well. In the long run it's simply not flexible.

Harris: The open source movement is a perfect example of allowing customers to build equity with you. Customers will build the functionality that they need into the software. By allowing the customers to do development work, open source software allows them to build equity with the product and ensure greater loyalty, because mass-market software producers will not be as responsive to customer needs.

Young: The biggest single challenge facing Red Hat was marketing because we were going after markets dominated by IBM and Microsoft and I didn't have even a tiny fraction of their resources. How was I going to convince people to use my technology?

Harris: So what did you do?

Young: So we gave it away. By promoting the GPL (General Public License) and by promoting this concept that you could use this technology for whatever you needed to use it for, we became the trusted supplier. In the [software] industry, average consumers and particularly sophisticated consumers were thoroughly pissed off with their suppliers and it didn't matter whom their supplier was. No one liked any of the suppliers. Read any of the consumer columns in any of the trade magazines about how technology product support is so bad – there's a theme to all of those articles. It was always so bad because the vendor kept control over the technology. It's as if you had bought a car with the hood locked shut and you allowed the vendor to retain the only key. It's not so much that you want to be able to get your ratchet out and fix your own car, it's that by being able to open the hood of the car, you've got control over the car. If the guy you bought it from doesn't do a good job looking after it, you can take it to 10,000 other shops. That doesn't make you any happier with the original vendor who didn't look after you, but it does solve the frustration problem. You end up being blasé about the vendor who didn't look after you because you can go and find someone who will. In the technology world you don't have that option. You have basically handed the keys to the future of the technology within your corporation to the supplier. That was the benefit we were selling by promoting the GPL. The GPL broke the highly profitable economic model of the proprietary industry. I wasn't going to make money anyway, competing with Microsoft. By breaking the model, I get all this huge marketing effort that I don't have to pay for.

Harris: In *The Art of War* Sun Tzu says, take your opponent's greatest strength and turn it into their greatest weakness. Microsoft's incredible profit engine is based on not releasing source code to the customer thereby you attack what is their core strength – what is their core strength now becomes their core weakness.

Young: We had none of that figured out. The only thing we did recognize was that Microsoft owned a monopoly and that if you were going to compete with a monopoly you were going to have to change the rules under which that player was able to achieve and maintain its monopoly. To a certain extent it didn't matter if the rules that we were adopting made no sense, as long as they were different. People ask, "How did you get the courage to take those risks?" Not taking a risk would have been much more courageous than taking radical risks (by industry standards) because we knew the status quo did not work in our favor. In fact, the status quo guaranteed our failure. So the idea of adopting a set of rules that made no sense was not a particularly difficult decision. I love the F. Scott Fitzgerald quote I read in Tom Peters' *In Search of Excellence*: "The sign of a first class intelligence is the ability to keep two opposing concepts in mind at the same time and retain the ability to function." You absolutely have to throw out all the old rules. It might look like you're being wild and crazy and undisciplined, but you have to adopt all the intellectual and commercial disciplines of learning how to make your new set of rules work.

Harris: I'm trying to get at the Red Hat advantage. You can't get into the guts of Microsoft's operating systems, but you can with *Linux*. In my opinion, that literally addicts your customers to Red Hat. They wouldn't leave to go back to a proprietary system because of the sense of freedom and control they have to shape their own destiny and solve their own problems. It is such an addictive tool that they won't go backwards.

Young: We won the Info World Product of the Year Award for operating systems. We actually tied that year (1996) with *Windows NT*. We then went on to win the Info World Product of the Year award the next three years in a row, four years altogether. They have since discontinued that particular category, because I guess they don't like giving it to the same company five years in a row. The thing that most shocked us about this, the reason I was having a hard time believing that they would do such a thing was that we were up against *Windows NT* which was the obvious alternative. Microsoft had started their *NT* project in about 1989/90, when Dave Cutler was recruited from Digital. Cutler was the architect who masterminded Digital's *VMS* operating system. That was four years before Red Hat was even launched and Microsoft had invested of a billion dollars and had at least 1,000 of the world's smartest operating systems engineers working on it. At that time there were a total of 27 of us at Red Hat, including receptionists and telephone order takers. You sort of wonder, "Who had rewritten the rules of economics?" that 27 kids in the hills of North Carolina, with a budget of maybe $200,000, could tie Microsoft with a billion dollar budget, a four-year head start and 1,000 of the world's smartest operating system engineers. And the answer is that this [open source] customer feedback loop meant that we actually had a bigger engineering team than even Microsoft or IBM could afford to assemble. That's the value of giving the users control. Not all of our customers contribute to making our product better but we've got enough customers that all we need is one out of a hundred of them contributing a bug fix, or adding a feature, or actually becoming a member of the open source engineering teams, that we end up reducing our costs of engineering to a small fraction of what the traditional proprietary binary model. So in those areas that we get some market momentum, our momentum, that positive feedback loop, becomes very exciting for us, because we build new technology even faster than Microsoft.

Harris: And it means that you improve faster.

Young: That's right and we become much more reliable. In other words, in Microsoft's case they may have 1,000 guys working on stuff, but when they launch the thing out the door, the only people who are allowed to make changes to it are the people employed by Microsoft. So the Microsoft bug fix model works that they ship a beta out to 1,000 or 10,000 users (pick a number) all of whom discover problems and send back a bug report saying this is broken or that is broken. Microsoft then compiles (pick a number) a list of 1,000 or 10,000 bug reports and then they have to actually go back and find that there is a bug and not a feature, in other words, that the user understood what the code was supposed to be doing. Then they have to prioritize it – how important a bug is it – then they have to allocate resources to fixing the bug, then they have to test the bug and then they have to go through another whole product cycle. The only people allowed to do any of that work, to do the testing, the prioritizing, the fixing, or the new revision, are people employed in Redmond, Washington. I don't care how big a team it is; it is a limited size. In Red Hat's case, when we publish a new version of Red Hat *Linux* we give every single one of our users a complete source code and a license to do whatever he needs to do with the source code. So instead of getting bug reports saying that this is broken or that is broken, we get a bug report saying, oh, by the way, this is broken, and here is how to fix it.

Harris: You empower users to co-develop code but don't you end up with four different bug fixes? Moving forward in the next version, which one do you chose?

Young: Red Hat ships the official version, giving customers an assurance of standardization. Using your example, there are four different ways of fixing a problem and the one that Red Hat chose addressed the needs of the majority of the market, but unfortunately for machine tool controllers it wasn't the optimum fix. So machine tool controllers would be pissed off at Red Hat because they introduced this bug and the fix didn't fix it, but instead made it worse. In a proprietary binary executable model, the machine tool controllers would be out of luck. In the open source model, all those patches are still out there and so if you don't like the Red Hat patch or the one that we incorporate as the standard patch, use the machine tool controller patch. The way we avoid the bottleneck in the open source world is to keep in mind this is not monolithic technology. Curnahan and Ritchie were the architects at Bell Labs who wrote the original *Unix* kernel. Their key innovation was to build a highly modular operating system because they knew that they couldn't get everyone to agree on what should be in that operating system. Some people wanted more features, other people wanted fewer. They also knew that they had no way of predicting the future, no way of knowing what features, five years or ten years into the future, people were going to consider essential in an operating system. So the only way to deal with that was to strip down the operating system to its necessary components and simply provide interfaces into the kernel and the various pieces, so you could build a highly modular operating system. In the *Linux* operating system case, the *Linux* kernel is 16 MB of the 800 MB operating system that companies like Red Hat build. So when we ship a copy of Red Hat *Linux*, it actually consists of in excess of 834 MB that consisted of 779 different programs. Each program is, on average, a little bigger than 1 MB of code. So each of the teams working on those different programs had a relatively manageable amount of code (a megabyte of code is still a good chunk of code), but nonetheless it's a relatively manageable project. So Red Hat's job as a clearing-house is we're responsible for the installation code, actually some big chunks of code, the compilers, all the software packaging and networking code, but in actual fact, the majority of the code we ship to our customers we inherit from other teams across the Internet and our job, when we get a bug, is to feed that bug report back to the maintainers of that particular piece of code.

There are probably more like 300 teams and the teams typically have an average of two and a half projects that they are working on. At Red Hat, for example, of those 779 projects that they're working on, in fact Red Hat is fully responsible in terms of being the primary maintainer of maybe 45 of those programs.

OPEN SOURCE AND THE OLD ECONOMY COMPANY

Between 1993 and 2001, the price of gold slumped from $450 to $250 per ounce. A small Canadian gold mining company's innovative approach to mining resulted in the company's share price increasing tenfold. Goldcorp beat all major North American stock indices, including the Dow, NASDAQ, and TSE300, as well as the blue chip companies IBM, GE, Berkshire Hathaway, Nortel, and GM. The company attributes its success to abandoning traditional practices and synchronizing the old economy with the new.

"We believe unconventional thinking is one of our key competitive advantages," said Goldcorp Chairman and CEO Robert McEwen.

The company had operated a mine at Red Lake since 1948, but by 1995 it had been starved of capital and conventional wisdom said the mine was finished. In 1996, when the workforce went on strike, the cost of production was $360 per ounce and the mine had an annual production of 53,000 ounces. With the price of gold at $380–400 an ounce in June 1996, it was an unprofitable mine. The strike lasted 46 months and rather than accept an agreement, the United Steel Workers union chose to voluntarily decertify. McEwen speculates it was because they were afraid of setting a precedent for other collective agreements.

Today the mine is highly profitable, producing 475,000 ounces of gold a year at a cost of $70 per ounce, a 45-fold improvement over 1996. The industry average for production costs in 2001 was $160. More than 80 percent of Goldcorp's results are due to the performance of the Red Lake mine.

Investing in new technology and pursuing a philosophy of making public proprietary information has turned the mine into the company's key asset. Forecasts for 2001 show that gross and net after-tax profits will be 70 percent and 30 percent respectively, while the industry as a whole worldwide is at break even.

Goldcorp installed a fiber-optic network in the mine connecting the surface to underground and relaying video, voice, and real-time mining data. This system allows geologists above ground to continually analyze ore richness and make real-time decisions on where to mine. The real-time data provides geologists with a "window" into the mine, significantly reducing the time to make decisions.

"The fiber-optic network has enabled us to remove communication barriers with the mine," notes McEwen, "Geologists no longer have to wait hours for a report." Operating expenses have fallen as more analytical work is conducted above ground. Also, with less people on site, safety has improved.

In March 2000, Goldcorp posted its entire geological database of the Red Lake mine, including all drilling and seismic results, on its Website and announced the "Goldcorp Challenge." The contest invited geologists, anywhere in the world to analyze the data, and suggest where the company should next focus its mining efforts. Goldcorp also posted analytical software that any professional or amateur geologist could download to help analyze the data. The mine data and the three-dimensional rendering program combined was 400 MB. The site had 475,000 hits and the 400 MB file was downloaded 1,400 times with queries originating from 50 countries.

Contestants had five months to analyze the data and submit suggestions and reasoning. The first prize was $95,000 for the best geological plan. Goldcorp retained all rights to submissions and any subsequent geological findings.

When examining the data, contestants were asked to highlight important clues that might lead to discovering another high-grade ore body at the Red Lake mine. Throughout the contest, Goldcorp posted updated information on its Website.

Goldcorp received confirmation of its proven and estimated reserves, and the models submitted have generated more than 100 new exploration targets. Goldcorp continues to work with licensed three-dimensional graphic software, greatly enhancing the ability of geologists to visualize and model the mineralization of most target exploration efforts.

The contest idea came to McEwen during an IT course at MIT in 1998, which highlighted global brainstorming. McEwen set out to apply the concept to Goldcorp. McEwen estimates that if he had had to hire all the consulting expertise that was brought to bear on the contest he would have paid two to three million dollars.

The Goldcorp challenge proved so successful that the company launched a new contest in March 2001 called "Global Search Challenge," bringing property owners and geologists from around the world together online.

Goldcorp believes the online showcase will help it identify and participate in the world's next major mineral discoveries. Public and private owners submit properties to the contest and explain why they feel theirs offers the most potential for mining development. Owners list geographic coordinates, commodity, and ownership details, and provide executive summaries, exploration results, claim maps, and any geochemical surveys. Data can be submitted digitally or by mail.

The registered users – natural resource companies, geologists, and prospectors from around the world – can freely browse through the information on prospective properties and assess their potential. Users can ask property owners questions.

The Challenge also allows investors to closely examine properties they might not have otherwise investigated. The forum forbids the exchange of personal, corporate, or other confidential information in order to prevent side deals from being struck outside of the contest. This stipulation is designed to ensure that Goldcorp will broker and potentially participate in any eventual deals that are struck.

Finally, vendors are asked what type of financial agreement they desire, and the estimated cost of the next stage of development.

Rewards total $2 million in prizes, awarded three times a year, over a two-year period to the five best submissions as determined by Goldcorp geologists. The top prizes are cash awards of $30,000 and the possibility of equity financing. The equity may be as substantial as $300,000.

"To win we must innovate. To innovate, we must leave the safety of the herd," said McEwen.

Goldcorp brings new meaning to the term "data mining," and highlights how the open source concept applied to software development – a new economy venture – can be applied to one of the most traditional old economy companies. What is required is an openness to explore new concepts. The financial results for Goldcorp have far exceeded traditional mining companies still mired in old ways of thinking.

LORENZO'S OIL

Lorenzo's Oil, starring Nick Nolte and Susan Sarandon, was released in 1992 by MCA Universal. The film tells the true story of two parents who saved their child from a fatal illness when doctors could not help them. *Lorenzo's Oil* highlights why an open source philosophy is essential for accelerating medical discovery and saving lives. When medical professionals share information cures come faster.

Augusto and Michaela Odone were mystified when their five-year-old son Lorenzo began showing alarming behavioral problems in 1984. After seeing many doctors, Lorenzo was diagnosed with adrenoleukodystrophy (ALD), a terminal brain disease that affects boys between the ages of five and twelve, and until that point, had always been fatal.

Despite resistance from the medical community, and resentment and opposition from parent organizations of children with ALD, the Odones discovered a cure for their son, and then shared that with other parents. Even in sharing the cure they were opposed by the medical profession and parents. Their story is a fascinating one.

ADRENOLEUKODYSTROPHY (ALD)

Our brains work by using neurons that transmit signals. Nerve fibres are protected by a fatty covering (called a myelin sheath), much like a coated electrical wire. In ALD, the myelin sheath is stripped from nerve fibres in the brain. As this happens, the neurons "short out" and the brain cannot send or receive messages.

Lorenzo began having behavioral problems and lost the ability to speak, see, hear, and walk. Less than a year after diagnosis, Lorenzo was confined to his bed, unable to move or even swallow on his own.

Extremely high levels of saturated, long-chain fatty acids cause ALD. In normal children, an enzyme breaks down these fatty acids, but this doesn't happen in ALD sufferers. As the medical community offered little hope, Augusto and Michaela Odone took it upon themselves to find a way to save their son's life. They spent hours researching medical texts and journals.

Augusto and Michaela postulated that if high levels of fatty acids caused the myelin to be stripped (a process called demyelination), then removing fatty acids from Lorenzo's diet would stop the destruction. They put Lorenzo on a very strict diet, eliminating foods that contained long-chain fatty acids. Despite the diet, however, his levels continued to rise. The Odones realized that the body, which also creates these fatty acids, was overproducing these to make up for the lack of them in Lorenzo's diet.

Michaela found an obscure 1979 reference in the *Polish Journal of Biology* that showed that when rats were fed oleic acid, their levels of short-chain, unsaturated fatty acid increased and long-chain, saturated fatty acids decreased.

Oleic acid lowered the level of long-chain fatty acids in Lorenzo's blood, but it was still higher than normal. The Odones experimented by adding erucic acid to the oleic acid. With both acids present, Lorenzo's saturated fatty acids declined to normal levels. The resulting mixture was called Lorenzo's Oil.

Today, Lorenzo's Oil is used as a treatment for ALD and can be effective when administered at the onset of symptoms. However, Lorenzo's Oil cannot restore myelin that has been stripped from nerve cells. So while Lorenzo's parents were able to stop further degeneration, they were not able to reverse the disease.

Lorenzo is now 23 years old and is able to communicate by moving his eyes and wiggling his finger. He remains bedridden and is unable to see or speak. Michaela Odone died of lung cancer in June 2000.

The Odones formed the Myelin Project (www.myelin.org) to bring researchers, parents and patients together, encourage the sharing of research information, and fund research into finding ways to regenerate myelin. This research will also benefit people who suffer from multiple sclerosis, autism, and Lou Gehrig's disease (amyotrophic lateral sclerosis, ALS).

The Myelin Project brings parents and patients face-to-face with medical researchers. In trying to find a treatment for their son, the Odones discovered that the motives of medical researchers are always clear.

"Lay people think that researchers are in their business to find remedies and treatments. Some of them are, actually, but most of them are not. Their motivation has nothing to do with finding treatment. Their motivation is rather to stick their name on an article, and publish in one of the main journals, like the *New England Journal of Medicine*," said Augusto Odone. By holding those researchers who receive funding from the Myelin Project accountable to patients and parents, their findings will be useful to the patients and not just science for science's sake. "I've been preaching for 12 years, that parents should be proactive and try to direct research towards practical goals," said Odone.

The Myelin Project also works to promote collaboration amongst researchers. Patients lose when medical researchers work in isolation from each other, unwilling or unable to share information. Instead of sharing information, researchers often compete with each other for publication in prestigious journals and patent applications. "I would do anything to promote collaboration rather than competition, particularly nowadays where to solve problems you really need teams," says Odone.

In the process known as peer review, medical researchers submit articles that they wish to publish to a group of their peers to validate their findings and approach. Given that those researchers who challenge medical orthodoxy often find their work ridiculed – as in the case of Dr Barry Marshall – this process is fraught with problems. In addition, peer review delays the publication of new research and information – sometimes for years. This is one of the systemic barriers that retards the rapid advance of medical knowledge.

Another is medical prizes which typically reward individuals, thereby promoting competition rather than cooperation among researchers. Rather than share new insights that will speed medical discovery, researchers hide them until they can gain recognition for their discovery and publish an article. Until the public that funds research demands new systems that create alignment with the interests of advancing knowledge as fast as possible, medical research will not advance as fast as it could. Odone argues no medical prize should ever be awarded to an individual – instead prizes should be awarded to groups who share knowledge and advance research.

The Internet has dropped the barrier between patients and medical researchers. A patient can use the Internet to look up research on a particular medical condition, access the databases of the top medical journals, and e-mail researchers directly. The Internet has the potential to become a powerful collaboration tool for researchers, but Odone has found that this hasn't happened yet. Deming noted that 94 percent of problems were due to bad systems and structures, not bad people. Medical researchers do care about curing diseases but they work in systems and structures that create disincentives to share information widely and readily.

AMAZON.COM EMPOWERS CUSTOMERS

Amazon.com was founded in July 1995, and sales have grown to $3.12 billion in 2001, making it the largest online bookseller.

Amazon allows customers to write reviews, create lists of favorite items, and even share their purchase information. Customers can contribute reviews, and frequent reviewers whose insights other customers rank as being helpful can become one of Amazon's Top 1000 Reviewers. Customers can also create lists, sharing what they think are the 10 best books on any given subject.

All of these initiatives allow customers to build equity with Amazon. Among book buyers there is a heavy book-buying segment. I call them bookaholics. These are consumers who delve widely and deeply into their areas of interest. A disproportionate number of these bookaholics are attracted to Amazon, in my opinion, because average bookstores (even superstores) cannot carry the breadth and depth of books in every subject area required to retain bookaholic customers. Through its wide selection and by not only allowing, but encouraging bookaholics to actively get involved in its site, Amazon builds equity with this most profitable customer segment and deepens its relationship with these most important customers.

Amazon became profitable for the first time in its fourth quarter ending December 31, 2001. Since its inception in July 1995, Amazon has lost $3 billion, leading some analysts to dismiss the company. But by capturing over $3 billion of sales, the majority of which would otherwise have gone to traditional bricks-and-mortar bookstores, Amazon has changed the bookselling ecosystem. What were once break-even and marginally profitable bookstores have gone bankrupt. In turn, the loss of bricks-and-mortar stores accelerates online book buying. By capturing a disproportionate number of highly profitable bookaholics, has Amazon further changed the bookselling ecosystem.

Thus while some critics dismiss Amazon because it was unprofitable for its first six years, it has nonetheless blindsided traditional booksellers.

CONTROL AND CREATIVITY: JAVA

How can organizations recognize trends earlier and respond faster? How can organizations anticipate where the market will move? How can they reinvent themselves? I asked James Gosling, the creator of Java, a Sun Microsystems vice-president and a Sun Fellow. Java is a programming language that greatly reduces complexity for programmers, by promising, "write once, run anywhere." This means programmers can write code that will run on any system rather than having to optimize code for every platform their program runs on (Windows, Mac, Unix). Java allows all kinds of systems to talk to each other, from smart cards to supercomputers, regardless of the underlying hardware or software. By 2004, 60 percent of all enterprises will have adopted Java applications and technology.[7] Gosling said:

> The central thing for us was distance from the mainstream. We had a group of a half dozen people that had been intimately associated with various parts of the company. We rented space a few miles away from Sun and cut the umbilical cord from the rest of the company. We weren't even on the corporate e-mail. We went to great lengths to make sure that nobody in the company actually knew what we were doing because we were afraid that the corporate antibodies would come after us and tell us what to do.
>
> We had a mandate to spend a couple of years thinking about issues and trends in computation that could affect Sun's business over the next five to ten years. We did it without connections and restraints. We needed time to just think and not just to come up with the occasional idea, but try them out, to build something.
>
> We pretty quickly zeroed in on what was happening in consumer electronics and began working with consumer electronics companies. We identified all sorts of interactions and as part of trying to explore these interactions we decided to actually build a device. That was very educational, it exposed a number of issues. My part of the project was to deal with tool problems and that is what became Java.

Companies don't do this nearly enough. The definition of research for most companies in the computer field is their product development.

Gosling went on to say that companies that are successful in changing the course of their industry have taken key people and allowed them to think several years ahead. Their mandate is not product development, but to perceive new opportunities that technology provides and anticipate where the market will move. The environment in which that happens is one in which,

> . . . taking a risk is a good thing. Failures are okay. In fact not failing often enough is as bad. Because if you are not failing often enough, you are not trying things that are sufficiently innovative.

There is an axiom in software engineering companies that the organizational chart tends to mirror the structure of the software they are working on.

THE ROLE OF CONFLICT

There is a statement in the Bible that has always puzzled me. Christ says: "Do you suppose I came to establish peace on earth? No indeed, I have come to bring division."[8]

Many people believe that peace is the absence of conflict. Conflict makes me uncomfortable, and therefore I tend to avoid it. At times, however, my conscience requires me to engage in conflict.

The most successful individuals and organizations are mission and vision driven. On a personal level, my mission and vision serve to focus and guide my activities, bring meaning and purpose to my life, and give me a sense of fulfillment. But pursuing my mission and vision actually brings me into conflict with other people, organizations, institutions, governments, and at times society as a whole.

To take an extreme example, living in South Africa during the apartheid years might require a conscientious person to be involved in protests. These actions would require tremendous courage, and would increase the sense of conflict in the individual's life, not decrease it. Such a course of action would require a greater tolerance for discomfort, ambiguity, and tension. But the individual would gain a sense of peace, accomplishment, and fulfillment from right living.

Within an organization, serving the mission might compel an individual to campaign for changes that will increase customer satisfaction levels. This requires effort and working against the status quo. It may bring the individual into conflict with people who gain their sense of security from "knowing" and enforcing the rules.

> *What most companies want is homogeneity. They want 150 trumpets playing in unison. But homogenous teams have blind spots; they move like a herd and often in the wrong direction. What's needed instead is complexity, the team as a jazz band that both harmonizes and improvises.*
>
> **Dave Marsing**
> **vice-president, Intel**

Love is both a verb (action) and a noun (feeling). People often confuse the two. When we talk of love, we are often talking about the feeling (noun) – a sense of joy, bliss, well-being and caring for someone else. But paradoxically, the only way to gain the feeling is through the action.

Shawnessy Johnson, our web designer and chief marketer at Strategic Advantage, just gave birth to her first child – Spencer McKenzie Johnson Band. For Shawnessy the action of love (verb) – involves getting up in the middle of the night to feed Spencer, change his diaper, and soothe him if he is crying. She engages in the *actions* of love regardless of her sleep depravation or *feelings*. In other words, mothers are loving in their action despite not always having the feeling. In the same way, people confuse the feeling of peace (noun) with the verb of peace.

As a verb, peace signifies a peaceful way, one that recognizes diversity of experience, opinion, and values these differences. A peaceful individual is comfortable with conflict and approaches difference with an openness, curiosity, willingness to learn, and compassion. A peaceful way values the search for truth over the ego's need for "being right."

When someone says, "I disagree with you," the language is incorrect. A more accurate statement would be: "I disagree with what you said." I am not my ideas. I am separate from them, can stand apart from them. Fred Kofman, a management consultant, says, "If you disagree with my idea, then I disagree with my idea." The discipline of being able to stand aside from my idea or position, and look at it from someone else's perspective, is powerful. This does not mean I have to give up my opinion, assumption, or idea, just temporarily set it aside in order to evaluate it.

"He who wrestles with us," wrote Edmund Burke, "strengthens our nerves, and sharpens our skills. Our antagonist is our helper." He who wrestles with us also has the potential to teach us.

Many individuals and organizations hold a dangerous mindset that there is only one "best" way to approach a problem or opportunity. To use a musical analogy, if there is only one way to sing a song, every voice will be in unison. Harmony, by contrast, is infinitely richer and more robust. It's the difference between homogeneity and heterogeneity.

What many organizations define as "peace" is unity on the surface – the apparent absence of conflict – where there is only one way, one strategy, one accepted doctrine. But underneath the surface conflict will roil.

Having only one approach increases an organization's chance of being blindsided. Nature doesn't take one approach to a problem. For instance the skunk, tortoise, and porcupine are all small animals yet each has a distinct strategy for keeping predators at bay. By embracing a multiplicity of strategies nature ensures it can't be blindsided. Diversity is security. Microsoft doesn't have only one strategy it has many: *Windows 2000, XP*, MSN, MSNBC, single applications, *Office*, a games division, the X Box, *Back Office*, etc.

If organizations need to embrace greater diversity to increase security and lessen the chance of being blindsided, they will have to embrace more conflict and more division.

So how can organizations and individuals increase conflict while decreasing friction? By increasing courage at the personal level and putting on training conflict resolution courses that teach empathetic listening. Most importantly, though, leaders have to model different behaviors.

The US constitution is based on rugged individualism. But an individual seldom accomplishes anything on his or her own. I have learned that the whole is more important than the individual parts. In other words, I have to be willing to accept what the group thinks as a whole. I have to allow them the right to be wrong, as long as group members are not proposing something that violates my ethics or principles. On the other hand, I have to be willing to stand up to the whole group when I think it is wrong, and engage in constructive disagreement.

We confuse "peace" with complacency and ease. In fact peace is having a discipline to live comfortably amid tension, ambiguity and discomfort. The serenity prayer reads:

God grant me the serenity to accept the things I cannot change;
The courage to change the things I can;
And the wisdom to know the difference.[9]

CONCLUSIONS

The ability to think beyond the current structure of your business is going to become an essential skill as new technologies will create radically new ways to do business and serve customers. Just performing better within the existing structure isn't enough.

REFLECTIONS

- How comfortable are you with conflict?
    - Personally?
    - Departmentally?
    - Organizationally?
- How can you increase tolerance for conflict – debate about ideas – without animosity between individuals?
- How could you apply the open source paradigm within your organization? What would it threaten?
- What are the dominant paradigms?
- How would that change:
    - Your products and services?
    - The way you develop new products and services?
    - The way you conceive of a product road map?
- Does your organization do an adequate job of sharing internal knowledge?
- Identify any systems, structures, and behaviors that discourage employees from speaking their minds. What could be changed to help employees develop greater courage?

CHAPTER 8

From Chaos to Order: Maximizing Opportunity and Minimizing Decision Risk

How can groups make decisions better and faster? What are the classic causes of failure in group decision-making? How can you align your organization with the needs of your customers? How can you uncover customers' unarticulated needs? Why do traditional methods of customer research fail?

In 1977, Dr Clifford Saunders began working for Bell Northern Research (BNR) as a design engineer after working in Saudi Arabia for five years. During his time away, design projects had grown exponentially more complex in scope, team size, and design features, but teams were still using the same decision-making tools.

Between 1985 and 1988, Saunders participated in three design projects. The first, named SLIC, was an integrated voice response computer system. The project involved more than 250 engineers and the architectural team alone comprised more than 50 engineers. The project cost more than $100 million to develop and was a commercial failure. As a result, Saunders was "revectored" – the human resource buzzword at the time for reassigned – to another design team.

This new design team spent $100 million trying to achieve 40 percent of the goals of the failed SLIC project while incorporating 60 percent new goals. It failed. Reflecting on it, Saunders notes, "It was just like the English when they travel abroad and want to be understood – they simply speak louder and slower." Only 10 systems were sold and the company didn't even recover its development costs.

So Saunders was revectored to a *third* project that was different than the other two and attempted to take on IBM, head to head, at the peak of its power. The project, titled DNS, was an attempt to design a new type of computer that was networked and would compete directly with IBM mainframes. It was another $100 million project and 50-person team. One system was sold but had to be bought back from the client.

Saunders had misgivings about the decision making, but felt uncomfortable questioning the process. After all, he was only recently returned from overseas, and as the "new kid on the block" he didn't have the political clout to question the way things worked. In fact, people who continually questioned and challenged the project leader were considered troublemakers and revectored.

Saunders didn't often air his reservations and discounted his own ideas, in the face of certain individuals who spun glorious stories of future success.

"Further, I didn't have evidence to support my views, while those in the cheerleading section had snazzy presentations and 'estimated sales' numbers on spreadsheets to support their claims."

Saunders began to reflect on the dismal product development projects and a number of shortcomings of group dynamics and the way groups make decisions. He began to study complexity and a tool to resolve complex situation called interactive management (IM) and one of IM's processes called interpretive structural modeling (ISM).

Today, the problems are so complex, the future so uncertain, that the only way to go is with teams. But most teams don't work optimally. How can you be certain that teams in your organization are making the best decisions?

The future is impossible to predict accurately. And creativity and innovation are not clean, linear, or simple processes. These facts highlight the need for successful teams and organizations to: (1) recruit divergent thinkers; (2) foster an environment where open, honest debate is the norm. But most people often are uncomfortable openly criticizing others' ideas. New tools, outlined later in this chapter, are helping teams to work more optimally, allowing individuals to challenge each other without offending each other. Few organizations have adopted these new approaches because what is familiar is more comfortable. Many executives prefer a command and control style – which often relies on "experts" to solve problems (industry analysts or management consultants). While I am not opposed to using these professionals, I believe that in most cases most of the knowledge, experience, and talents required to solve an organization's problem reside within the organization. The challenge of leadership therefore is to put in place systems and structures that facilitate the solving of complex problems by cross-functional teams. Relying primarily on external experts is not only disempowering, but experts are fallible:[1]

"An amazing invention, but who would ever want to use one?"
– US President Hayes, after participating in a trial telephone call in 1876.

"Everything that can be invented has been invented."
– Charles H. Duell, commissioner, US Office of Patents, urging President William McKinley to abolish his office, 1899.

"There is no likelihood man can ever tap the power of the atom."
– Robert Millikan, Nobel Prize winner in physics, 1920.

"Who the hell wants to hear actors talk?"
– Harry Warner, Warner Brothers, 1927.

"I think there is a world market for about five computers."
– Thomas J. Watson, chairman, IBM, 1943.

"640K is enough for anyone."
– Bill Gates, chairman, Microsoft, 1981.

THE FAILURES OF GROUP PLANNING

Leadership

Individuals who made strategic assumptions headed the design teams. If these assumptions were flawed, the whole project was doomed.

Secondly, even if the leaders often had a clear idea of what they wanted, they were unable to communicate it to others.

Thirdly, even if the leaders did have a clear idea, and did communicate it, the vision often changed during the project. Known as "scope creep," this is a phenomenon where end-users request new features and benefits be added during the course of the development work.

Culture and Contradicting the Boss

The culture we grow up in greatly influences the way we behave in groups. In Asian cultures, for instance, it is highly impolite to contradict your boss. It would result in a loss of face for both the subordinate and the boss. Most people, in general, feel uncomfortable contradicting their boss – regardless of culture. Imagine being in a meeting and the boss gets up and says, "Here is how we are going to do this," and you think that is the stupidest idea you have ever heard. It's going to fail for this, this, and this reason. How comfortable do you feel pointing this out in front of your peers?

Most people feel uncomfortable and don't speak up. Therefore, the key to getting at the best ideas is to enhance conflict. This is not conflict on the personal level, but rather the conflict of ideas.

If you actually share your reservations, the group may still go ahead with the plan, but strategies can then be put in place to mitigate the risks you have identified. At the very least they will have been raised and people will be aware and on the lookout for early warning signs. Speaking the truth gives other people the permission to do the same. If you are thinking something, the chances are others on the team are as well.

Individual style (i.e. Myers–Briggs[2]) and cultural differences (Asian deference to authority in group settings) ensure that in an average meeting not everyone will contribute. Instead, outgoing individuals will tend to dominate the group discussion and decision making. Those individuals holding back may have important information for the rest of the group. Any process that is designed to improve decision making will have to include methodologies to draw out these types of people.

Force of Personality

Often in a group there is one individual who is popular, persuasive, or stubborn to the degree that they wear down their opposition.

Individuals like this can often sway a group to follow a line of action. An individual who is shy or reserved may not wish to contradict someone who has a forceful personality.

Honesty

Why are we not absolutely open and honest in organizations? We all know the expression "don't shoot the messenger." The information senior executives receive is filtered, distorted, and sanitized, because no one wants to be the bearer of bad news. Does our tendency to "edit" what we truly believe enhance or retard the security of the organization?

Personal Styles in Dealing With Uncertainty

We all have different styles when it comes to dealing with uncertainty. Some people are more comfortable sharing hunches that they have, while others wait for more proof.

As adults we don't like to be proven wrong and our egos work to make sure that we always appear in a good light in the eyes of our peers. So often we would wait and see if we are right, rather than share a tenuous idea.

Consensual Reality

As individuals, we often do not listen to ourselves. We may have a small voice in the back of our mind telling us one thing, but because we do not see that opinion reflected or accepted in the wider society of our immediate peer or work group, we do not feel it is valid. This phenomenon is consensual reality.

This is one of the reasons that the stock market takes such huge swings. In a bull market, the prevailing wisdom is that it is "A good time to buy." This is sound advice as "A rising tide lifts all ships."[3]

However, during a rising market, commentators who warn of the danger of unreasonably inflated price–earnings ratios are dismissed as being out of touch with the times.

While aligning with the major market movements, the best stock traders also remain open to contrarian thinking, so that when the market reverses its trend they willingly and quickly reverse their positions, rather than defend them (and their egos' need to be correct). They quickly take small losses, while unsuccessful traders hold onto losing positions and lose much more.

Dynamics of Large Groups

Think of a design team of 50 engineers. How many ideas can they discuss at once? How efficiently do these groups operate? Think about your own experience in large group meetings. I personally find them boring. Most of the time people aren't talking about issues that interest me.

Usually the personality of the leader or a few people will dominate the group. The answer is not fewer meetings. It is changing the *kind* of meetings that we have.

MEMORY LIMITATIONS

Psychologist George Miller discovered in the 1950s that the maximum number of items the human brain can retain in short-term memory is seven, plus or minus two.[4] This means that most people can only remember seven items that they are introduced to without aid. This is very important in the area of complexity because complexity overwhelms this human limitation. As you will see later, the greatest number of problems ever facilitated out of an interactive management session was 678 by Henry Albert, working to redesign the US Defense Department acquisition system.[5] But 678 problems are overwhelming: where do you start? Given this limitation of our brains, we need new tools to help us deal with complexity. What is required is a process to sift through these problems. Pareto's Law holds that 20 percent of the factors will cause 80 percent of the headaches. IM identifies the most important ones and then allows the group to prioritize this smaller subset.

COMPLEXITY

The world is growing more complex. Complexity is growing exponentially. Alvin Toffler coined the phrase "the Information Age" and Peter Drucker told us that we had become "knowledge workers," but knowledge and information are no longer enough. The amount of information available to us across the Web is doubling every 18 months, and knowledge has a half-life. Microsoft's programmers assume that half the code they write today will be replaced within three years because the tools will be so much more powerful.

The assumption underlying the hierarchical command and control organization that comes to us from the Catholic Church and the military was that one individual or a small group of individuals would do all the important thinking and everyone else would merely carry out the orders. This can no longer be the case. The world is too complex, the rate of change too swift and markets too volatile. *Organizations that use the old mechanisms for decision making are failing to respond as quickly and accurately as possible to change in the market.*

Product developers must continually wrestle with complex trade-offs. Which would the consumer rather have, more features or faster running software? Is it better to be first to market with a product that meets 80 percent of the consumers' needs, or release a product a year after your competitor has stolen the market and established the standard? On the other hand, you can't rush out the release too quickly because it has to have enough new, exciting features to compel most users to upgrade. And you can't release software too quickly, because there is a competing need to spend the time to debug it and have as few bugs as possible.

Complexity applies to the amount of information, the speed at which the market is changing, the number of people who must be involved in the decision making and the complexity of trade-offs. Organizations that try to make all these decisions using just pens and flip charts will find themselves seriously disadvantaged.

PROBLEMS OF GROUPS

Many people consider meetings unproductive. To begin with, in a meeting of 20 people one person is speaking and 19 are listening. It is like having a 20-cylinder engine but using only one cylinder at a time. How can more creativity and power be released in meetings? How can more creativity and power be released through the planning process? How can an organization generate more employee commitment to change? The IM workshop uses a number of parallel processes so that all people are thinking and working at the same time while their reactions to issues are being captured simultaneously. This increases the amount of discussion, input, and commitment.

Departments often plan independently but operate in an interdependent reality. The marketing department heavily advertises a new product and production is overwhelmed. While marketing executives are getting bonuses, customer satisfaction with the organization is plummeting.

DEGREE OF FEELING

When we vote on an issue we typically vote yes or no. This doesn't get at the degree of feeling that people have. In a group of 19 people if 10 people vote yes, but are only marginally in favor (say at 51 percent), whereas the nine who vote are completely opposed (at 0 percent), then those in favor are in the majority. A voting system that took into account the degree of feeling would show that no one was strongly in favor and many were vehemently opposed to the issue.

If a group votes to do something but no one is really committed to it, will the project be executed? Likely not, in that people have to have a passion to carry a project out, in order to overcome the inevitable roadblocks that they will encounter. In the case above, of 10 people who feel 51 percent that things should go ahead, no one will champion the project and it will have a number of vehement detractors. The quality of decisions is based on the decision-making system.

STAKEHOLDER ANALYSIS

Different stakeholders often see issues in very different ways. Sales departments see things differently than marketing. Finance has different perceptions than shipping. The IT department has a different agenda than the executive team, and the HR department has a different orientation than manufacturing.

When debating issues, there is no easy way to keep track of the degree of feeling different stakeholders have on different issues.

UNDISCUSSABLES

Certain issues are "undiscussable" in groups, notes Harvard Business School professor Chris Argyris. The fact that there are undiscussable issues is itself undiscussable! Executive teams, departments, and whole organizations are then caught in a double bind. You can't solve a problem until you can see it or admit to it.

The challenge for decision makers is not *problem solving*, it's *problem seeing*. Managers have honed the practice of problem solving. What decision makers need to do now is better develop their *problem seeing* and *opportunity perceiving* capacity.

To help a group identify its blind spots, I ask people to identify as many undiscussables as possible – writing each one out separately on an 8½ × 11 sheet of paper. Participants then post their responses on a wall outside the seminar room. (I ask the most senior decision makers to remain in the room while everyone is posting to protect the anonymity of those posting.) Everyone reads all the postings and common ones are lumped together. Each participant then receives three colored dots (red, orange, yellow) and votes for the three most threatening undiscussables. Like fire, red is the hottest or most threatening undiscussable, orange is second and yellow is third. After the voting the items are scored (red = 3 points; orange = 2; and yellow =1). The undiscussables now become discussable because the silence has been broken. The exercise unleashes a tremendous amount of energy within the group, as participants have what they formerly felt were undiscussable issues validated as being of concern by others. They feel empowered to speak freely about what once seemed forbidden.

For those who know it, this is a variation of the open space technology pioneered by Owen Harrison.[6]

This highlights the principle that we must have new systems and structures in order to achieve new results. By definition, people will not talk about undiscussables. So by asking them to anonymously identify them in writing and vote on them, the process – or system – creates new results.

IN THE THICK OF THIN THINGS

Do meetings you are involved in often get bogged down in minor details that have little or no importance? Have you ever been bored out of your mind when people repeat the same point of view over and over again? How is it that many groups end up spending so much time on issues that are of so little importance? This may be a product of frustration and certain individuals wanting to use the meeting to gain a sense of self-importance. This raises the whole issue of what motives drive human behavior and are these motives the best for the organization?

NEW TOOLS FOR NEW TIMES

Decision making in most organizations has not fundamentally changed in millennia. But the problems organizations face have grown infinitely more complex. As Einstein said, "We can't be at the same level of thinking as when we got ourselves into the problem in the first place." We have to employ new tools.

In 1988, Clifford Saunders created software, called *Ballot Resolver* (hereafter called *Resolver*), that would eliminate many of these problems and help groups optimize decision making.

The first problem is that we cannot evaluate or keep track of more than seven issues at a time in our mind. So, how can we keep track of dozens of issues and rank them? Saunders designed software that will keep track of up to 200 issues at a time.

THINKWARE

Given our limitation of only being able to remember 7 ± 2 issues in short-term memory, complex problems are unsolvable using traditional tools such as pen and paper. If the individuals or groups are given powerful new software tools, they can solve complex problems that, without the tools, would have remained unresolved.

Groups can handle a certain amount of complexity unaided, but soon also reach a limit. Using a skilled facilitator and pens and flip charts, the groups' capacity is greatly increased. But Saunders realized that if a group is given a powerful, computer-based *thinkware* tool, software that increases the group's ability to think about complex problems, along with a skilled facilitator, they could often solve "insolvable" problems.

Saunders began searching for solutions, and discovered Professor John Warfield's work on *interpretive structural modeling* (ISM), a qualitative, computer-assisted way to structure complex situations. Most problems can be analyzed in terms of elements, sets, and relations. From these, models can be built. The ISM process consists of five stages: preparation, brainstorming, voting, model construction, and model interpretation.

The preparation phase consists of formulating trigger questions to stimulate the generation of issues and criteria to study the relationship between these issues. In the brainstorming phase, issues are generated. The voting phase ranks the issues. The software builds the model from the voting, which the facilitator helps the group to interpret.

Each participant in the group receives a wireless numeric keypad, which sends signals to a radio receiver. Once everyone has voted, the results are tabulated instantly and are displayed on a screen.

The number of people is solved by using wireless keypads. Our short-term memory limitation is solved by the fact that the computer remembers. The difference in language and mental models is solved by a trained, experienced facilitator.

MASHED POTATOES

When Saunders was a little boy he used to mash potatoes for his mother. His mother would tell him, "Now you mash them well, Clifford." At five, wanting to do the best job possible, Cliff would mash and mash and mash those potatoes. It didn't matter how long or how well Saunders mashed them, his mother would always mash them a few more times.

In Saunders' mind it was because he was only five and didn't know better and mothers know so much more. The lesson is powerful. If in a system we put in energy, time, and enthusiasm and receive no reward, we become frustrated. To put it another way, when we try all sorts of different strategies and the outcome is always the same, the result is frustration.

In the 1940s, psychologist Dr Norman R.F. Maier conducted numerous studies on frustration using lab rats. Maier trained rats to solve a simple maze. There was a standing platform and the rat could jump to the left or the right. On one side was a red card and the other was a blue card. Behind one of the cards was a piece of food. The rats quickly learned it was behind the red card. Maier then moved the cards so the red was on the left instead of the right. The rats learned it was behind the red card regardless of its position. Then Maier changed the rules again. He began putting the food behind the blue card. It didn't take the rats long to figure it out. Then he began changing the rules more often, and eventually not putting any food behind the cards at all. No matter how hard they tried, the rats could never win. The rats got so frustrated, they stopped playing the game.

Maier applied electric shocks to the rats forcing them to jump from the platform. The rats went crazy because they were forced to play a game they knew they could not win. They rolled themselves up into a ball, or bit themselves and their handlers.

This is exactly what happens in organizations when people are forced to participate in a system that they know makes no sense or could be improved, but they feel powerless. The result is frustration and cynicism and it is this sentiment that gives rise to the popularity of the Dilbert cartoon strip.

THREE LEVELS OF PROBLEMS

In working with clients over the years, Saunders discovered three distinct levels of complexity of problems. Level one problems involve collecting and analyzing the opinions of many decision makers, from potentially many stakeholder groups, and measuring the depth of agreement or disagreement on issues. Level two problems are clearly defined, but to solve them requires deciding from among a large number of possible strategies which is the trim tab. Level three problems are not clearly defined. The first task of the group, therefore, is to decide how to define the problem(s), and once that is accomplished, it becomes a level two analysis.

Level One Problems

Level one problems are the simplest of all as they involve collecting data. It could be impressions from a focus group, an executive team, or delegates at a conference. There are also real-time applications.

Data gathering sounds simple, but how, for instance, can you swiftly and accurately find out how 1,700 people at a conference feel about a number of issues? In the past, you could vote by show of hands with all its inherent limitations, such as how group dynamics biases results, or you had to use a time-intensive, cumbersome, paper-based voting system. With the new system, however, you can vote on up to 200 issues, with up to 10 answers per question, and segment the group by up to 10 stakeholders. The data is collected, analyzed and displayed instantly!

The following are examples of how complexity-resolving software can be applied to level one problems.

HIGHLIGHTING HOT SPOTS

Saunders and I were working with a management team. We broke it up into two groups: the five-member executive team, and the general management – a group of about 40 people. Each group registered separately as different stakeholders. The whole group was then asked a series of questions about issues facing the organization. When the perceptions of the executive team differed from the general management, Saunders asked for different points of view. The software highlights with whisker hairs around averages the degree of agreement within the group (Figure 8.1)

For instance, the two dots above could be the responses of the two stakeholder

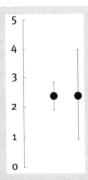

Figure 8.1

groups – the management team and the executive team – to the question "Is accessing capital a problem?" The management team's responses were averaged in the first dot and the executive team's in the second. (Answers were based on a five-point scale, with five being in complete agreement and zero in complete disagreement with the statement.) The whisker hairs around the first dot are very tight – showing that among the management team answers there was very little variation in their answers – most voted with a four or five. But the wide whisker hairs on the second dot show that the executive had very divergent answers. While the average was 1.8, four voted one, while the other voted five. The wide spread in the whisker hairs highlights the spread in thinking. One person voted it was very difficult while the other four voted that it was very easy. While the average was 1.8 (easy) there was significant disagreement within the group.

So Saunders asked, "Someone who voted that access to capital is easy, please explain your point of view." And one of the executives replied, "We've been doing it for years, it's not a problem."

"Okay," replied Saunders, "Now who voted that it was hard?"

The reply took us by surprise, "It's not hard to raise capital. It is hard to distribute it. To make the decision as to which operating unit to invest it in and where it will be most beneficial. That's the hard part."

So for the executive team, raising capital wasn't an issue, but distributing it was.

The general management perceived raising capital was difficult. The voting showed that senior executives were not concerned about raising capital. Further discussion may have highlighted the need for managers to prepare better cost–benefit analysis cases to present to executives.

Quantitative vs. Qualitative

The software quantifies people's opinions on issues. It tells you to what degree they agree or disagree with a statement, or how much they like or dislike a new feature.

However, it doesn't tell you *why* they like or dislike it. That information is qualitative and that is the job of the facilitator to determine.

The facilitator is just as important, if not more important, than the software tool. An experienced professional facilitator can improve group decision making with only a pen and flip charts. The complexity-resolving software adds no value on its own. But when used by an experienced facilitator the software can help groups resolve situations that were irresolvable before.

Creating Instant Interaction in Large Groups

Conferences are often boring, especially technical ones. Typically, papers are delivered and there is little or no interaction. It's one-way communication. The organizing committee for the 1997 International Switching Symposium surveyed delegates and found they were tired of the same old kind of conference. They wanted to be more involved in each session and they wanted the conference to be interactive. But how do you make a conference with 1,700 delegates interactive? ISS 97 hired Saunders to bring in his technology and facilitate plenary sessions. The presenters were told to prepare questions for the 1,700 participants following their presentations.

Saunders divided the participants into seven stakeholder groups: satellite, regulator, cable, old telco, new telco, and wireless. Each presenter was challenged to involve the audience in his/her presentations. Vinton Cerf, the senior vice-president of Internet Architecture and Technology for MCI WorldCom and the "Father of the Internet" was one of the presenters. He asked the participants, "What percentage of voice traffic will be carried over the Internet as data by 2001?" Within seconds, the conference knew the answer. Regardless of the stakeholder group they belonged to, delegates felt the answer was 50 percent.

It was a completely interactive meeting where presenters could craft questions on the fly in reaction to answers that may have surprised them. The organizers had hired controversial commentators who interpreted the results and often provoked discussion.

The technology became transparent quite quickly. In other words, people began to look at the value of the feedback, rather than focusing on how cool the technology was. After the session, Cerf said, "I don't think people realize what you have done at this conference of 1,700 people. Your technology has done today what the spreadsheet did for personal computers."

Differences in Perception

Resolver software can also highlight where there are differences in perception among different stakeholders. For instance, the CEO at a company-wide meeting of departments announces that he wants to launch a major new initiative and wants to get the reaction of the senior management team of 200 people. All the different departments feel positive about the initiative except the IT department that overwhelmingly feels it will fail. Discussion reveals that the IT department is not even meeting its current objectives and deadlines because over one third of its resources are currently dedicated to a major reengineering effort. Without the allocation of additional resources, or of dropping projects already committed to, the IT department cannot be involved in the launch of any new projects.

Politicians Go High Tech

A level one problem can also have some unique applications: a presidential candidate wants to refine his message, so a videotaped speech is played for a random sample or specific target group of voters in a room, each with radiofrequency control. As the candidate talks, they react to the messages by moving a slider to the right if they like the message and to the left if they dislike it. The degree of movement corresponds to the individual's degree of feeling. The software compiles the reactions in real time and overlays it on a video of the speech for the researchers so they can then determine what the group liked and disliked about the talk.

Level Two Problems

Level two problems are still complex, but operate within a defined area. For instance, a CEO sets the goal for the organization of increasing market share by 3 percent and profitability by 5 percent. How will the management team execute the goal? Or how can the organization improve customer satisfaction? The challenge is clearly defined; the group needs to figure out how to accomplish it.

The following are examples of how complexity-resolving software can be applied to level two problems.

CANADA REACHES CONSENSUS

We have so overused antibiotics, that some bacteria have developed a resistance to them. Certain strains of tuberculosis (TB) have developed a resistance to a number of drugs. Doctors can now take three of our strongest antibiotics, combine them in a chemical cocktail, give it to a patient with multiple drug resistant TB and it will have no effect.

TB is a contagious disease and an individual who has multiple drug resistant TB must be kept away from the general public. The only treatment really is to confine the individual in a hospital until they recover or die.

In 1996, the World Health Organization (WHO) criticized Canada for being the only developed country in the world with no national TB policy. Between 1977 and

1997 Canada had no such policy because each province considered this area of health policy its own purview. So, in 1997 the federal government brought all the stakeholders together – senior officials from each provincial and territorial ministry of health, officials from the immigration department, federal ministry of health officials, representatives of the First Nations, HIV-positive groups, senior TB academics, and laboratory testing people – a group of 110 people in all.

For 20 years this group had not been able to reach any consensus on this issue. In two and a half days the group passed 120 separate resolutions with the support of more than 80 percent of the representatives. What it took to reach national consensus on TB was a new way of working. Everyone could see the facts, and while the proceedings were emotionally charged at times, the process was open and transparent which increased trust between groups that had been antagonists before.

Aligning Organizations with Customer Needs

Organizations can survey prospective and existing customers, asking them to rate 40 or 50 points of service, including price, service, quality, product features, delivery, billing, and promptness of response. (1) Rank each service in terms of its importance to your overall satisfaction. (2) How well or how poorly is the organization meeting each need?

Point A is something the organization is doing exceptionally well but that customers do not value. For example, if a hospice had built a sound system into every room, it would have spent thousands of dollars needlessly. Point B is something like a telephone in every room. It's exceptionally important to customers but the organization's original plans didn't call for it.

Using this information, plot the results on the two dimensions (importance and performance), as shown in Figure 8.2. First, we will plot importance. Everything above

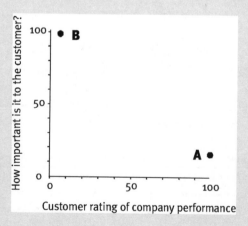

Figure 8.2

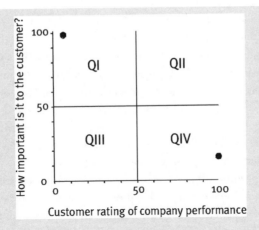

Figure 8.3

the horizontal mid-point line is important to the customer. Everything below the line is unimportant.

Everything to the right of the vertical mid-point line means the organization is doing well in the customer's opinion and everything to the left indicates the company is doing poorly (see above).

We now get four quadrants (Figure 8.3). The top-left quadrant (QI) contains items that are very important to the customer but on which the organization is doing poorly. The top-right quadrant (QII) contains items that are very important to the customer and on which the organization is doing very well. The bottom-left quadrant (QIII) contains items that are not important to the customer and on which the organization is doing poorly. The bottom-right quadrant (QIV) contains items that are not important to the customer, but on which the organization is doing very well.

Quadrant IV activities are clearly a waste of money. The organization is doing a great job, but customers don't care. The activities don't add value from the customers' perspective. Quadrant III really doesn't matter. The organization is doing a bad job, and thankfully the customers don't care. Quadrant I is the quadrant of crisis. It contains items that really matter to the customer but on which the organization is doing poorly. The organization needs to stop investing in the activities in Quadrant III and IV and invest all the savings of time, energy, and money into points of customer service in Quadrant I, thereby pushing the ratings on those dimensions of customer service into Quadrant II. Simply put, the organization should do best what customers value most.

Rationalizing Improvements

Complexity resolving software allows organizations to expand this two-dimensional model (importance versus performance) and add other variables:

- How much will it cost to improve each feature?
- How much time will it take?
- What percentage improvement is possible? For instance, on a 0–100 scale can a feature be improved from 10 to only 15 or from 10 to 90?
- What is the competitive positioning? Are there certain features or benefits that no other competitor has that if we were to include in our next product release would compel users to switch to our product? Are there certain features of our competitors' products that are so compelling that their customers will not switch products unless we match them?
- Call center priorities. While it may not seem obvious, given that each call costs a company an average of $32.74 and that technical support calls can cost as much as $400 an hour for a senior technician, it is important to eliminate the classic problems that product users have. Finding what the top 10 list of call center problems, and resolving these in the next product release not only will increase customer satisfaction but cut costs.
- Programmers/designers – what are the innovative product features that new technology enables that programmers and designers find exciting?
- Usability labs (see description below).
- Unarticulated needs (see description below).

These new dimensions, added to the initial two, give a more complex analysis. Saunders designed *Resolver*Ballot*, software that can collate input from individuals' impressions on up to eight variables that can then be plotted against each other. *Resolver* can find the "sweet spot" among eight dimensions. The graph on the above page is two dimensional, and I can imagine a three-dimensional tic-tac-toe game – but I can't imagine and eight-by-eight dimensional graph. *Resolver* solves the challenge of finding the features that will make the biggest different to customer satisfaction, at the least cost, with the fastest development time, that will make the biggest competitive difference, and eliminate the biggest possible burden from the call center. In other words, helping decision makers maximize the return on investment, by seeing more clearly through the fog of competing priorities.

Dell Computer Corporation

Dell Computer Corporation twice a year holds a "platinum council," inviting the Chief Information Officers (CIOs) from its largest customers to an off-site technology summit. PC analysts and partners such Intel provide insight into the future of technology, and CIOs get to mingle with each other. Dell uses the forums to gain insight into what customers want. The engineers at Dell had been building ever-faster machines, but at one of these platinum councils the customer feedback was,

We really don't care if the computers are two percent faster or three percent slower.

What is more important to us is reliability and consistency of the product line. After four years of buying Dell systems, our technicians have to support ten different kinds of video cards, five different kinds of hard disks. You keep changing components, because this one is marginally faster than that one. This increases the complexity of our network, increases the total cost of ownership of each PC and means our technicians have to work on low-level, unexciting conflicts – so it is hard to motivate them and retain staff with this kind of boring work. What we really need is reliability, backwards compatibility and consistency.

So, the result of Dell engineers' efforts had actually been creating problems for customers.

Using keypads, you could get a focus group of customers to vote on up to 200 points of customer service in terms of how important they are to them (e.g. price, speed of computers, reliability, service response time) and how well the organization is serving them on these points. With this data, you can plot how important an issue is to customers against how well we, as a company, are doing.

The results are often surprising. The organization may be investing all sorts of time and effort in an area that is adding no customer value, or worse yet, upsetting customers, whereas there may be things the customer deems to be very important where the organization is doing little or nothing. Such an analysis allows the organization to reorient itself to the customers' preferences.

As consumers, we make complex decisions based on criteria that we are not even fully aware of. Customers will often tell you that they want everything: better price, faster service, higher quality, more features, greater ease of use. But what do they feel is most important? The researchers need to pit points of customer satisfaction against one another to create a hierarchy of needs. If the organization had only one additional dollar to spend per customer, what investment would yield the greatest delight? The process is called forced ranking.

Some interesting research was done by a jet manufacturer a number of years ago. Executives who bought corporate jets were asked a series of questions, "Would you like mahogany paneling in the interior?" *Yes.* "Is it important to have a faster plane?" *Yes.* "Would you like wider seats?" *Yes.* "Would you like built-in cellular phones?" *Yes.* "How about longer-range planes?" *Absolutely.*

When executives were asked, "Would you be willing to pay an extra $250,000 for these added features?" Their tune changed. *"No way,"* they said. Customers will typically say yes to every feature you propose. But what are actually the most important features or benefits? This is why force ranking is so important.

So the executives were asked, "If you had to chose between a mahogany paneling and longer range, which is more important?" *Longer range.* "Which is more important faster planes or built-in cellphones?" *Faster planes.*

It all boiled down to, "Just make the planes as fast as possible and with the longest range – everything else can be add-on features." Executives who buy these jets spend a lot of time traveling. What they want is to spend less time in the air. Therefore, range is important because refueling requires landing and creates the potential for delays. So all engineering efforts were invested in increasing the range and speed. Not surprisingly, these jets have sold extremely well.

The method of forced ranking outlined above is called paired comparison. We have a keen sense of comparison and we can usually decide out of two choices, which is more important to us. Paired comparison is a powerful way to sort out a complex mess of criteria by pitting all of them against each other in a systematic way. In the end it creates a hierarchy of needs or desires.

Getting consumer input in this systematic fashion is critical to help engineers and designers in making trade-off decisions while developing new products and services.

WHY TRADITIONAL CUSTOMER RESEARCH METHODS FAIL

Traditional methods of customer research such as focus groups and broad surveys fail for a number of reasons.

Unarticulated Needs

Often customers cannot even articulate what it is they really want. For instance, a really good researcher interviewing a car buyer would not just ask about potential improvements but would also ask about upsetting instances while driving. I would relate a real-life story of an accident I witnessed. A car in the fast lane and a truck in the slow lane of a three-lane highway both move into the center lane 100 yards in front of me. While the drivers may have looked in their rear-view mirrors, they obviously didn't look side to side. They hit with tremendous force. The car began doing 360-degree turns and crashed into the guardrail facing the oncoming traffic, while the truck careened to the outer edge and flipped upside down in the ditch. And all of this happens in slow motion – it's a surreal experience – with adrenalin pumping I realized that this could be my last moment on earth.

What I am really saying to the researcher is, "I am absolutely terrified of colliding with another vehicle in my blind spot. What I really want is four infrared or sonar sensors in the four corners of my car that proactively warn me when I am about to hit something in my blind spot." But it is unlikely that an average consumer will be able to articulate what they want (positive feature or benefit) but they will be able to articulate their classic fears or frustrations (negative). It is therefore up to highly creative individuals and organizations (1) to elicit classic fears and frustrations from existing and potential customers and (2) then to create new products or services that meet these unarticulated needs.

The laws of physics that would enable the telephone to be invented existed prior to the telephone's invention. Similarly we as consumer had a need for the phone prior to its creation – it's just that we didn't know it. Our needs exist before we realize them. It's up to creative individuals and companies to uncover these needs and then invent products and services to meet them.

Therefore organizations must work to uncover what upsets customers and then create solutions to these problems in the form of new features, products, or services.

Usability Labs

Focus groups are useful for incremental approaches to refining existing products and services, but they are inadequate when dealing with new products and services because consumers cannot understand how to use a new product or service, or how it will impact their lives until they have used it.

In order to gain deeper customer insight, software companies employ usability labs. Michael Dell recounted a story about Dell's usability labs in an interview: Dell researchers find an average person on the street who has never used a computer and will bring them into the usability lab. The interactions are videotaped so that product designers can learn from the consumer behavior.

In one case, researchers handed a subject a Dell shipping box containing an expensive new notebook computer. The guy opened the box, couldn't figure out how to get the notebook out, so he lifted the whole box up and quickly flipped it up side down, so that the $8,000 notebook fell crashing to the floor.

Obviously the man off the street didn't know that dropping a notebook on the ground from a height of six feet isn't a good thing. The researchers showed the videotape of the incident to the guy who designed the packing box. The designer felt he'd designed the best packaging possible, but obviously it wasn't good enough for new users. So the company redesigned the shipping box: an instruction sheet that uses step-by-step cartoons now covers the entire top of the box, and once the instructions are removed, lifting handles are apparent.

Declumping

I was speaking at a risk managers' association conference and I asked the 600 delegates to work in groups and list what they perceived to be the risks that they faced as risk managers. During the break these were collected and entered into a computer system. Using keypads, the delegates then voted on the items in terms of how likely they were to occur and how severe their impact could potentially be. Each delegate had a radiofrequency keypad and the results were tabulated instantly. The group perceived all of the threats to be both likely and severe. Now the group faced a "clump" of threats and was no further ahead.

The software provided by the conference organizers only was able to measure two variables against each other (in other words likelihood vs. severity). This does not really add value. This is where it becomes critically important as to *which software tool you are using*.

Resolver can analyze up to eight variables that can then be plotted against each other. This significantly enhances the value of the tool, and avoids non-productive "clumping" of results.

Focus Groups

As consumers, we know what we want and we make trade-offs in our own minds on what is important, but we can't always articulate how we make those decisions.

In Figure 8.4, a researcher (A) is asking a question of someone in a focus group (B). There are three conversations going on – conversation two is the public conversation. Another conversation is going on in the head of the researcher (conversation 1) and another in the head of the person being interviewed (conversation 3). Which is the most important conversation?

Software tools allow a researcher to explore how individuals are thinking

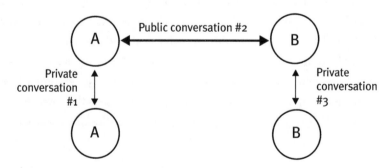

Figure 8.4 The most important conversation?

and feeling and get a level of agreement from every other focus group participant. This allows deeper insights than the traditional focus group techniques do.

The problem with the way focus groups are traditionally conducted is that one loud or very opinionated individual can bias the result of the whole group, because the researchers are really not getting at what each consumer in the group is thinking.

Another research approach is to get away from the academic focus group environment and interact with consumers in their normal environment. In conducting research for a clothing company, this might involve taking a hand-held video camera to a customer's home and having them open their wardrobe, and talk about why they like their favorite clothes. The video captures all sorts of clues that the individual consumer might never even articulate.

Level Three Problems

Level three problems are messy. These are difficult to describe, have undefined boundaries, and are very confusing. In a level three problem the problem itself has not yet been defined, nor have the strategies for resolving it.

Complex problems involve many issues, are influenced by existing and emerging trends which may conflict, and the data is confusing. Solving a messy problem requires a team. The more complex the problem, the more people with technical expertise have to be involved in solving it. This further complicates the problems because each individual has different mental models or paradigms of the problem, interprets the data and trends differently, and evaluates importance by different criteria. Manufacturing will interpret the problem differently than engineering, accounting or the information technology group. And each group will argue strenuously for the optimum solution as they see the problem (Figure 8.5).

Here's a simple exercise. What comes to mind when I say, "Fast car?" Answers typically are a Porsche, Ferrari, or Indy 500 pace car. To one individual it might be a Mercedes Benz such that on the autobahn at 200 kilometers an hour, the coffee doesn't jiggle. To me it might mean a Miata with the top down. Now a Miata is not actually a fast car – but being so low to the ground, with the wind whistling through what remains of my hair it *feels* fast. Do you see the danger? We all speak English so we *assume* that we understand what "fast car"

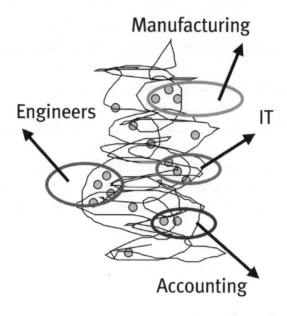

Figure 8.5 How different functions analyze a complex situation.

means, but it means *very* different things to different people. If you think a fast car is a Mercedes, and I think it's a Miata, and you come into a car dealership asking for a fast car and I start trying to sell you a Miata, I am not going to be a successful salesperson.

How can a group solve complex problems? Saunders' thinkware uses the salami approach. Issues are identified, clarified, sorted – highlighting the most important ones. This group of issues becomes the salami. Salami is easiest to eat one thin slice at a time. Thinly slicing for the group of issues means isolating and evaluating the relative importance and interdependence of two issues at a time. Based on these comparison judgments, the software builds a model that prioritize problems thereby facilitating decision-making and helping to create the most effective solutions possible. The complex problem is solved one slice at a time.

In this sense the software is a trim tab factor – it is a system that takes the complexity out of complex situations making it easy for decision-making teams to spot the trim tab issue(s) that will result in the greatest organizational improvement. When a group solves a level three problem it feels like magic to them. The group feels they have solved the insolvable.

RESOLVING A COMPLEX SITUATION

One of Saunders' clients wanted to develop a greater understanding of their present environment : how it was changing, what the key leverage points were, and how the organization could be better positioned to take advantage of new opportunities, while minimizing future risks. The session began with brainstorming around identifying major risks. The group then evaluated 11 risks by four criteria: amount of risk, likelihood of it transpiring, adequate controls (are we prepared), and the future strategic importance of this (do we anticipate a shift in importance over time?) The purpose was to create an in-depth understanding of each risk and to build a risk map.

The next step was to determine which risks were the greatest relative to each other. Under normal circumstances, it is difficult for a group of people to know what to do with so many risks. It is at times overwhelming, and people don't know where to start. By pairing each risk and asking if risk A were to actually occur, would it make risk B more likely? The software sorts out all the relationships and creates a map or flowchart called a problematique.

For instance, an executive team may identify a number of potential threats, such as attracting the best people, developing new products and services, having the right information technology (IT) infrastructure, having the best partners and creating alignment with strategic partners. The problematique will show how participants perceive the relationships between the issues. If we pay higher salaries or offer people equity in the company, we will be able to attract and retain the best and brightest people. These people in turn will not only develop the new products and services, but select our IT infrastructure, and help us identify and negotiate strategic alliances that are in alignment with our vision. It shows that some problems are symptomatic and others are root causes.

All of the tools discussed in this chapter work to highlight what Saunders calls the BAATM, the best answer at the moment. Our perception of situations as individuals and groups will change over time as new information becomes available and as the market changes. But these tools give groups the ability to identify what the best answers at the time are.

APPLICATIONS

The software and process can be used in strategic planning, project management, software or product development, conflict resolution, consumer research, resource allocation, and risk management. It has numerous benefits. It:

- Pulls out the ideas and contributions of *every* participant.
- Highlights areas of agreement and disagreement immediately. The group can then use its time to focus on issues of most importance.

- Shortens meeting time by up to 40 percent.
- Active involvement increases retention of meeting content by up to 70 percent.
- The system protects confidentiality by allowing participants to get comfortable in being honest. Over time this helps create a cultural change in the organization.
- People feel that the process is open, transparent, and unbiased. This increases the commitment to the final outcome.
- Allows individuals to get quick feedback on new ideas in brainstorming sessions.
- Keeps participants focused on the issues.
- Increases ownership of final results.
- Activates new levels of creativity from participants.
- Generates a statistical measurement of support for each idea. The process is transparent so it creates buy in and adds credibility to decisions.
- Allows unbiased evaluation and criticism.

DECISION DOCUMENTATION

By having a recordable history of decisions, groups can go back and evaluate them. For a toymaker, Christmas season is a make it or break it time, with up to 80 percent of the annual sales being crammed into this period. With the fickle market and unpredictable consumers, it is just a guess what craze is going to be hot this year and what is not. This is critical because production for items can't be in real time. In other words, you have to predict nine months in advance what is going to sell well this year. Wouldn't it be useful to have the debate between the designers recorded, so that you could go back after the Christmas season and begin to build a predictive model? Person A has been right 65 percent of the time on production volumes. Person B has been right 50 percent of the time, and Person C has been right 70 percent of the time. Therefore in the future when making decisions we will apply different weightings to each of their estimates. As their accuracy changes over time, we can change the weighting.

CONCLUSIONS

The increasing complexity of problems requires new ways of solving them.

Top-down decision-making doesn't work anymore. Organizations are too complex and markets changing too fast to centralize decision making at the top of the organization. As Lou Pritchett, the author of *Stop Paddling and Start Rocking the Boat*, asks, "Have you ever noticed that bottlenecks are always at the top of the bottle?" *The role of leadership is to ensure that the systems and structures are in place to ensure optimal decision making by individuals and teams.* Ensuring the right systems and structures are in place is the trim tab of leadership.

Deciding what is the system that will make the most difference will vary from organization to organization, as different industries have different capital intensities, distribution models, etc. The key then is to have a system or methodology that will help decision makers identify what the trim tab is for their industry. Complexity resolution software is one tool that can help you decide what the trim tab is for your organization.

Complexity resolution software helps create an environment where people are encouraged to voice their feelings about decisions, regardless of their position within the company, and where conflict is welcomed. And it helps companies align with the true needs of customers.

REFLECTIONS

- Is your organization open to using new tools, such as the software described above, to reach decisions and solve complex issues?
- How do you know that your organization is meeting the real needs of customers? Do you know what their real needs are? What have you done differently in the last 12 months to explore your customers' needs?
- How could usability labs help improve your products or services?
- What methodology does your organization follow to uncover new value?
  - List ways in which you can anticipate their needs in five or ten years time.
- How could you improve the time-to-competence learning curve within your organization? In what ways have you worked to improve your customers' time-to-competence learning curve?

CHAPTER 9

Strategic Scenarios: Planning and Preparing for Possibilities

How can executives and teams prepare for the future? How can you discover your own blind spots? What tool will help you identify leading indicators that forewarn when your company or whole industry is about to be blindsided? What one personal character trait will help individuals avoid being blindsided?

Herman Kahn (1922–1983) coined the term "scenario planning." In the late 1940s he worked at the Rand Corporation, a US military think-tank, studying how a nuclear war might play out. Using analytical techniques such as game theory and system analysis, applied to military theory, he developed potential outcomes of nuclear war based on different military decisions.

One of Kahn's neighbors worked in the movie industry. Kahn was wondering what to call the stories about alternative futures that he was developing. His neighbor pointed out that in Hollywood a plot was called a "scenario." Kahn adopted the term.

Kahn's ideas were so distasteful and upsetting that one journalist, Gerard Piel of *Scientific American*, coined the phrase "thinking the unthinkable" to describe Kahn's approach.

Kahn liked the phrase so he used it as the title of his next book. Kahn believed that the best way to prevent nuclear war was to avoid the cultural blind-spot and think through what would happen if war occurred. What if it *did* happen? What kind of world would survivors face? *Dr Strangelove*, played by Peter Sellers in Stanley Kubrick's classic 1964 cold war satire, was modeled on Kahn.

"Thinking the unthinkable" is a profound and exceptionally powerful concept. Why don't we think about the unthinkable? What prevents us? I find it horrifying to think of nuclear war, population explosion, environmental collapse, species extinction, or ozone depletion. I don't think about the unthinkable because it makes me deeply uncomfortable, it's morally objectionable, distasteful, and ultimately threatening, and it is diametrically opposed to what I feel *should* happen.

Therefore I cannot begin to ask, what conditions would lead to these events occurring? What danger signals would lead me to believe the likelihood of these terrible scenarios is increasing? By refusing to think the unthinkable, I voluntarily create blind-spots for myself.

PERSONAL REACTION

It is as if I am identifying what I believe with my sense of who I am (identity or self-esteem). In essence I am saying, "I am what I believe." Even entertaining the possibility of these unthinkable scenarios so challenges my fundamental beliefs that I feel threatened. Put another way, "Attack my beliefs and you attack me."

I am drawing my sense of self-esteem and security from what I know. The practical impact of this is that I can't stand aside from my ideas, examine them in the harsh light of reality and, if they are found wanting, set them aside and adopt new ones.

This is one of the fundamental reasons that change is so difficult. People tie what they "know" to their sense of identity. I put know in quotation marks because I feel it is based on an illusion. We all change our ideas, because otherwise we would all still have the opinions of a six-year-old.

ALL KNOWLEDGE

When conducting a seminar, I ask the audience to imagine a pillar from floor to ceiling representing all knowledge in the universe, both the knowledge we have uncovered as the human race and knowledge we have yet to discover or uncover. What portion of the pillar would represent all human knowledge as a percentage of all knowledge? Would all human knowledge be close to the top, bottom, or middle? Invariably people answer the bottom, often right at the floor.

Then I say: "Now lets take all that human knowledge, that little fraction of all knowledge, and imagine that it is stretched out from floor to ceiling. Where would my knowledge as one individual or your knowledge fall on that scale?"

After highlighting the fact that LexisNexis has almost three billion documents indexed, the 2.3 million English books in print in North America, and the 550 billion Web pages in 2001, people invariably answer, "Close to the bottom." Well, if I only know a fraction of a fraction, am I not in a dangerous position to hold tightly onto to my ideas?

CLASSIC SCENARIO PLANNING

In the 1970s, the planning group at Royal Dutch/Shell began using scenario planning to prepare for the future. The team spawned a host of disciples, including Peter Schwartz, Pierre Wack, Arie de Geus, and Kees Van Der Heijden, who spread the word through books and lectures. Major corporations have adopted the method.

The classic case of scenario planning is cited by Peter Schwartz in *The Art of the Long View* and by Kees Van Der Heijden in *The Art of Strategic Conversation*. The benefits of scenario planning are: (1) more robust decisions; (2) better thinking about the future because scenarios challenge participants' mental models; (3) enhancing corporate perception and better recognition of patterns of change and their implications; (4) improved communication by using scenarios to provide context for decisions; and (5) as a way to provide leadership to the organization.

At Shell, the planning group thought about the future of the oil industry and the company's position to the year 2000. It anticipated the energy crisis of the 1970s, the reduction in the demand for oil, the evolution of the global environmental movement, and even the breakup of the Soviet Union. Having developed contingency plans based on these scenarios, the company was able to move swiftly while its competitors were overtaken by these events. Shell was able to respond quickly and effectively to the 1973 oil crisis.

DELPHI TECHNIQUE

The purpose of scenario planning is to expand the mental models (paradigms or perceptions) of decision makers about the future. One way to do this is to begin the exercise with a Delphi. A Delphi is a survey technique, first developed by Rand in the 1950s, for soliciting the wisdom of experts. A number of experts from various fields are asked to rate the likelihood of a series of trends and the results are tabulated and circulated. Then, the participants are asked to vote again in light of what their peers responded in the first instance. The technique can also be used in a more open-ended way, inviting the experts to make future predictions, with respect to certain issues or in response to certain triggering questions. The answers are collated, synthesized, and fed back to the group as a whole for their opinion. The idea is to tap into the wisdom of a wide range of experts to assess what global trends might occur.

Every expert gets to read what everyone else has said and in turn add his or her opinions. After two or three rounds the opinions begin to coalesce in agreement around certain points while diverging on others. A Delphi synthesizes expert opinions on the probability of certain future outcomes. This is a rich input for the scenario planning exercise and will stretch the minds of those participating, helping them to look at the world with new eyes.

Today, the Internet increases the speed at which a Delphi can be conducted and the technique is being used to involve more than just experts. Some organizations are now involving customers and suppliers, as well as key internal and external experts. A vital question is, "To contribute maximum value, is the expert group diffuse enough to generate depth of insight?"

Participants determine which trends, technologies are certain to occur (such as Moore's Law will hold till 2014, Metcalfe's Law ensures Internet growth will continue, world population will grow). These trends will color every scenario that is developed. The group then examines uncertain trends. The group can then cross them in a two-dimensional graph by answering two questions: "Which of these trends is most likely to occur? Which would have the biggest impact on our organization?" The group chooses which uncertainties to explore and develops three or four different scenarios.

WHY SCENARIO PLANNING?

Scenario planning is not about *predicting* the future. It's about *preventing* it. Scenarios are powerful planning tools because the future is unpredictable. The purpose of scenario planning is to reduce the number of surprises for decision makers, companies, and industries. Scenario planning is grounded in uncertainty, and looks at a number of different options as to how the future might turn out. Companies have "blind-spots" in their planning. Too often organizations set strategy based on "The Official Future " – an articulated or unarticulated view of the future that dominates thinking within the organization. The view of the future is based on a desired outcome or set of goals. Underlying this view is an assumption that the executives, or corporation is in control.

They assume one future and plan for it. When that future does not happen, they panic and their capacity to change and adapt is reduced. This single scenario of the future is the trap that most companies fall into.

Organizations that presume a predetermined outcome fail to test strategies and decisions against other possibilities, and fail to look for the signs that indicate a different future. They are in fact "blind" to reality and caught up in a dream of the official future. Blind companies are easily blindsided.

The point of scenario planning is to create plausible scenarios. The ultimate goal is to create mental agility, and flexibility and the ability to respond to whatever situation unfolds.

Scenario planning forces to the surface assumptions that individuals in the planning group have about the future, allowing the group to examine them, determine which are valid, and discard those that aren't.

Once a group has developed the scenarios they can put themselves into the future and "backcast" or look back and ask the question, "What were the signs that we knew were leading to this scenario?"

If the music industry executives of one of the major record labels had developed a digital music future scenario in a scenario planning exercise, they could have backcast and said what is preventing this file-swapping future from emerging? They would have identified a couple of things:

- *Bandwidth* – The average connection speed for individuals in 1993 was 9,600 baud (9.6 kbs) and if you had a really fast connection it was 14.4 kbps. At 9.6K a four-minute song, 40 MB in size, would take 10 hours to download. At 14.4K that would drop to 6.3 hours. So it wasn't unreasonable for music executives to dismiss a digital music future as a possibility.
- *Compression technology* – Prior to 1997, when the MP3 file format was developed, a four-minute song took almost 40 MB of space to digitize. These huge files could not be readily moved across the Internet.

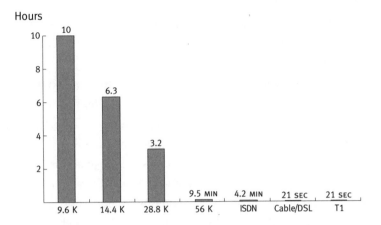

Hours

Figure 9.1 Time to download a four-minute song. Prior to 1997 without compression file = 40 MB. From 56K on, after 1997, using MP3 file = 4 MB.

In other words, looking at the possibility of a digital music future in 1993, a group doing scenario planning might conclude that triggers indicating the increased likelihood of a digital music scenario would be: (1) if bandwidth expanded 100-fold and was widely available at a reasonable price; (2) if compression technology improved 100-fold, so that files were 100 times smaller; (3) a combination of (1) and (2), such as a 10-fold increase in bandwidth and a 10-fold decrease in file size due to new compression technology. Figure 9.1 shows how the download times fell.

As music executives then witnessed these triggers occur within the market, they would already be prepared for the future.

Great leaders are like great chess players, notes Graham Crawford, executive vice-president of Gilmore, an internationally recognized, award-winning training and development firm based in Toronto. A great chess player doesn't think about the next move only. He "thinks implicatively" – thinking out into the future, "If I do this, the other player might do this, and then if he does that then I would do this." Grand-master chess players typically think 10 moves ahead. [1]

Crawford believes that most executives aren't thinking more than one or two steps ahead. This is dangerous because as events accelerate and become more complex, "our thinking system has to be faster and more complex." There is a danger that organizations can be blindsided.

But most executives aren't concerned about being blindsided. "It's like teenagers," notes Crawford, "They read about stuff, but take risks anyway. They don't believe it's going to happen to them."

Companies do the same. Even when presented with information, executives think that they can't be blindsided, or it will be different for their organization or industry. "In this economy it's a big problem if you can't spot patterns quickly and develop your responses based on implicative thinking."

"If you ask executives, 'Have you heard of scenario planning?', a huge percentage will answer, 'Yes!'" notes Crawford. "If you ask, 'Have you participated in the scenario planning session?', a smaller, but measurable percentage will answer, 'Yes.' And then if you ask 'When's the last time you led a scenario planning session?', the drop off is alarming."

GROUPTHINK

Groupthink is a concept that states that individuals will disagree with the group when discussing an issue on their own, but in the group will concur.

In other words, individuals moderate or censor their opinions because of some social pressure within the group. This is a powerful reason for using technology that allows individuals to vote anonymously, as discussed in the previous chapter. A classic case of groupthink is the Bay of Pigs invasion. While individually many of the decision makers had serious reservations about the invasion, as a group they supported the decision to go ahead.

AIRLINE INDUSTRY BLINDSIDED

On September 11, 2001, two hijacked US commercial airliners crashed into the World Trade Center within 18 minutes of each other, causing both 110-storey towers to collapse. A third hijacked plane crashed into the Pentagon, and a fourth, suspected to be aiming for Camp David or the White House, crashed in Pennsylvania. Rescue efforts began immediately, but there was little hope that survivors would be found in the rubble of the buildings. More than 2,800 people were reported dead.[2]

Could the tragedy have been avoided? If US aviation officials had used scenario planning that including terrorist hijacking of domestic flights, all US airlines could have instituted security procedures that Israel's airline, El-Al, has always used. The cockpits of El-Al jets are sealed behind two virtually impenetrable, locked doors and armed, plain-clothed sky marshals fly on every flight. Unlike all the other airlines in the world, El-Al actually experienced an increase in passengers on its international flights after September 11. Travelers felt more comfortable flying with an airline that hasn't been successfully hijacked in 30 years. Had the US implemented El-Al's security measures, the events of September 11 wouldn't have happened.

CALCULATING THE COST OF SEPTEMBER 11

The reaction after the attacks was immediate. In an unprecedented move, the US Federal Aviation Authority (FAA) closed US airspace, diverting inbound planes to Canada or Latin America, and grounded all commercial flights for four days. Tens of thousands of travelers across the US scrambled to get home or find accommodation.

The US economy had gone into a mild recession in March 2001, but the attacks pushed it deeper into recession. Their impact has been staggering:

- The aviation industry laid off 200,000 people 2001, over 125,000 of them in the US.[3]
- Airlines around the world lost a combined $14 billion in 2001,[4] according to the International Air Transport Association (IATA), a trade group representing 266 airlines worldwide. This is almost three times as large as the previous worst combined loss of $4.8 billion in 1992 following the Gulf war.[5]
- About 1,200 aircraft, 10 per cent of all commercial jets worldwide, have been grounded since September 11, according to IATA.[6]
- Air traffic worldwide fell 6 per cent – or by 60 million passengers – in 2001.[7]
- Major airlines continue to face a cash crunch, and more bankruptcies and mergers are expected as few airlines are predicted to make money before 2003.
- $150 billion of planned North American airport construction projects were cancelled.[8]
- American Airlines, the largest in the world, as of February 2002 continued to lose $6 million a day, while the second largest, United Airlines, lost $10 million a day in the fourth quarter of 2001, losing a total of $2.1 billion in 2001, more than any other airline ever.[9]
- The attacks and their aftermath "had a staggering effect on our overall financial performance, producing the largest quarterly loss" in the company's history, said Don Carty, CEO of AMR, American Airlines' parent company. "We are in the midst of the worst financial crisis in the history of the industry."[10]
- The September 11 attacks were the costliest ever for the insurance industry,

and total claims estimates range from $20 billion to $70 billion. In comparison, 1992's Hurricane Andrew resulted in $18 billion in claims.[11]

- Airline insurance premiums are expected to hit $9.5 billion by the end of 2002, more than six times the $1.5 billion airlines paid in 2000.[12]
- Smith Travel Research said the worldwide travel industry lost an estimated $3.5 billion in room revenue in 2001.[13]
- Almost 500,000 workers have been laid off by hotels, tour operators, restaurants, and theme parks in 2001.[14]

Analysts believe that bankruptcies among US carriers are inevitable, as most US carriers are not expected to make even "modest" profits until 2003. Only two US carriers, Southwest Airlines (see Chapter 5) and New York-based JetBlue, made money in 2001.

The airline industry laid off 200,000 people in 2001, including 30,000 cut by Boeing. By November, four airlines had gone bankrupt: Ansett in Australia, Canada 3000, Sabena in Belgium, and Swissair (although it was revived by a government bail out and renamed Swiss).

Airline lay offs since September 11

American (& TWA)	20,000
United	20,000
Delta	13,000
Air Canada	12,500
Continental	12,000
US Airways	11,000
Northwest	10,000
Swissair	9,000
British Airways	7,000

As Americans cancelled plans for travel and holidays, the ripple effect spread throughout the economy, affecting tourism, hospitality, travel agents, and transport companies such as taxi drivers.

When flights resumed in the week after September 11, airline bookings declined about 70 percent. And most US airlines can't cope with even a small fall in revenue. They are capital-intensive, high fixed-cost businesses. North American airlines, which typically require 65 percent capacity just to break even, were flying with only 30 percent loads for a couple of weeks after the incident, due to consumers canceling flights out of fear. Airplanes cost up to $200 million each and even a fall of 5 percent in traffic can wreck operating economics.

Wider Impact

Stock market trading halted for four days, the longest market shutdown since the Great Depression. In the week following the attacks, the US stock market lost $1.38 trillion dollars of value.

The two largest trading partners in the world are Canada and the US. Every day 37,000 trucks cross the US–Canada border carrying $1.4 billion in goods. More than 70 percent of all Canadian exports are delivered to the US. The impact of the attack was delays in border crossing due to increased security checks. Trucks were waiting 12 hours to cross the border and line ups were up to 24 kilometers long. As they say, "time is money," and the financial impact of these delays has yet to be calculated, but it will be staggering.

September 11 had an impact on the US economy and in turn the world economy. The US officially went into a recession in March 2001, but the effects were greatly accelerated by events on September 11. As the world's economies are increasingly interdependent, the effect of the US recession has had a spillover effect and Europe and Asia.

TOO LITTLE, TOO LATE

The first security improvement made by UK and US carriers following September 11 was to reinforce cockpit doors. This simple, low-cost solution could have been identified as a vulnerability by using scenario planning, in my opinion. Secure doors would have been a trim tab factor in preventing the events of September 11. British Mathematician Alan Turing said that any sufficiently interesting computer program is in principle unknowable. Turing's theory applies to the future. The future is sufficiently interesting and complex that by definition it is unknowable. No one can accurately predict exactly what will happen next year, let alone in five or ten years. In the 1980s and 1990s companies still engaged in five- and ten-year strategic planning exercises. The speed of change has rendered such practices obsolete.

With such a capital-intensive business as the airlines, where even a small shift in consumer behavior can have such large impacts on the bottom line, it is all the more important to engage in scenario planning.

A scenario planning exercise with the airlines would have to look at a number of trim tab factors that could blindside the industry: videoconferencing, fractional jet ownership, and the spoke and hub structure.

Airlines remain profitable because of frequent flier business travelers. As mentioned earlier, business travelers account for only 8–10 percent of commercial airline passengers, but produce over 40 per cent of revenue.[15] But executives who travel constantly hate to be away from their families so much. By 2005, I predict that we will have full-motion videoconferencing across the Web for free. What will happen in 2005 if executives take 30 percent fewer trips because they feel videoconferencing offers a superior alternative? What will happen to airline profitability? Airline rationalization? Do you think that in strategic planning sessions, airline executives are looking at Intel and vendors of high-speed Internet connections (T1, cable modem, and DSL) as their competition or are they benchmarking against other airlines? Because of the videoconferencing analysis above, since 1998, I have been saying that if I were an airline executive, I would be keeping a very clean balance sheet, not buying or leasing any new planes, preparing for the ultimate industry rationalization when I could buy cheap capacity from competitors on the verge of bankruptcy. In 2002 that opportunity is now a reality, as 1,200 planes have been grounded since September 11.

Don't misunderstand me: the airline industry is not about to end, but more airlines will fail or have to merge to survive. The fare structure will have to change significantly. In 2001, a mid-week (with no Saturday night stay) full-fare economy (not business class) return ticket from Toronto to Vancouver cost over $C3,000! You have to sell a lot of tickets to Cancun, Mexico at $C699 for every business traveler taken out of the mix.

Given the disproportionate profit that frequent fliers represent, US airlines have done little to focus on their most important customers in the wake of September 11. To qualify as the top-tier frequent flier an individual typically has to have flown 100,000 miles the prior year, that's 200 hours of flying, on between 60 and 120 flights. Add to this the time to travel to and from the airport, check in, clear security, clear customs and immigration, and pick up bags and wait for transportation: that adds two to three hours per flight. Multiply by 60–120 flights and you get another 120–360 hours a year. So top-tier frequent fliers are spending between 320 and 560 hours a year – or 8–14 average work weeks a year involved in some aspect of air travel. Add to this the fact that executives are already overworked and see their families little if at all, and *surprise* – frequent fliers no longer want to be frequent fliers. The airlines have failed to understand what their most important customers experience.

The result? I was standing in a check-in line-up with a CEO talking about this. He told me that he had just installed a videoconferencing system because of flying delays. So the events of September 11 will accelerate videoconferencing system sales.

A second consequence of the increased delays for travelers is that frequent fliers who formerly flew on commercial airlines are increasingly turning to private jet charters and fractional jet ownership. While passenger volumes on US commercial airlines have fallen by 20 percent between September 11, 2001 and February 1, 2002, private air charters and fractional jet ownership is up by as much as 26 percent.

Fractional ownership is a time-sharing method for private jets. In 1986, Executive Jet pioneered fractional aircraft ownership with its NetJets program. NetJet guarantees owners availability 365 days a year with as little as four hours advance notice. For a higher or lower hourly rate, owners can also get larger or smaller aircraft. And unlike those who own a single aircraft, NetJets clients can get more than one airplane per day and jets of different types at different locations. Between 1997 and 2001, Executive Jet grew by about 35 percent a year. Heightened concern about safety, security, and convenience has bolstered sales since then.

Executives using private charters and fractional jets save time by: (1) bypassing check in; (2) bypassing airport security; (3) avoiding delays due to passengers whose bags are in the cargo hold but don't board the plane; (4) bypassing delays at immigration and customs when flying to a different country; (5) reducing air time by flying directly point-to-point, as opposed to using the spoke and hub method employed by most US airlines.

Good scenario planning would highlight these factors in advance, and if and when an event like September 11 occurred, the airlines would immediately respond to lessen the impact of delays on their most important customers. For instance, by implementing express lanes at security, customs, and immigration for frequent fliers. Frequent fliers would still have to go through these procedures like all other travelers, but would not experience long delays, as airlines would work with federal regulators to create express procedures. In the five months following September 11, US airlines have still not instituted these measures for their frequent fliers.

Once a company buys into fractional jet ownership, the commercial airlines have lost highly profitable customers forever, because the executives who made the decision to purchase a fractional ownership have to justify their decision to shareholders. So corporate executives will *only* ever fly on a commercial flight as a last option. With each fractional jet ownership commercial airlines are not loosing just one, but potentially many frequent fliers from a corporation.

But the most important point is the way most US airlines are structured – using the hub and spoke architecture. Rather than being able to fly directly from Kansas to Hilton Head, SC you might fly on two different flights: Kansas to Chicago and Chicago to Hilton Head. Indirect flights greatly increase the chance of delays due to weather, and now security. While the airlines are diligent in matching passengers with their bags on the initial flight, they are not required to do so on connecting flights. If this requirement changes, as it likely will due to increased security concerns in the wake of September 11, this will further increase delays and increase the defection of frequent fliers to videoconferencing, private jets, and fractional jet ownership.

Good scenario planning would highlight the tension between the hub and spoke structure of most airlines and the point-to-point philosophy of Southwest Airlines. Scenario planning would highlight how point-to-point is better suited to win market share in every scenario, including a post-September 11 environment. Knowing that one structure inherently will do better regardless of what happens in the future would help airline executives to realize that they are in a losing game by employing a hub and spoke structure and have the courage and discipline to go through the change of converting the bulk of their operations to a point-to-point structure.

Elements of scenarios can help organizations prepare for a number of futures. For instance, the lessons learned from developing a scenario involving a sudden downturn in airline business travelers because of videoconferencing would have partially prepared an airline for the sudden downturn caused by the terrorists attacks on September 11, 2001.

Given that we can't accurately predict the future, corporate executives in strategic planning sessions need to explore their understanding of the future, identify the unconscious "paradigms" they have about their industry, their products and services, and their competitors.

As Peter Schwarz writes in *The Art of the Long View:*

In the scenario process, managers invent and then consider, in depth, several varied stories of equally plausible futures. The stories are carefully researched, full of relevant detail, oriented toward real-life decision, and designed (one hopes) to bring forward surprises and unexpected leads of understanding. Together, the scenarios comprise a tool for ordering one's perceptions. The point is not to "pick one preferred future," and hope for it to come to pass (or, even, work to create it – though there are some situations where acting to create a better future is a useful function of scenarios). Nor is the point to find the most probable future and adapt to it or "bet the company" on it. Rather the point is to make strategic decisions that will be sound for all plausible futures. No matter what future takes place, you are much more likely to be ready for it – and influential in it – if you have thought seriously about scenarios.

In other words scenario planning is not about predicting the future, *it's about predicting possibilities*, and then taking action on what Saunders calls BAATM – the *best answer at the moment*. Saunders' method of scenario planning forces executives to answer the question, "What completely unexpected events could change the structure of our industry?"

A group engaged in scenario planning can choose to take the planning to quite a few different depths. The simplest way is to draw a trumpet (see Figure 9.2).

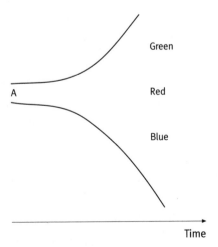

Figure 9.2

Point A is here now. The present has been created (another way of perceiving it is as constrained) by an infinite combination of factors.

Because most corporations do not employ a disciplined approach to collecting customer feedback (FedEx, for example, surveys 2,100 randomly selected customers every day for 90 days) or employee feedback (such as Sun Microsystems mentioned earlier) or competitive intelligence, many corporate executives do not have an accurate sense of their current reality.

Executives who employ real-time systems in these areas are further ahead, but don't know what kind of world they are going to face two or three years from now. The further out into the future you look, the greater the fog, and therefore, the wider the mouth of the trumpet. They could face the rosy future that you read about in their annual reports, they could meet an icy Blue world of price erosion, collapse of their market, the introduction of some new technology, or a competitor out of left field. Or they could go through a world that they had no idea could ever happen – some Green world they never even conceived.

Using scenario planning is not so much about predicting the future, but preventing it. Knowing in advance that digitization of music could allow for file sharing over the Internet would have enabled music executives to quickly launch their own digital music services as Napster's popularity became apparent.

BACKCASTING: LEVEL I SCENARIO PLANNING

For executive teams that claim they don't have a lot of time to do full-blown scenario planning, backcasting is a powerful method to get them thinking about scenarios and their implication to the organization. Saunders will randomly divide the team into three groups – Green, Red and Blue. Each group meets separately, and projects itself three years in the future. For instance, the Green team will look back and work out what shocking turn of events created this Green future that no one could have predicted. The groups wrestle with the question, "What factors caused this to happen?"

Once all the teams have developed these scenarios, they present them to the whole group. The Green team will present its scenario.

Then the Blue team will get up and say, "Wasn't that a fantasy, listening to the Pollyannaish view of the Green team? Now let's tell you what *really* hap-

·

pened." The Blue team's story will bring tears to your eyes. "We'll tell you how everything went downhill."

For instance, a group of airline executives in the Blue scenario might report, "Well videoconferencing did drastically affect our business, eliminating 30 percent of our high-margin business travelers. The result was devastating for the industry-intensive competition for the fewer frequent-flier business travelers. Discounting was inevitable. Some airlines tried to identify new niches. Boeing and Airbus sales fell dramatically as airlines halted long-term purchases. In this environment, cost cutting has been the key to survival. We further embraced our global alliance with other national airlines, sharing check-in services, first-class lounges, and route sharing, significantly reducing costs while maintaining or increasing services levels as perceived by customers. The global alliances have meant that successful airlines have grown stronger while the weaker have perished.

"We finally had to recognize the superiority of Southwest's point-to-point model. The stock market had been telling us this all along, but we somehow were able to ignore it. In November 2001, Southwest's market capitalization of more than $13 billion was slightly less than that of American, United, Delta and Northwest, *combined and then doubled!*[16] The fact that the company had 29 consecutive years of profitability was too much for us to ignore, especially since it remained profitable in the wake of events on September 11. We began the goal of moving 50 percent of all flights to point-to-point within two years, and 75 percent within three. The changes to the airline were tremendous.

"We kept a clean balance sheet by leasing planes rather than buying them outright. We have refitted planes rather than buying new ones, and delayed new purchases for five years on average. In the last three years, 10 percent of airlines worldwide ceased to exist either through bankruptcy or being bought out. We predict that another 10 percent more will fail in the next three years."

Then the Red team relates its scenario. With no technology, backcasting can be a striking exercise for people. It's not about which scenario actually transpires. The purpose of the exercise is to open people's minds to possibilities.

TRIGGERS: LEVEL II

After each group has presented its findings, the teams are challenged to determine which triggers will warn them that they are moving towards that scenario.

What events would suggest that the Green world was going to happen? What signs in the market would be a harbinger of the Blue world for the airline executives? One trigger might be sales of desktop cameras, which are required for videoconferencing. When camera sales explode, the possibility of the Blue scenario increases. Similarly, an increase in bandwidth, such as the penetration of cable modems in North America, or the launch of the telcos' ADSL, might be other triggers.

When executives begin to see these triggers actually occurring in the market they know what to do and can alter course accordingly, implementing strategies that prepare for the scenario's unfolding. Forewarned is forearmed.

CROSS-IMPACT MATRIX: LEVEL III

Again, scenarios are not about predicting which future will happen, but about preparing for all possibilities. The next step is to prepare a cross-impact matrix:

	Red	Green	Blue
Red			
Green			
Blue			

What happens if we think that we are headed for the Blue scenario and the Red actually transpires? Or the Green? What happens if we prepare for the Red but the Blue transpires? What happens when we expect Green but end up in Blue or Red? Would we be prepared?

Imagine a telco executive team preparing for the eventuality of a Blue scenario – planning for long-distance calls to be 3¢ a minute by 2004 and having 50 percent of all corporate voice traffic traveling as data across the Internet by 2001. Revenues plummet by 40 percent. In this environment, managing costs is essential, but by strange forces the company ends up in the Green scenario that no one expected. No one could foresee the elasticity of demand. While long-distance calls in North America fell from an average of 15¢ a minute in 1998 to 3¢ a minute in 2004, volumes rose 80 percent. No one could have predicted that. With the launch of ADSL, and an insatiable appetite for faster access to the World Wide Web, Internet traffic has increased 6,400 percent over three years. Telcos are now selling videoconferencing equipment to residential and business customers. Because of the radical increase in processor power and advances in compression technology, full-motion videoconferencing is now possible over regular phone lines. Because of this new technology, people are now making more long-distance calls than ever before, and while the cost-per-minute for long distance has fallen so significantly, revenue has increased because of the exponential increase in demand for videoconferencing.

If you know you are going to be in the Blue world, you can organize it so that you manage your costs and plan for an ultimate meltdown. But the market is better than you thought. Have you cut yourself so lean that you can't take advantage of the new opportunities presented by heading for the Green world?

You learn a great deal by going through the cross-impact matrix, and examining the six combinations. Usually it becomes apparent that some elements are common, regardless of what happens. For instance, it may be that in every case the company needs extreme flexibility in the workforce.

So the executive team can ask:

Do we have the flexibility we need? Do the bulk of employees have an entitlement attitude? Do they recognize that the nature of their work will be continually changing? Have we hired people who are comfortable with change and uncertainty? Have we trained our people to be flexible in their work and is our workforce capable of being redeployed in new areas quickly? Have we been honest with employees? Are we continually telling them that we are uncertain about the future – we don't know whether it will be a Green, Red or Blue? Should we have a greater reliance on contract workers? If we don't have the flexibility, what steps do we need to take?

The cross-impact matrix also helps executives to realize that part of all three scenarios could happen. If this part of the Blue scenario came true, we could end up in the Green scenario predominantly.

Ultimately scenario planning is all about flexibility. Saunders talks about MSUing (making stuff up) as we go along. If people have seen the thing before and they have already rehearsed what they would do, they can react quickly. Just telling the story begins to open the mind.

TRENDS: LEVEL IV

It is the interaction of various trends that creates these different scenarios.

Scenario planning should create an atmosphere of self-reflection – to make conscious information that will be of use. For instance, if currency traders were one of the factors in the Asian currency crisis of 1997,[17] we can expect new currency crises with other countries in the future, as currency traders will continue to pursue economic gain by betting against currencies that are weak. The capital flow represents trillions of dollars a day, so financial turbulence will not likely get better, but may get worse. Collectively, currency traders, if they act in unison, are more powerful than national governments.

The group works to answer the question, "What are all the trends that may influence the future of our industry? Our products? Our services? Our company?"

As the group will be predicting where the organization is going in the future, it is a good idea to identify and involve stakeholders in the organization, those who will be affected by the various worlds. After the planning sessions, these individuals carry this work on within their own departments. For instance, above we identified that a flexible workforce might be key and this would affect how human resource policies are devised, how the legal department contracts work, and hiring practices. Individuals from all these areas would benefit by being involved and would contribute to the proceedings.

It is important to make sure that the group is not too inwardly focused, wrestling with issues and trends from outside the standard discussions within the organization. If the budget allows, Saunders will bring in one or more of the following: a futurist, an economist, or a consumer researcher. The group may be composed of the right stakeholders, but they may not have experience outside of their area. For instance, scenario planning for the airline executives might require bringing in a mathematician or a computer programmer in a little-known field of compression algorithms. A compression program takes a very large file, such as video data, and compresses it into a small file so that it can be sent quickly across the Net. The expert(s) would describe in easy to understand terms the potential of the technology and predict when computers will be powerful enough to engage in real time video compression to enable full-motion videoconferencing across regular phone lines.

Another example would be a group of bankers discussing the future of the physical check. Such a group might need a mathematician to discuss the progress of optical character recognition and validating financial transactions across the Internet. Security in the future will not be based on a password but on biometric data such as a fingerprint, handprint, voice scan, or a scan of your retina. These forms of verification are infinity more reliable than passwords, which are easy to guess.

Identifying trends can be difficult. Often a group will resort to experts outside the organization and use the Delphi technique. Whatever process is used to generate the trends, once you have identified them, you need to determine which are the really important ones. It is critical to narrow these trends down, otherwise it will overwhelm the group. It is quite common to have 80–100 different trends identified by the end of the session.

Using radio frequency keypads, Saunders asks the group "Let's take trend number one – supposing it did happen, would it seriously impact the scenarios? And if it didn't happen what would its impact be?" Inconsequential trends produce little impact on the scenarios regardless of whether they occur or not, but important trends show tremendous impact whether they happen or not. Using this method you can eliminate 80 percent of the trends as being unimportant.

To further reduce the number of trends Saunders asks, "Of the important trends, which are certain and which are uncertain?" For instance, Moore's Law will continue to hold true in the foreseeable future. So it is an important and certain trend. The political climate in China, however, may be important but it is uncertain. From an initial 80 trends the group may be left with 20 important trends, 10 of which are certain to occur and 10 which are uncertain.

The important and certain trends become the backdrop for *all* the scenarios. While the group selects the most interesting important and uncertain trends to use as fodder to develop scenarios. A full scenario planning might involve analyzing all 10 important but uncertain trends. But most executives will focus on a smaller subset of these 10 trends.

IMPORTANT AND UNCERTAIN TRENDS IMPACT: LEVEL V

If time is short the group can just intuitively guess which two of the 10 important and uncertain trends will have the biggest impact on the organization. Then the group does a 2 × 2 cross-impact matrix. This compares the interaction of the two trends. For instance, global economic health (great or terrible) crossed with

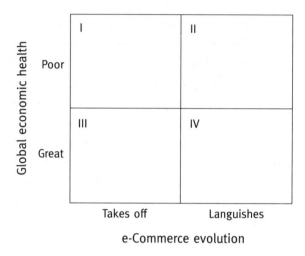

Figure 9.3 Cross-impact matrix.

e-commerce evolution (goes well, doesn't take off) (see Figure 9.3). The group is then divided into four groups. Each one takes one of the four scenarios and projects themselves three to five years into the future and backcasts. For instance, "What would happen if the economy tanks but e-commerce takes off?" (quadrant I in the cross-impact matrix). The group might come up with the following rationale – as we all know, the year 2000 saw the worldwide economy slowdown, and in the worst recession since the depression, it was e-commerce that kept things moving. In fact, the crash forced companies to embrace new ways of working to significantly lower costs in order to offer less expensive products. Consumer spending was at an all time low. So if a company wanted to survive, it had to be a low-cost producer in its product or service category.

The other three groups present their backcast scenarios and the group develops tremendous insights into their business, given the assumptions that are highlighted.

If the group has more time, Saunders will use one of the software packages he designed, called *Resolver*Ballot*, which can measure up to eight variables against each other. Each criterion can be plotted against the other seven. In this approach each of up to eight trends is paired against the other seven, by asking: "If trend number one were to actually occur would it make trend number two more likely?" Using the keypads, people vote. The software sorts out all the relationships and creates a map or flowchart called a problematique. It identifies which trends have the most influence over all the others. In other words some trends are root causes of others, which can be seen as symptomatic.

INDIVIDUAL PERCEPTION

People viewing the same situation will almost always have different interpretations. *Roshomon* is a classic 1951 Japanese film that explores the relative and elusive nature of truth. Directed by Akira Kurosawa, *Roshomon* tells the story, or stories, of a murder, as recounted by four witnesses and participants. With help from a spirit medium, even the victim's version is told. These different characters all relate the same event – but with different outcomes. The audience sees the event from all four viewpoints. Yet at the end, they find themselves wondering what really happened.

It is not that one interpretation is right or wrong, the story simply helps show us how our perceptions can vary. The way each character interprets the events highlights more about his or her perception and interpretation than it does about the story itself.

Scenario planning works in the same way, highlighting the interpretations that different people place on the same event. By forcing these different assumptions to the surface, the executive team can explore the different assumptions and develop a mutual understanding, and ultimately greater alignment in the organization. Hashing out all these differences before a crisis strikes means the group can respond with less internal conflict and greater synergy.

Scenarios deal with two worlds," wrote Pierre Wack. "The world of facts and the world of perceptions. They explore for facts but they aim at perceptions inside the heads of decision-makers. Their purpose is to gather and transform information of strategic significance into fresh perceptions. This transformation process is not trivial – more often than not it does not happen. When it works, it is a creative experience that generates a heartfelt 'Aha!' from your managers and leads to strategic insights beyond the mind's previous reach."

Look at the two lines below. Which line is longer?

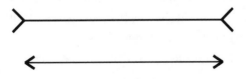

Use a ruler to check your answer. Even after measuring the lines, most people still do not believe that they are the same length! This is the classic Müller–Lyer optical illusion. The point being is that we cannot always trust our perception.

GOING ALL OUT: LEVEL VI

Interactive Management (IM)

Interactive Management (IM) should only be used when a situation is complex. A complex situation is by definition one in which no one individual has all the information, knowledge, intuition, anticipation of trends, or perspective to be able to resolve it. IM should only be employed after normal problem-solving methods have failed.

If applicable, a level VI would begin with a Delphi, and participants would read the Delphi report as background for the exercise.

IM brings together a cross-section of individuals from different departments who are involved in the complex situation. The assembled individuals should have a good understanding of their department and perspective on the complex situation from their departmental perspective.

At the start of an IM session the individuals are given a triggering question. For instance, what are the problems that are preventing us from resolving this problematic situation (whatever the situation is)?

The facilitator would then employ a technique known as the *nominal group technique* (NGT), where each participant silently generates answers to the triggering question. The triggering question could be "What might prevent us from achieving our target of 20 percent growth?" or "How can we shorten cycle time within manufacturing?" But the triggering question strikes at the heart of the complex situation.

Every 5 or 10 minutes the facilitator can collect these sheets and have a typist key them into a computer so that they are projected on the wall where everyone can see them. When participants see other people's ideas, it triggers more responses. After 30 minutes of silent generation the next phase can begin.

The process then moves into clarification, where in a round robin format, individuals talk about their ideas. The first person would talk about his/her first idea. Others in the group could ask questions. A statement should contain only one idea so there should be no "and/or" in the statement.

The second person would then talk about his/her first idea. This process continues until everyone has clarified all his or her ideas. This process can take up to three days, as in the case when groups identified upwards of 700 problems that they were facing. There is tremendous learning at this stage as people from different departments begin to appreciate how other people in other departments see the situation.

During the clarification process ideas can be added or modified. Some statements will be broken up into two statements, while ideas from different individuals may be combined.

As each statement is clarified, it is numbered, printed out, and hung on the wall surrounding the group. Ideas are clarified and modified by the group as a whole. Ownership of the ideas shifts from the individual to the group. In this spirit, ideas are numbered as opposed to attributed to the original author.

At the end of the clarification process, the group will have literally hundreds of ideas surrounding them on the walls of the workspace. The clarification creates a better understanding from a holistic perspective, system perspective, or 10,000-foot view.

At this point, individuals are asked to vote for the top five ideas that they feel are contributing to the complex situation. This reduces the number of issues. Pareto's law applies to complexity: 20 percent of the issues will cause 80 percent of the problem.

The group might end up with 60 issues, but that is still overwhelming given our short-term memory limitation (7 ± 2). These issues have to be structured.

Spreadthink

Most of us think that we see things objectively. However, within any group there will be "spreadthink." Often we think that there is just one root cause to a problem and hence just one solution. So we search for the simple solution, the magic bullet. But spreadthink proves that everyone sees the problem a different way. Once you have taken a group of 20 individuals from different departments, who are each intimately involved in a complex situation, and have spent three days in an IM session to identify all the contributing problems, you will have a list of hundreds of problems. Each problem has been discussed and clarified so that there is a shared understanding of all of them in the group.

Ask each of these 20 individuals to vote on the top five problems and you will end up with more than 50 different answers. This is spreadthink: each of us has a different perception of what the situation is, and each of us will rank factors in different hierarchies of importance in our effort to resolve a complex situation. If traditional problem-solving methodologies are used to resolve complex situations, most of the group's time will be unproductive and spent arguing over which strategy to employ. Without understanding each other's points of view, the group's members will never understand the complexity and never resolve it effectively.

After three days of clarification and discussion, which promotes mutual understanding, everyone in the group votes for the top five issues. If there were perfect alignment of thought in the group everyone would vote for the same five issues. Spreadthink guarantees that members of the group will still perceive the problem differently. The following equation predicts the number that will be raised with the following formula:

$$\text{Items} = \frac{\text{participants} \times \text{votes per participant}}{2}$$

For instance, if there are 20 participants and each gets to vote on which are the top five issues, the number of issues to be structured will be:

$$\text{No. of items} = \frac{20 \times 5}{2} = \frac{100}{2} = 50$$

Groupthink

Groupthink is the concept that individuals disagree with the group when discussing an issue on their own, but in the group will concur.

In other words, individuals moderate or censor their opinions because of some social pressure within the group. This is a powerful reason for using technology that allows individuals to vote anonymously because it moderates these social forces.

Structuring

Interactive Management is the discipline of studying complexity and *interpretive structural modeling* (ISM) is the process that generates a pictorial diagram showing the relationship between problems. By creating a model, or picture, highlighting the inter relationship of problems, a decision-making team can decide which problem(s) to tackle first.

While our minds cannot sort through all relationships implied by 60 variables, we could easily compare two. For instance, you could ask, "Does problem 411 – the fact that we do not grant stock options" significantly aggravate problem 47, "attracting and retaining the best computer programmers?" If the majority of people in the group answer "Yes," there is a positive correlation between 411>47.

Most relationships are transitive. That is if A>B and B>C and C>D, then A>D. Now there are exceptions to every rule. For instance, if Liz loves Tom and Tom loves Mary, does Liz love Mary? This example is not transitive, because it deals with emotions as opposed to facts.

The relationships in an IM session are transitive. Because of this the computer software can eliminate 80 percent of the questions required to sift through all the relationships of 60 variables. Because of this fact, IM offers organizations incredible leverage. What the group ends up with is a diagram (Figure 9.4).

The diagram (called a problematique) in Figure 9.4 shows the relationship between different problems. For instance, problem 2 and 117 are in the same box – meaning that they are self-reinforcing: 2 reinforced 117 and 117 reinforces 2. Organizations will often tackle a problem in isolation. In this case, if an organization tackled 2 without tackling 117, then once the organization stopped investing time, money and effort in solving 2, it would reappear because the organization had not resolved 117 at the same time.

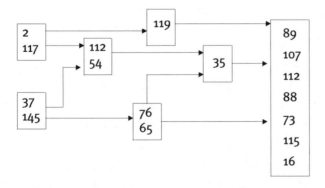

Figure 9.4 The graphic portrayal of a problematique.

The problematique also shows the upstream/downstream relationship of problems (i.e. (2 and 117) and (37 and 145) make all other problems worse). Whereas problems like 89 are mostly downstream. (John Warfield notes that terms like cause and effect are not useful, because there could always be new problems not evoked in the NGT which would be further to the left – such as not taking enough time to do strategic planning and using new tools.)

Problem 89 may be bad morale within the organization. The human resource department might want to put on a company picnic or hold an employee appreciation day bringing in a motivational speaker. But the underlying problem is a lack of real-time data. The picnic or motivational speaker, while a nice thought, won't improve morale. But most organizations have no way of seeing the inter-relationship of challenges they face.

THE POWER OF IM

To ascertain all the relationships in a group of variables would require creating and filling a matrix with $N(N-1)$ cells where N is the number of items that is to be structured by the group. So if the group had 60 items that have to be structured, the number of matrix cells to be filled would be $60 \times (60-1) = 60 \times 59 = 3,540$. In other words, the facilitator would have to ask the group 3,540 questions. This would take an incredible amount of time.

But because of the software, the group only has to answer 20 percent of these questions – or 708 questions. This still seems to be a lot. But to put it into perspective, remember that the group was originally dealing with a far larger universe of questions, before each individual voted for the top five. Amid this larger universe – say the 678 problems – to examine all the relationships between all these variables without using inference would be truly overwhelming.

To structure them would require asking $678 \times (678-1) = 459,006$ questions of the group. Assuming each question took one minute to answer, the group would be there for 7,650 hours – or 956 eight-hour days – or 191 weeks – or 3.8 years. However, because the NGT boils down the issues to the most critical ones by having the group select only the top five problems per individual, and assuming maximum spreadthink so that each individual selects five different problems and ends up with something like only 60 problems. Structuring these without the inference engine of the software would mean $60 \times (60-1) = 60 \times$

59 = 3,540 matrix cells – or less than 1 percent of the former number. Doing it this way, assuming one question answered per minute, would mean 3,540 minutes – or 59 hours, or 1.5 weeks. But because of the inference engine of the software, it reduced 80 percent of the required questions – resulting in just 708 questions – 708 minutes, or 11.8 hours – roughly two days.

The less effort, the faster and more powerful you will be

Bruce Lee
martial arts expert

Using Pareto's law that 80 percent of the results can be determined by looking at 20 percent of the issues, then this process is exceptionally high leverage because it engages in two reductionistic processes that saves 99.998 percent of the time required. What could be a higher leverage activity?

To put it another way, imagine we could say to you – give us three days of your time with a group of 15 people from departments across your organization and what we will give back to you is the equivalent of 413.5 times more time. So investing three days with 15 people is 45 person days. Imagine that the results were equivalent to 18,608 person days – or in other words 9.3 person years of planning time. Would that be a high leverage activity you would be interested in?

SINGLE AND DOUBLE LOOP LEARNING

Argyris coined the phrases single and double loop learning. Single loop learning is when I learn something and at the end of it I am the same individual I was before, only now I have a new skill.

In double loop learning, not only I am learning a new skill, my perception changes as well. IM is a powerful example of double loop learning.

IM changes a participant's perception in a number of ways. At the outset participants appreciate only their own perspective on a complex situation. From their own analysis they may have come up with what they perceive to be "the problem." But in going through the NGT, they discover all the other perspectives, and realize that others see the complex situation differently. The participant is further exposed to these differences in opinion over the next few days during the clarification process. One of the changes in perception is that participants begin to realize that their views are not as objective as previously thought.

A second double loop learning occurs when the concept of spreadthink is exposed. Most participants are staggered that even after three days of discussion that people's thinking and perception of the problems are still so divergent.

When the IM is finished and the group interprets the pattern, the participants perceive the interrelatedness of problems and how they compound one another.

Finally many individuals are overwhelmed at the power of the IM process once they have been through it. Numerous groups are brought to deep emotions – of gratitude, joy and relief to find a process that is capable of embracing diversity and through consensus arriving at an action plan.

Most problem-solving methodologies must deny complexity in order to deal with it. In other words, they must be reductionistic to reach a solution. By contrast, IM embraces the diversity as the only way of resolving complexity. The process therefore creates tremendous buy in from the participants.

I believe that IM would have helped Microsoft identify the Internet as a trend it would have to address earlier (see case study in Chapter 2). IM would have allowed individuals within Microsoft to amplify their concerns about the Internet, helping Bill Gates and other senior executives within the corporation to recognize the threat earlier and respond faster.

HOW CAN WE KNOW WHAT WE DON'T KNOW?

Fish Discover Water Last

A Taoist story tells of a fish that asked an elder fish, "I keep hearing others talk about this thing called water. Just what is water?"

The elder fish replied, "Water is what surrounds you."

Aghast, the little fish asked, "But why can't I see it?"

To which the elder replied, "Water is within you and all around you. You were born into it and you will die in it. Water envelopes you like your own skin."

To paraphrase; "Fish discover water last."

Similarly, many executives are living amid complexity, but are unaware of how it affects them. How the systems and structures built in the early industrial era are completely out of touch today.

One characteristic more than any other will help executives avoid being blindsided – humility. This essential character trait (the "self" level of the 10S model) coupled with curiosity and search behavior will help to ensure your orga-

nization is not blindsided. But working at the personal level, while necessary, is insufficient. Executives need (1) to understand the unique and inherent challenges in trying to resolve complex situations; (2) to be aware of paradigms and paradigm shifts; and (3) to implement a systemic solution such as employing IM as a tool to resolve complex situations.

CONCLUSION

Scenario planning helps individuals and teams to not so much predict the future, but to prevent it. By identifying potential threats and opportunities, a team develops greater flexibility in responding to whatever change occurs, identifies triggers for different scenarios, increasing the speed with which they recognize and respond to market shifts. Scenario planning reduces the risk of being blindsided and increases the chance that organizations will be able to take advantage of new opportunities before their competitors perceive them.

REFLECTIONS

- How can you find out what you don't know?
  What are the industry orthodoxies?
  - Which of these no longer make sense given the new technology?
- If you were beginning a company from scratch, in your industry today, what would you do differently?
- As an organization, how can you prepare for an unimaginable future?
- What percentage of time is spent focusing on long-term issues? Short-term issues?
  - Personally?
  - Departmentally?
  - The whole company?
  - The executive team?
  - To thrive in the future, how will you have to change the balance?
- How could your organization be more flexible and faster to respond? What are your metrics for flexibility? Speed?
- What might an exercise in scenario planning or backcasting identify for the organization?

- How can you make sure that executives are adequately concerned with the threat of being blindsided?
- In the decision-making process, what prevents individuals from presenting their true opinion?
- On a scale of 1–10, how would you rate your organization's discipline of self-reflection/correction?
- How could you create a discipline of focusing on double loop learning in your organization? (Rather than fighting fires, reflect on deeper questions – what is causing fires? How do we prevent fires? How do we redesign systems and structures to eliminate fires altogether?)
- Is there a systematic discipline in place where individual teams can think several years out?

PART III

This final section of the book will provide individuals with tools, philosophies and approaches that they can personally use to help deal with the speed and amount of change.

Being and Becoming

What strategies and techniques help individuals to accept and thrive in this fast-changing environment? How can we evoke the highest potential from each other? Is there any value in challenge and pain? Can individuals create a sense of security that cannot be threatened?

An organization is nothing more than a collection of individuals. While executives can make daily pronouncements about the need for change, if no one in the organization actually changes, the organization as a whole will not change.

However, if the organization is blindsided, all the individuals will have to change, either because they are laid off, or because they remain within the organization as it scrambles to realign with market forces.

Being blindsided threatens all organizations, unless they are continually adapting to external business environment changes. As my friend Lou Pritchett, author of *Stop Paddling and Start Rocking the Boat*, says, "If the rate of external change exceeds the rate of internal change, disaster is imminent." To avoid being blindsided, individuals have to continually change.

Below are a series of approaches, tools and an understanding of how to personally deal with change.

APPLYING PARETO PERSONALLY

Pareto's Law, the 80/20 rule, can be applied at the personal level. In my own activities 80 percent of the value I add for my organization will come from 20 percent of my activities. Do I know what those 20 percent of activities are? And similarly looking at my modification of the 80/20 rule: the 20/60/20 rule (Chapter 6), 20 percent of a my activities will generate 80 percent of the value to the organization; the remaining 60 percent will generate 40 percent of the benefit; and the remaining 20 percent of my activities will generate 20 percent negative value. Am I able to distinguish between these different activities? And then what can I do to eliminate, automate or delegate the low leverage activities?

LAW OF LEVERAGE

I use the law of leverage with entrepreneurial groups I work with. In theory an individual works 40 hours a week, 50 weeks a year, or 2,000 hours a year. A CEO of a small company with $10 million in sales or a manager in a large organization responsible for a department with a $10 million budget can then calculate the law of leverage by dividing the top line by the number of hours ($10,000,000 ÷ 2,000 hours = $5,000/hour). So this CEO or department manager is responsible for top-line revenue of $5,000 every hour they work and this is based on last year's results, so it doesn't take into account any growth. If he wants to achieve 10 percent growth this year, he should earn $5,500 every hour.

The individual then needs to evaluate every single activity as to whether it will yield $5,500 of top-line revenue. If not, the individual has to stop doing it, either by delegating it, or eliminating it through work redesign.

Another way of looking at the same situation is asking, "What alone can I do?" In my case I ask, "Can my assistant write my next book?" No. "Can my assistant book my travel?" Yes. "Can my assistant work out at the gym on my behalf?" No. "Can the office manager negotiate with suppliers?" Yes.

Use the Law of Leverage and ask the question, "What alone can I do?" I can use trim tabs to help me stay disciplined and focused on what is most important and where I can add the most value.

THE FASTER WE GO, THE MORE WE NEED TO SLOW DOWN

We are moving faster and faster in our society. We have pagers, cellphones, e-mail, and voice mail overload. As the Queen of Hearts in Lewis Carroll's *Through the Looking Glass* says, ". . . it takes all the running you can do, to keep in the same place. If you want to get somewhere else, you must run at least twice as fast as that!"[1]

While *Blindsided!* advocates moving faster while implementing systems and structures that allow for faster recognition and response to challenges and opportunities, we also need to implement systems and structures that allow us time to slow down. The faster we go, paradoxically the greater the discipline we need to set aside time to slow down.

But in our busy lives, we don't take time out individually or organizationally to think and reflect. I believe the key to individual and organizational security is self-reflection and self-correction. Therefore, we need to institutionalize self-reflection and self-correction. In other words, create a discipline of quieting down, slowing down, reflecting, discussing and then, based on the insights gained, make course corrections.

An airplane is off course 98 percent of the time because winds are constantly buffeting it. The pilot or autopilot has to constantly make minor corrections to ensure staying on course.

Self-reflection and self-correction will not be effective if they are applied in a haphazard way. They need to be applied in a disciplined, rigorous way. On an individual level this might mean writing a diary, meditation and discussing problems with colleagues and friends.

Some people will chafe at the notion of discipline. Opposing comments often are: "It isn't spontaneous. It limits freedom." I would argue exactly the opposite. The discipline of self-reflection and self-correction is the very process that expands freedom, choice, and spontaneity. In other words, freedom comes from discipline. The freedom to act based on choice, as opposed to reacting, comes from developing proactive muscles and continually clarifying how I/we see the situation.

Discussion is a key element. I find that it is through discussion that I learn and see alternative viewpoints. It is through discussion that I gain insight. My challenge is to put myself in discussion with people whom I admire and whose opinions I respect. Even people who I don't admire or like, alter my opinions as I come to understand their viewpoint.

On a group level, a discipline of self-reflection and self-correction involves discussing problems and analyzing them to find systemic causes and solutions. For complex problems it would involve using new tools like the complexity tools described in Chapters 8 and 9. These tools take time, and managers, such as the Ford manager referred to in Chapter 2, will often say, "I can't afford to give up 20 of my key people for three days!" As a result, those managers continue to remain mired in a complex situation like the one at Ford where hundreds of engineers had been wrestling unsuccessfully with a problem for seven months.

Which is the best choice between these two options: doubling your speed or heading in the right direction? The obvious answer is heading in the right direction. Doubling your speed while heading in the wrong direction only means you'll fail twice as fast. In other words, we can't substitute efficiency (speed) with effectiveness (correct direction). As management guru Peter Drucker said: "Efficiency is concerned with doing things right. Effectiveness is doing the right things."[2]

On an organizational level, a discipline of self-reflection and self-correction would involve having quarterly executive retreats to ensure that everyone was onside with the vision; Using new tools such as scenario planning to resolve complex situations; and taking time to involve stakeholders in strategic discussions.

Fred Kofman, a consultant, uses a metaphor that helps me understand the paradox of speeding up and slowing down at the same time. He talks about a wheel. At the edges it can be spinning very quickly but at the center it will be still. The faster the wheel turns the more important it is that it is perfectly balanced at the center. When driving, if the wheels are unbalanced, the faster you go, the more violently the car will shake. Similarly, the faster I go in life, or the faster corporations work, the more important it is to be centered on the mission, vision and superordinate goals of the 10S model.

STRATEGIC DISCUSSION

Alan Webber, the editor of *Fast Company*, argues that learning and knowledge are the key business assets.[3] While knowledge flows through the technology, it resides in people and it is people learning together (in discussion) that creates new knowledge. Therefore, a commitment to learning conversations and communities are key to creating new knowledge and process improvements. Therefore, the role of leaders is to design infrastructures that create, foster, and support learning communities. "Conversations are the most important form of work," says Webber, "So much so that the conversation is the organization."

At a group level, the discipline of self-reflection and self-correction involves discussion. In the 10S model these discussions should begin with analyzing stakeholder needs and scouting trends and technology. This implies a series of ongoing conversations with stakeholder groups and individuals involved in cutting-edge information and systems.

MEDITATION

While some may find it puzzling or even disconcerting to talk about meditation in a business book, I am going to anyway. I was at a conference entitled Authentic Leadership in June 2001 where I met Fred Kofman, whose talk at the conference is included in this chapter. The conference was put on by the Shambhala Institute,[4] which combines organizational and meditation practices. At the conference we meditated every day for one hour, which involved a 20-minute lecture followed by 40 minutes of meditation.

The experience had a powerful effect on me. One of the metaphors taught in the sessions was to think of a mountain. In the winter snow comes. And the mountain just is. And spring comes. And the mountain just is. And rain comes. And the mountain just is. And summer comes. And the mountain just is. And the sun shines on the mountain. And the mountain just is. And mountain goats walk on the mountain. And the mountain just is. And fall comes. And the mountain just is.

It is a powerful metaphor. Thoughts come and go, emotions come and go. Good thoughts come. We still are. Upsetting thoughts come into our mind and we just are. The metaphor highlights the transient nature of thoughts, emotions, and life events. The deeper lesson is that we pass through them. It's like the expression, "This too shall pass."

I have taken to meditating for 15-minutes every day. The economics of meditation and spirituality are paradoxical. If I take 15-minutes out of my busy schedule to meditate, paradoxically I find I have more time in the day and get more accomplished because I am centered. I know where I am going, and what I want to achieve in any given day. I am not as easily distracted. Meditation and the process of self-reflection and self-correction are high leverage activities. A trim-tab factor. The more centered I am the better the quality of my life and the more time I have for other areas of my life.

I have found that the practice of meditation seems to change my experience of time. Meditating slows things down. It increases awareness. Try this exercise: Sit in the center of a large rectangular room facing one of the long walls. Turn your head so that you are looking over your right shoulder at the center of the short wall and then slowly begin turning your head in a 180-degree arc until you are looking over your left shoulder at the center of the other short wall. Take four minutes to complete the process and concentrate on being aware of every bump in the wall, hanging picture and texture of paint. Paradoxically, the more I slow down, the more time I have, the more I notice, the better my response will be in a fast changing environment.

Dr Fred Kofman[5] *gave the following talk on June 11, 2001 at the "Authentic Leadership" conference in Halifax, Nova Scotia.*

FINDING OUR TRUE SELVES

I like climbing mountains; it's a spiritual practice for me. Last January I went to South America to climb Aconcagua. Most people thought I was crazy. Aconcagua is about 23,000 feet, the tallest mountain outside of the Himalayas. Above 20,000 feet, it's not pleasant anymore, the air gets pretty thin, the nights get pretty cold, and there's the possibility of "killer storms" with winds of 80+ miles an hour.

I remember waking up on summit day and telling one of my friends, "You know, I have never felt so shitty in my life. I feel so bad. I can't even pinpoint what hurts. It's systemic. Everything hurts." It was awkward. I was feeling terrible, but at same time the experience was exhilarating. I was so close to the roof of the Americas that I could taste it. It didn't taste pleasant or unpleasant; it tasted intense, like a spicy dish.

As I walked up the mountain I meditated. It was a long 20-day walking meditation. It was a purification of sorts. The mountain eats away at you, it grinds you. Literally. Not only do you lose weight, but you also start dropping old baggage. More and more things become irrelevant. Life gets very simple: Did you eat? Did you go to the bathroom? Can you breathe? Do you have a headache? Are you getting sick? Do you have any blisters? Are you able to move? A few basic things matter and everything else doesn't. And friendship, I found out, was one of the things that matters most.

Three of my best friends and I summitted together. It was very touching. As soon as we got to the top we started crying uncontrollably. The guide was puzzled, "Why are you sad? We made it." But we were not sad; we were overwhelmed. My friends and I had taken the climb as a spiritual quest. It was so moving to reach our goal. We were just crying, not out of sadness, or even joy, it was just raw emotion coming out of our eyes. And meanwhile, other people were reaching the summit plateau and high-fiving each other; they stared at the four of us hugging and crying like babies. It was a rather strange scene.

Anything that pushes one's boundaries, such as climbing, is a spiritual practice. The key is staying present in the midst of a difficult situation. The ultimate goal is not the summit but the moment-to-moment focus on staying conscious and alert. Although I wanted it, I wasn't really fixated on getting to the top. My goal was to get to my edge, the limit of my physical strength and see what laid beyond. I was going to get to the top or I was going to faint. Several times on summit day I thought I would faint before getting to the top. And it would have been okay for me to faint and turn back to high camp. I would have given it all I've got; that's the ultimate integrity, regardless of success. I didn't faint so I didn't find my edge. I was very happy to summit. But I am still wondering, how would I have responded if I had had to turn back? Those who turned had their own spiritual challenge, which was to acknowledge their limit and go back down. And in a way that may have been harder than getting to the top. That's an experience that I'm still missing, so I guess I have more mountains to climb.

I want to start with a story that I find very moving. It is a story from the Sufi tradition which Andrew Harvey, a wonderful writer, mystic and storyteller, presents in *The Way of Passion: A Celebration of Rumi*. The story is about a pregnant lioness. The lioness is looking for food. She is hunting and she sees a flock of sheep. So of course she goes for them because the sheep are easy prey, and lions are not very good hunters. Many times they fail to catch their prey. She was happy to find the sheep, goes for the sheep and actually kills one. But she has bad luck, the effort of running and chasing after the sheep makes her give birth and she dies.

The little cub is born completely alone in the world. The mother is dead. He doesn't understand anything. The only thing he sees around is sheep. And his first impression of mommy is sheep. There is the flock of sheep and there is this lion cub thinking, "I must be a sheep." The cub joins the flock of sheep and the flock takes the cub as one of them. He walks around like a sheep. And baaaahhhs like sheep. The cub is just another sheep. They spend their time eating grass and talking about the stock market; complaining about the hard work at the office and that life is boring – you know the stuff sheep do all the time.

Life goes on and the cub develops into a young lion. You can imagine what a ridiculous sight it is: a grown lion walking in the middle of a flock of sheep, eating grass and acting like one of them.

One day an old lion that is standing on top of a mountain sees the young lion in the flock and is outraged. This is a shame for the whole lion race. "What the hell is that guy doing down there?" he thinks. "He should be eating them not eating *with* them."

So he runs down to the valley and kills a couple of sheep – while the rest of the flock scatters. He then goes after the adolescent lion. He grabs the young lion, who is shivering like a frightened sheep, sure that the older lion will kill him.

But the old lion doesn't kill him. He takes him to a pond and forces him to look into the water. The young lion is startled because of what he sees. He thinks he is going to see a sheep's face, but he doesn't; he sees a lion's face. Then, the older lion grabs a piece of a dead sheep and feeds it to his younger brother. He is horrified, because this is like cannibalism to him. But under the pressure of the older lion, he eats it. Surprised, he notices that after a couple of bites, the sheep's flesh doesn't taste so bad.

Finally, the adult lion commands: "Now you are going to roar like this." And he gives the most incredible roar: "ROARRRRR!!!!!!" And then says, "Now you do it." The young lion utters a feeble: "Roar-bhaaaa."

"No, no, no!" despairs the old lion. So they work at it a long time. And after many attempts, the young lion manages to give a great RRRROOOOOOAAAAARRRR.

That is the roar of awakening. The Sufis say that it is the roar of a human being who discovers his true nature.

We could think of the adult lion as an authentic leader. His methods are not what we would call "very compassionate," perhaps, but they are certainly effective.

There is a question I want you to consider. What are the skillful means through which each one of us learns about our true nature? And I want to propose an exercise involving personal stories that you will share with your table's partners.

Think about a time in your life when you learned something very, very significant. Something very important about yourself, about who you are, about your place in the world. Just think of a very meaningful event, something that you would say was life shaping for you. And something that you would feel comfortable telling to the other people at your table. Share that story. Then we will investigate some of the qualities of those events in order to discover what helps us to learn about ourselves.

[*After the exercise*] Think about the stories you've heard and let's distinguish two parts. We will call "The leading edge of learning" the beginning of the story – before you had your learning experience. We will call "The trailing edge" the end of the story – what happened after, or as a result of your learning experience. For example, if my story is about my climb of Aconcagua, the leading edge would be the ascent, what happened before I learned whatever I learned, or had my peak experience. The trailing edge is what happened afterwards, including the way in which my experience influenced my later life.

What state (physical, mental and emotional) were you in during the leading edge? What was happening? What were you thinking? How were you feeling?

[*The audience answers: panicked, frightened, confused, pained, stressed, desperate*] Okay, okay, I think we get the point.

Now let me tell you about a discussion I had with the organizers of this conference. I said, "I'd like to help you make the conference a success by sending the potential participants the following letter:

Dear Participant,

We have designed this experience for you to achieve maximum learning about yourself. This will be an event that you remember for the rest of your life. So we have created a 'development oriented' environment where you will feel panic, fear, confusion, pain, stress and despair.
RSVP.

If you had received this letter, would you have come? Who would have signed up for this conference?

[*People laughing*]
I know, I know, I am a marketing genius.

Think about it. It's amazing. If someone told you what was going to happen in a true "learning" event you would never go. That is exactly the kind of place you *don't* want to go. And yet, years later, when somebody asks about a time in your life when you learned something very significant about yourself, you recall a story that starts with panic, despair, confusion, fear. Why? Because that is the ground on which the soul grows. That is where you discover who you really are. In the face of difficult challenges.

You see, I am not that crazy about climbing mountains, it is a cheap way of getting that feeling of panic, confusion, fear and feeling bad. I mean, some people work for corporate America. I take my hat off to them! Some people work with people that have AIDS. Some people chose to put themselves in situations where they have to find something very deep about themselves or they won't survive. The point is to seek situations where you have to find something very deep about yourself. For me, that is the basis of all leadership.

Why on earth would you choose to do something crazy like that? Well, first, we don't choose. And thank God we don't have to choose. We would never do it. The blessing is that we get these learning events whether we want them or not.

In *Fiddler on the Roof*, there is a scene when Tevie, the milkman who plays the central part, is talking to God. He says: "Dear Lord I know that being poor is no shame but couldn't you give me a little more money? Couldn't you make me a rich man?" And then he sings his famous song "If I Were a Rich Man." Sometimes I feel very similar to Tevie, I want to tell God: "Dear Lord, I know that learning is a blessing, but I have learned enough, okay? I know you are very kind and have given me all these wonderful learning opportunities and I really, *really* appreciate it. But couldn't I take a little break? Like for the next 200 years . . . ?"

Haven't you felt like that sometimes? "Enough of this learning crap! I need a rest." I have a friend who calls these situations AFGOs: another frigging growth opportunity.

What is the saving grace, the redeeming value of these AFGOs?

There is only one thing that is so powerful, so important, and so meaningful that would lead us to want to experience these. There is something in our soul that wants to experience the fullness of our true nature – and that is what happens in the trailing edge of your learning experience.

What are some of the things that you felt after your learning peak? At the end of your own story?

[*Answers yelled out: Courage. Insight. Exhilaration. Inner strength. Compassion. Wisdom. Connection. Happiness.*]

Aren't these the things that make life living worth? I mean life worth living?

These are the things that really touch us. That light fires in our souls. But whoever is not ready to pay the price of knowledge will not get the knowledge. To attain such state, you must put everything you think you know about yourself at risk. And that is why this is so scary, because the price of this kind of knowledge is the sum of all your fears: "I may not be the kind of entity that I used to think I was." That is the ultimate fear. And when we glimpse the truth of this statement, everything shakes.

I was in Berkeley during the 1989 earthquake. I was on campus, which is on bedrock; nothing shook very much there. But when I was driving back home I saw the disaster and thought, "Oh, my God this was pretty bad." Then I turned on the TV and got really scared. It had been much worse than I thought. For several days there were aftershocks. Being in an earthquake is a very disconcerting experience. We tend to think that the ground is solid. Well, I have some news for you: ground is not solid. If you have been in an earthquake you know that ground moves like the sea – there are waves. It's amazing. But the funny thing is that after such an experience you can't trust "the ground" any more like you used to. Your illusion has been shattered and it will not sustain you in your certainty as before. The final consequence of the experience for me was much bigger than the earthquake itself; it was learning that what you used to think was certain is not. And then, every certainty you hold begins to shake.

Antonio Machado has two poems that are absolutely fantastic. The first one says:

> Man has four things,
> That are no good at sea:
> Anchor, rudder, oars,
> And the fear of going down.

We think we are living on solid ground, but we are not. We are not on solid ground, we are at sea. And what is not good is the fear of going down, because if you have the fear of going down, deep into yourself, you cannot sail.

One of the tasks of an authentic leader is to provide the support that people need to get over the fear of going down. To get over the fear that it is inherent to each one of these learning experiences. Whoever is not willing to pay the price of knowledge will not get the knowledge.

If we are alone and all we have is our idea of ourselves, our little idea of our little selves, learning is just too scary. Too scary. Most people will choose not to learn. Not to pay the price of knowledge. So the leader is the one who can stand there and support each one of us while we go through that turmoil of discovering that who we thought we were is not who we really are.

Machado's second poem goes like this:

> Last night as I was sleeping I dreamt, blessed illusion,
> That I had a beehive inside of my heart.
> And the golden bees were making white combs and sweet honey
> Out of old bitterness and failure.
> Last night as I was sleeping I dreamt, blessed illusion,
> That it was God what I had inside of my heart.

Machado's is a different notion of God. It is not one of a God that is outside, that tells you what to do and what not to do. For me, this is the God of authentic leadership. The God of the golden bees that each one of us has inside our true heart. It is the capacity to take every bitterness, every failure, every fear, every challenge that we face and turn it into white combs and sweet honey. That is exactly what you did in those situations you have recalled.

Now there are very many situations in which that did not happen. The shit hit the fan and it flew all over. There was no saving grace. There are situations like that. But one can ask: "Is that the end of the story?" Or perhaps those situations are nothing more than the leading edge of a learning story, which has not yet ended. If you start thinking like that then even the worst things that you can be living right now are a call to grow your heart, so it has enough transformative capacity to get the goodies, the juice that is in that story. Because the more the grief, the more juice you have there to transform into white combs and sweet honey.

Rumi is an awesome poet; he has produced some of the most loving, and most dramatic, mystical verses. "Whoever is not killed for love is dead meat," he says. Wait a minute, what do you mean, "If you have not been killed for love you are dead meat?" There is something about living a life of immediate pleasure – living a life of immediate gratification, a life without challenge, which actually ends up making you dead meat. The human being comes fully alive in the face of these challenges.

As a leader, your responsibility is *not* to make sure nobody has to face challenges, that would be deadly. That would be like if your kid came back from school saying: "Dad (or Mom) I don't understand these math problems." And you replied: "Okay, I don't want you to be traumatized, so let me do them for you." That is not helpful. That is disabling.

If, on the other hand, you give your seven-year-old a system of differential equations and say: "Deal with this challenge all by yourself;" he probably won't develop a passion for math.

Somebody asked the Jewish sage Hillel if he could summarize the Jewish tradition in the time he was standing on one leg – and he said, "Yes, love your brother as yourself. The rest is commentary."

I can summarize developmental psychology in the time I am standing on one leg: "You need an environment that provides both support and challenge for the person. The rest is commentary."

Development happens in this tension between support and challenge. What you support is not the old theory of the self as a leader. What you are trying to support is that which transcends any notion of self that the person has. What is *That*? As the Sanskrit holy saying goes, "Thou art *That*" which indicates we might call *That* the soul, the divine spirit, the divine nature, essence or pure presence. There are many names and no names for it. *That* is what is able to grow. *That* is what, as an authentic leader, you see, you support, and you stand for. And in standing for *That* you need the toughness necessary to allow the personality to burn.

In these trials, the personality burns. The soul is singing while the personality is crying tears of blood. That is what Rumi describes so passionately. He is saying, look, I love your soul, and that means I am not going to have any pity for your personality. Because it is your personality which is blocking the growth of your soul. And your soul will blow up your personality from the inside. It will look for opportunities to break this shell. Just like a caterpillar will look for opportunities to break out of its cocoon and become a butterfly. Making sure that the caterpillar stays a caterpillar is not leadership. That is not love.

In Nepal, the little kids come up to you, put their palms together, do a little bow and greet you; "Namaste." I assumed it meant hello and goodbye, like the Italian "Ciao." I asked my trekking guide, "What's the exact meaning?" I was blown away. "Namaste" means, "I can see the divine light that shines in you." Imagine that instead of saying "Hello" when you greet people you say, "I can see the divine light that shines in you." And the other person would reply, "And I can see the divine light that shines in you." We would remind each other every time we meet, who it is that we really are.

I like to remember and remind others of *That*. That's why it is my pleasure to bow like this to you and say from the bottom of my heart: "Namaste."

Kofman's talk is powerful. I don't believe we know what we are truly capable of. Leadership then is helping people to discover their true nature, by providing both challenge and support simultaneously.

The following insight about honeybees powerfully communicates to me that I don't really know what my true potential is as a human being.

ROYAL JELLY AND THE QUEEN BEE

Nature is fascinating. For the honey bee, or *Apis mellifera*, life revolves around the queen bee. Pre-eminent in the hive's hierarchy, the queen bee is up to 60 percent larger than worker bees, and can live up to 40 times longer (six years compared to six weeks). She lays an average of 2,000 eggs a day, about two-and-a-half times her own body weight, and spawns more than 5 million bees during the course of her lifetime.

Both the queen and worker bees are identical at birth; however, their anatomy and physiology become radically different over a period of days. Worker bees are fed a dilute solution of honey, pollen, and nectar, whereas the larvae in the larger queen cells are continuously fed royal jelly throughout their lives. Any interruption in the diet would halt the transformation of the larvae into a queen bee.

Royal jelly is a creamy-white nutritional substance secreted by the hypopharyngeal glands of worker bees. Reserved exclusively for the queen bee, royal jelly is the source of her superior attributes.

When a hive becomes too crowded, the queen will leave with some of the workers to establish a new hive. The workers in the old hive begin feeding royal jelly to up to six fertilized eggs. The first queen bee to emerge from her cell will sting the other five developing queen bees to death in their cells. If two queens hatch at the same time, they fight until one dies, as there can be only one queen in the hive. When a queen bee dies the same procedure will occur.

Tibetan Buddhists believe in reincarnation, and that when the Dalai Lama dies, his soul is reincarnated within two years, as a newborn child. After the Dalai Lama dies, monks meditate hoping to receive signs as to where the Dalai Lama's spirit will be reborn.

The current Dalai Lama was found after a series of dreams and visions led senior lamas to a home in the northeastern province of Tibet. Asking the owners of the house for shelter for the evening, the group leader, Kewtsang Rinpoche, posing as a servant spent much of the evening observing and playing with the youngest child. The child called him "Sera lama." Sera was Kewtsang Rinpoche's monastery. In a few days the group returned, bringing items that belonged to the thirteenth Dalai Lama and items that did not. In every case, the child correctly identified items belonging to the thirteenth Dalai Lama, saying, "It's mine, it's mine." This convinced the search party they had found the new incarnation.

The parents, also convinced of the reincarnation, turned three-year-old Lhamo Thondup over to the Buddhist monks to raise as the fourteenth Dalai Lama. He was taught by the best Tibetan Buddhist teachers, and in an environment of unconditional love. In other words, he was fed a type of royal jelly.

While average individuals in society are not privy to such a rich learning environment, nonetheless incredible spiritual leaders such as Martin Luther King Jr, Mahatma Gandhi, Buddha and mystics such as Meister Eckhart, or poets such as Rumi emerge. I believe we all have the potential to develop far beyond what we perceive our capacities to be, but to do so requires us to put ourselves in a rich learning environment; one that would lead to exceptional and accelerated spiritual growth.

Certain conditions are required for this to occur. We must require a deep desire and willingness to learn. This implies a sense of awe, wonder and curiosity, or to use a Zen expression, a learner's mind. Secondly, we need to be self-aware, self-reflecting and self-correcting.

UNCOVERING

While there can only be one queen bee in the hive at a time, there can be many spiritually developed people on earth at the same time. Spiritually developed people revel and celebrate the development of others. The greater the spirituality exists, the more that can exist. It is not a zero-sum gain, but unlimited and infinite. Einstein's brilliance in no way detracted from Michelangelo's and Michelangelo's in no way diminished Einstein's. Competitive spirituality is an oxymoron.

Michelangelo's unfinished carvings are breathtaking to look at. In *Atlas the Slave* a perfect torso of a man is emerging from the untouched bottom of a block of marble, as if he is struggling to get free. Michelangelo said that before he began carving any piece he envisioned the figure he wanted to carve in every detail in the marble block. His job was to uncover what he already saw inside the piece.

It seems to me that we are all the same. We are born with certain talents, and our job in life is to uncover them. I believe we have no idea of what our real potential is. To find out what our purpose, our mission in life is, I believe we should follow Joseph Campbell's advice: "Follow your bliss."

All of these stories ("Finding our true selves," "Royal jelly and the queen bee," "Uncovering") raise the question, "How do we evoke or draw out the best in people?"

"One day when the subject of leadership was brought up by one of his staff, President Eisenhower took a small piece of string and laid it on his desk. 'Look,' he said, 'if I try to push it I don't get anywhere. But if I pull it I can take it anywhere I want.'"[6]

In the same way leaders need to evoke the best out of people in organizations. Communities need to evoke the best out of each other. I must work to evoke the best out of my spouse, and she out of me.

A similar question is, "How can organizations get maximum productivity from people?" Daniel Yankelovich coined the phrase "discretionary effort," which is the difference between the minimum effort an individual can make in a position and not get fired or disciplined from the maximum potential contribution that individual can make. Organizations must work to elicit or evoke this discretionary effort from employees.

One of the most exciting ways to elicit the most from employees is having a manager work with each employee to co-define their responsibilities. The goal is to match the skills and interests of individual employees with the organization's jobs and goals. While there will never be a perfect fit for every employee, it is important that the company actively works to maximize the intersection of personal and corporate interests. With a large pool of employees, big companies have a greater likelihood of optimizing this and creating a win–win for both employees and the company, than small companies. In large companies there are more opportunities for people to move around. The important point is that the companies have systems in place that guarantees employees will be happy.

Creating an ideal organization. It takes time. It is an organic process that evolves through continual discussion. Discussion has to be ongoing because markets evolve (1) as customer needs and preferences change, and (2) as employees' interests evolve and change.

Separating action from outcome highlights another important principle: I cannot do for someone else what he or she can do for herself or himself. For instance, I can't work out on someone else's behalf. I could go running, and I would receive all the cardiovascular benefit but they would get none. Now if they ask me, I can tell them *how* to work out, or *why* to work out. I could coach someone in working out, but I can't actually *do* it for that person. This ties in with the concept of leadership being like gardening. The plants grow themselves and leaders merely work on the context.

LIFE IS CIRCULAR

Here is a very simple, powerful model:

$$\textbf{Be} \longrightarrow \textbf{Do} \longrightarrow \textbf{Have}$$

In North America, we in essence say: Have–Do–Be. In other words, many people think, "If I win the lottery, I will *have* a million dollars, then I will be able to *do* certain things, then I will *be* happy." In other words, by winning I will have a million dollars and be able to afford a Mercedes Benz, and expensive vacations. Because of my power, property, and prestige, I will attract a perfect partner. Then

I will be happy. My internal state of being (happiness, security, self-esteem and sense of fulfillment) is a function of external circumstances, doing and having.

In work, people apply the same philosophy. If I *have* a certain job title, I will be able to *do* certain things, and then I will *be* successful.

It also applies on the organizational level. If we *have* a certain market share, we will be able to *do* more research and development then we will *be* innovative.

Or on a personal level, if I *have* a spouse, we will *do* certain things together, and then I will *be* happy.

This outside-in approach inherently creates insecurity. If my security comes from people, places or things, and circumstances change , I lose my security. If I was an Olympic athlete and I defined my self-esteem by my physical prowess and I lost my legs in a car accident, who would I be? A candidate for suicide.

In 1999, my mother-in-law, Marg, discovered she had breast cancer and underwent a radical mastectomy and then chemotherapy. She showed tremendous courage through the whole experience and I am happy to report the cancer is in complete remission. As Marg says, "My breasts don't define me." Not even the physical body I inhabit defines who I am.

If I derive my security from what I do or have and these are taken away from me (I don't get the promotion, I lose my job, my spouse dies, or the house burns down), then I lose my security, happiness, and sense of self-worth. Grieving a loss is human and natural, but using it to define our existence is dangerous. Lasting security, stability, and happiness can only be a function of being, knowing who I am, and what values I believe in.

One of the reasons that I believe organizations have so much difficulty in implementing change is that people become so attached to their positions. They begin to feel they are their job description. Therefore, if you change my job description who am I?

But given that 80 percent of the technology we will use in our daily lives in just ten years hasn't even been invented yet, how can the union and management negotiate a job description that will remain valid for ten years, or five years or even one year?

I believe that the title of my next book will be *Being and Becoming*.

Because there is an interesting tension that exists between whom I am today and who I want to be. I am not all that I want to be. I am in the process of becoming.

Kofman uses a metaphor that our souls are like movie screens. All sorts of images are projected onto the screen, but at the end of the movie the screen is still white. In life we have all sorts of experiences, but they do not color or taint our souls. Our souls are inviolate.

THE FISHERMAN

Western countries have never experienced a higher level of material wealth, and yet people still do not seem happy. One way to avoid being personally blindsided is to root my sense of security in *being* as opposed to *having* or *doing*. The following story is a favorite of mine:

One day a fisherman was lying on a beautiful beach in the Caribbean, with his fishing pole propped up in the sand and his solitary line cast out into the sparkling blue surf. He was enjoying the warmth of the afternoon sun and the hope of catching a fish.

A businessman who was on holiday came walking along the beach and noticed the fisherman. The businessman decided to find out why this fisherman was so relaxed and not working harder. So he went up to the fisherman and said, "You're not going to catch many fish that way."

The fisherman smiled as he looked up, and the businessman asked, "How do you spend your days?"

The fisherman smiled and replied, "Well, I get up in the morning and play with my children, have breakfast with my wife, then I come out to the beach where I fish until I catch one. Then I go home play, with the kids and have dinner. In the evening I go out to the square where I talk with the other men in the village and we play music. Then I come home, make love to my wife, and then we cuddle and go to sleep."

"Well, it's your lucky day," said the businessman, "because I have my MBA from Harvard and can help you improve your life. You see, you have to work harder and catch more fish," said the businessman.

"Why?" replied the fisherman, "I only catch what we need to eat."

"Well if you caught more fish you could take the fish you didn't need to the market and sell them. With the money you could buy a second fishing rod."

"Why?" asked the fisherman quizzically.

"Because then you could catch more fish."

"Why?"

"Well with the additional money you could buy a boat."

"Why?"

"Aha!" said the businessman with pride, "With a boat you can be location independent and you can fish anywhere offshore."

"Why?" asked the fisherman, still smiling.

"You can buy a bigger boat, and hire people to work for you!" he said.

"Why?"

"Well, by reinvesting your profits in the business and through hard work and dedication, you can build up to a fleet of boats. And invest in sonar technology to more accurately track fish and you'll really increase your catches!"

"Why would I want to do that?"

"Well then open your own canning operation here on the island. This way you'll have vertical integration and even greater profitability."

"Why would I want to do that?" asked the fisherman, smiling yet puzzled.

The businessman was beginning to get a little irritated with the fisherman's questions.

"Eventually you can build your business to the point that you can open an import business within the US selling fish directly into US markets. And I would go for the Japanese market too, the Japanese love sushi and are not price sensitive."

"Uh huh."

"And here is where it gets really exciting," continued the businessman. "You work to generate lots of media buzz around your company, and *yes*, wait for it – then do an IPO on Wall Street and make *millions* of dollars!!!" said the businessman who had whipped himself up into a frenzy of excitement.

"Why?"

"Don't you understand??!! You can become so rich that you will never have to work a day in your life! You can retire, play with your children, fish in the day, play music in the square at night and make love to your wife!"

Using Be–Do–Have as a tool helps me to realize what is truly important in life.

THE VALUE OF PAIN

Very few people think of it this way, but pain can be very useful. The following is from *When Bad Things Happen to Good People* by Harold Kushner:

> Why do we feel pain? Approximately one out of every 400,000 babies born is fated to live a short, pitiful life which none of us would envy, a life in which he will frequently hurt himself, sometimes seriously, and not know it. That child has a rare genetic disease know as *familial dysautonomia*. He cannot feel pain. Such a child will cut himself, burn himself, fall down and break a bone, and never know that something is wrong. He will not complain of sore throats and strong aches, and his parent will not know he is sick until it is too late.[7]

In fact, pain is one of the gifts of life. I am not talking about the pain that people feel in car accidents or with fatal cancers. I am talking about the pain we often feel in life, such as when we are fired from a job. Perhaps there is a lesson I have to learn, such as being sensitive to other people. Or perhaps I have to learn that I am more than my job.

In a strange way, pain is a friend and a teacher. It is what stimulates us or motivates us to learn and grow. It forces us to move on. It pushes us out of our comfort zone. In fact, I might never move were it not for pain. Pain is built into the game of life. It is not that there is a right or a wrong, just that when we are in pain something is wrong.

The real question is can we make sense or purpose out of pain? Kushner writes:

> The pain of giving birth is creative pain. It is pain that has meaning, pain that gives life that leads to something. That is why the person who gives birth is willing to do it again. That is why the person who passes a kidney stone will usually say "I'd give anything not to have to go through that again," but the woman who has given birth to a child, like the runner or mountain climber who has driven his body to reach a goal, can transcend her pain and contemplate repeating the experience.[8]

In many companies, people fear telling senior executives bad news. This fear is often justified, as there is a natural human tendency to shoot the bearer of bad news. In my own company, I have to remember that if I react poorly to bad news – throw a temper tantrum, yell at people, etc. – that I will create an informal system that guarantees people will delay or avoid altogether telling me bad news.

If I don't get honest feedback, does that increase or decrease the likelihood of the company being blindsided? Whenever you introduce delays in feedback loops in a system, you increase the chance of being blindsided. To deeply understand this principle, imagine that you were taking antibiotics after having minor surgery and one of the bizarre side effects of the drug was that it introduced a 15-second delay in muscle response. While driving along the highway you witness an accident ahead of you, but you cannot apply the brakes or turn the steering wheel for 15 seconds. Does the delay in this feedback loop enhance or retard your security? It is the same with organizations. Anything that delays feedback loops greatly decreases the organization's security and increases the chances of being blindsided.

The systems in place in the organization could collect 360-degree feedback for everyone in the organization and no one could get a promotion unless they received good feedback from direct reports. Would that change the orientation of your organization?

At the strategy level, 360-feedback could be applied to all stakeholders, suppliers, customers and partners in the value chain.

At the structure level, the organization is oriented to discovering, uncovering and intuiting leading indicators. Some people are assigned to do this, like James Gossling the inventor of Java at Sun Microsystems.

Using the 10S model (Chapter 4) you can see how this works on many levels. On the personal level I must have the courage to confront situations, for instance, be willing to take bad news to the CEO. Similarly the CEO has to have a high emotional quotient to accept bad news without shooting the messenger. This would require developing empathetic listening, being able to stand aside from my opinions and not react while being given negative feedback. It is being able to say if you disagree with my ideas I disagree with the ideas.

In *Emotional Intelligence*, Daniel Goleman argues that emotional intelligence (EQ) is more important that IQ. EQ takes the form of self-awareness, altruism, personal motivation, and empathy. Goleman defines emotional intelligence as a person's ability to: (1) understand his or her emotions and use them to make good decisions in life; (2) manage negative moods and control impulses; (3) remain motivated and optimistic despite setbacks; (4) build positive relationships; and (5) persuade or lead others.

Goleman argues that EQ has a greater impact on job performance than IQ. An employee may have a high IQ and be highly skilled, but if they have a low EQ they will be unable to handle stress, work constructively with others, or lead a team. In fact, IQ contributes only about 25 percent of the factors that determine job performance.[9]

This is important because many studies have shown that a manager will tend to throw good money after bad when a project is failing. This highlights a low EQ because they don't have the humility to admit that they are wrong. Similarly, individuals with a high EQ are able to accept negative feedback, creating a more open and honest culture.

TAOIST FARMER

There is a powerful Taoist story that helps me deal with any challenge I am facing.[10] In a poor country village, there was a farmer who was considered to be rich. He owned a horse, which he used for plowing and for transportation. One day his horse ran away. The villagers said, "What terrible luck, you have lost all your wealth." To which the farmer simply replied, "Maybe."

A few days later the horse returned bringing with it two wild horses. And the villagers said, "What incredible luck, you have just tripled your wealth!" but the farmer just said, "Maybe."

The next day the farmer's only son was out riding one of the wild horses, trying to tame it, when it bucked him off and he broke his leg. (Three thousand years ago that was a life-threatening injury.) All the villagers said, "What terrible luck, your only son with a broken leg!" But the farmer just said "Maybe."

And the next week the Emperor's men came through the village conscripting every young man to fight in a war, taking every young man except for the farmer's son. They rejected the farmer's son because of his broken leg. When all the villagers said, "What incredible luck," the farmer simply replied "Maybe."

I have used this story very profitably in life. For instance, when I am driving on the highway in the fast lane and there is someone driving slowly in front of me, rather than get upset, I think they could be saving me a speeding ticket because perhaps there is a radar trap ahead. This then encourages me to slow down.

A second lesson from the Taoist farmer is understanding the Buddhist belief that all suffering is caused by attachment. When I am not attached to an outcome I can live life joyfully no matter what is happening.

All of these stories help me live comfortably, amid a rapidly changing world.

CONCLUSION

Some people might ask – what does the soul – or our true nature – have to do with avoiding being blindsided? As Joseph Campbell recommended, "Follow your bliss." If I am doing what I am meant to be doing in life – living out my full potential, my soul cannot be blindsided. The intrinsic rewards of living a fulfilling life give such a psychic or spiritual benefit that what I have, and what I do, fall into secondary importance. In this sense I cannot get blindsided. I can have a happy fulfilled life regardless of market conditions, and external change.

While this chapter has focused on strategies to help people cope with change, individual change is essential for organizational and societal change to occur. It is therefore fitting to finish a book that focuses on helping organizations to avoid being blindsided by focusing on the personal level – an area we all have the greatest degree of control over.

REFLECTIONS

- How will you personally apply this material?
- List the ways in which your fears have benefited you.
- Which disciplines of self-reflection and self-correction do you use to continually correct course and bring greater calm, peace, and balance to your day?
- What do you do to slow down? What do you do organizationally to slow down?
- How could you exhibit greater curiosity and willingness to learn new things?
- Is your personal happiness based on *Have–Do–Be* or *Be–Do–Have*?
- How can you encourage discussion within your organization?
- Are enough stakeholders involved in strategic organizational discussions?

- How might your organization do a better job of evoking the "discretionary" effort of its employees?
- Do you personally value open and honest feedback? Have you asked others to rate your openness anonymously – i.e. 360-degree feedback? How can you eliminate a *shoot-the-messenger* mentality within your organization, causing a feedback delay and, consequently, a reduction in response time?
- Do you take into account an individual's EQ when he or she is considered for a managerial or leadership position? Is it within your organization?
- What pieces of this book, if applied would most benefit your organization? If you want immediate response, what structures and systems will you create to galvanize the organization?
- For your organization to escape being blindsided, what long-term plan would you create and who would you include in its creation?

Epilogue

I would very much welcome your comments on *Blindsided!* Email me at jimh@jimharris.com – and if your suggestions are incorporated in a future edition of the book, I will thank you in the acknowledgements, and send you a complimentary copy of the subsequent edition.

Notes

Introduction

1   This book will often refer to companies but you can substitute organization or non-profit.

Chapter 1

1   Milken Institute, from data provided by the US Federal Reserve.

2   Microsoft Network press releases.

3   Napster Public Relations Department.

4   Joshua Cooper Ramo, "Welcome to the Wired World," *Time Special Report: The Networked Society*, February 3, 1997, p. 30.

5   *Worldwide Ecommerce Growth*, Forrester Research Inc.

6   This phrase was coined by James Gosling, the creator of Java and a Vice-President of Sun Microsystems.

7   Hoover's Inc., Austin, TX: *Hoover's Company Profile Database* – American Public Companies, 2001.

8   Eastman Kodak, "Third Quarter Earnings Transcript," November 1, 2001.

9   Anthony B. Perkins and Michael C. Perkins, *The Internet Bubble: The Inside Story on Why It Burst and What You Can Do To Profit Now* (New York: HarperBusiness, 2001, rev. edn).

10 Nortel Networks Networks, "Nortel Networks Sees First Quarter Below Expectations," Press Release, March 21, 2001.

11 Peter Elstrom, "Telecom Meltdown," *Business Week*, April 23, 2001, p. 100.

12 For detailed information about MP3 technology, visit the Fraunhofer IIS Website at www.iis.fhg.de.

13 Pearse Flynn, "Broadband Access," *Alcatel Telecommunications Review*, 4th Quarter 2000.

14 Bill Gates and Paul Allen licensed their BASIC computer language program for personal computers to MITS in 1975. MITS delivered the Altair 8800 that year. In 1976 Steve Wozniak and Steve Jobs created the Apple I computer and founded the Apple Computer Company, on April Fool's Day. And in 1977 Commodore unveiled prototype PET computer. In 1981 IBM announced 5150 PC Personal Computer.

15 Matt Richtel, *The New York Times*, "With Napster Down, Its Audience Fans Out," July 20, 2001.

16 Jupiter Media Metrix, "Users of File-swapping Alternatives Increase Nearly 500 Percent in the US, Surpassing Napster," Press Release, October 10, 2001. www.jmm.com.

17 Jeremy Heidt and Craig Havighustt, "In Napster's Wake, Enter Morpheus; MusicCity.com program lets Users Trade Copyrighted Files," *The Tennessean*, July 14, 2001.

18 This figure of 250 was provided by Matt Bailey of WebNoize in an interview, September 25, 2001.

19 Webnoize media release September 6, 2001.

20 Alan Cross, "Rage Against the Machines," *Saturday Night*, December 2, 2000. Alan Cross is the Program Director at Y95.3 in Hamilton, Ontario.

21 To learn more about ASCAP – American Society of Composers, Authors and Publishers visit www.ascap.com.

22 "Are We Promoting Piracy?" transcript of an interview with Tim O'Reilly and Open P2P.com. Http://www.openp2p.com, May 15, 2001

23 Robert Wright, "The Hole Truth on the MP3 Debate," *Toronto Star*, June 22, 2000, p. H3.

24 According to the International Federation of Phonograhic Industry. Contact them at www.ifpi.org.

25 United States Census Bureau, *1990 Census of Population and Housing*.

26 Interview with *Salon*, see www.salon.com/tech/feature/2000/06/14/love/index.html.

27 M. William Krasilovsky and Sidney Shemel, *This Business of Music: The Definitive Guide to the Music Industry*, 8th edn (New York: Billboard Books, 2000), pp. 21-22.

28 Jeffery Scott, "Will Federal Pact Slash CD Costs?," *Atlanta Constitution*, May 12, 2000, p. 1G.

29 Visit www.creativelabs.com/products/portable-audio/ to see their latest products.

30 From an interview with Hank Berry, August 7, 2001.

31 Scott Bowles, "High-rolling 'Eleven' bumps 'Potter' from No.1 Perch", *USA Today*, December 10, 2001, p. 1D.

32 Andrew Frank, "The Copyright Crusade," Viant Corp., White Paper, 2001, p. 17. The report can be downloaded at www.viant.com.

33 "2000 Attendance Survey, US Economic Review," Motion Picture Association of America (www.mpaa.org).

Chapter 2

1 This is the central theme of my last book, *The Learning Paradox* (Oxford: Capstone, 2001). It is an excellent companion to *Blindsided!*

2 Peter Sealey is a marketing professor at the Haas School of Business, University of California at Berkeley.

3 Leslie Walker, "Plugged in for Maximum Efficiency: Undaunted by Dot-com Flameout, Companies Move To Streamline Operations by Harnessing the Web," *Washington Post*, June 20, 2001, p. G01.

4 M. Mitchell Waldrop, *Complexity: The Emerging Science at the Edge of Order and Chaos* (Touchstone/Simon & Schuster: New York, 1992), p. 30.

5 Dr Clifford Saunders is a facilitator, software designer, and speaker (www.tooserious.com).

6 John Ezard, "Officers Dismissed Radar Warning of Exocet Attack on HMS Sheffield: Invincible Lost 19-minute Chance to Issue Alert During Falklands Conflict," *Guardian* (London) Sept. 26, 2000.

7 Waldrop, *Complexity*, pp. 304-5.

8 Joshua Cooper Ramos, "Welcome to the Wired World," *Time*, February 3, 1997, p. 30.

9 John MacIntyre, "Go Figure – Read all about IT," *Canadian Bankers Association–Canadian Banker*, vol. 107(3), p. 44 (September 22, 2000).

Chapter 3

1 Jean Lebreton and Ian McLaren, "Learning the Various Laws and Lessons of the e-Revolution," *Nation*, August 14, 2000. Lebreton and McLaren are with the Boston Consulting Group in Asia. Their paper highlights four laws: Moore's Law, Metcalfe's Law, Gilder's Law and Coase's Theorem.

2 Dean Takahashi, "Industry Group: Moore's Law Rules," *Wall Street Journal Interactive*, November 23, 1999.

3 "Gene Machines," *The Industry Standard*, June 8, 2001, pp. 38–43.

4 James Cook, "The Molting of America," *Forbes*, November 22, 1982

5 Julie Schmit, "Microsoft Faces Challenge from Internet Rivals," *USA Today*, December 5, 1995, p. 2B.

6 Microsoft Press Release, "MSN Hotmail Tops 100 Million User Milestone," May 14, 2001.

7 David P. Reed, "That Sneaky Exponential – Beyond Metcalfe's Law to the Power of Community Building," see www.reed.com/gfn.

8 George Gilder appearing on John McLaughlin's "One to One," broadcast weekend of May 26–27, 2001.

9 Scott McNealy, "The Net Effect," *The Industry Standard*, June 4, 2001.

10 George Gilder, "Moore's Quantum Leap," *Wired*, January 2002, p. 106.

11 Yankee Group, "Cable Modem Providers Continue to Lead the High-speed Internet Charge: The Yankee Group's Predictions on Consumer Broadband Services," September 4, 2001

12 Ibid., p. 7.

13   Ibid, p. 8.

14   David R. Kolzow and Ed Pinero, "The Internet Economy and its Impact on Local Economic Development," *Economic Development Review*, Winter 2001.

15   Forrester Research Inc., "Global Ecommerce Approaches Hypergrowth," Research Brief.

16   R. R. Bowker Co. which publishes *Books in Print* (www.bowker.com).

17   IDC, "E-mail Usage Forecast and Analysis, 2000–2005."

18   Messaging Online, "Year-end 1999 Mailbox Report".

19   Gartner Group, "Implementing an Integrated Document Management Strategy," February 20, 2001.

20   Cyveillance, Inc., "Sizing the Internet," July 10, 2000. Mark Gilbert, "KM and Content: Push! Pull! Publish! Profit?" Gartner Group (Presentation at Symposium and ITXpo), April, 2000.

21   Morgan Keenan, "ELearning: The Engine of the Knowledge Economy," Industry Report, p. 12.

22   An Intranet works the same as the Internet, but is only accessible within a company or organization, not to the general public. Oracle.

23   Alvin Toffler, *The Third Wave* (New York: Bantam Books, 1981).

24   http://www.ccsf.caltech.edu/~roy/dataquan/.

25   Press release from BrightPlanet www.brightplanet.com.

26   Michael K. Bergman, "The Deep Web: Surfacing Hidden Value," Bright Planet White Paper, 2001, p. 1.

27   Hal R. Varian and Peter Lyman, "How Much Information?," School of Information Management and Systems, University of California at Berkeley, 2000.

28   Ibid., Table 6.

29   Dave Reinsel, analyst with IDC, October 2001.

30   Hard drive cost per gigabyte data provided by David Reinsel, analyst with IDC Inc., October 2001.

31   IDC, "84 Million People in the US Will Plug into the Wireless Internet by 2005," Press Release, March 17, 2001.

32   Darryl Carr, "The Next Big Catch," *Upside*, March 2001.

33   Peter F. Drucker, *New Realities* (London: Butterworth-Heinemann, 1989).

34   Aire de Geus, *The Living Company: Habits for Survival in a Turbulent Business Environment* (Boston, MA: Harvard Business School Publishing, 1997), quoting a study by the Royal Dutch/Shell Group Planning, *Corporate Change: A Look at How Long-established Companies Change*, September 1983.

35   Simon Caulkin, "The Pursuit of Immortality; Corporate Longevity," *Management Today*, May, 1995, p. 36.

36   Jerry Useem, "Churn, Baby, Churn," *Inc. Magazine*, May, 1997.

37   *Information Week*. The complete rankings from 1995 to 2000 can be found on their Website at www.informationweek.com.

38   Clayton M. Christensen, Richard Bohmer and John Kenagy, "Will Disruptive Innovations Cure Health Care?," *Harvard Business Review*, September/October 2000.

39   Arie de Geus, "Planning as Learning," *Harvard Business Review*, March 1988.

40   Jim Harris, *The Learning Paradox* (Oxford: Capstone, 2001), pp. 67–79.

41   Marcia Stepanet, "Rewriting the Rules of the Road," *Business Week*, September 18, 2000, p. 86.

42   *Investor's Business Daily*, December 19, 2000.

43   P2P expert Clay Shirky at the Accelerator Group, quoted by Amy Cortese in "Masters of Innovation," *Business Week*, April 7, 2001, p. 194.

44   According to Bob Knighten, P2P evangelist at Intel in an interview, September 27, 2001.

45   Bruce Ubin, "Sharing Power," *Forbes*. November 20, 2000, p. 278.

46   For more information about SETI@home, go to their Website at http://setiathome.ssl.berkeley.edu/.

47   To download the client, visit www.intel.com/cure/.

48   "Top 100," *Red Herring*, May 1, 2001.

49   Jupiter/Media Metrix, "Global Top 20 Web & Digital Media Properties," June 2001.

50   Reid Kanaley, "Internet Experts Try to Measure Web Traffic Levels," *Philadelphia Inquirer*, September 27, 2001.

51   Michael Dell, "How 'E' Works," speech at the National Press Club Luncheon, June 8, 2000.

52   Alvin Toffler, *The Third Wave* (New York: Bantam Books, 1981).

53   The Quality of Working Life report is produced annually by the Institute of Management (IM) and the University of Manchester Institute of Science and Technology (UMIST). Since 1997 the report has sampled the same 5,000 chairmen, chief executives, managing directors, directors, senior managers, middle managers and junior managers who are members of the Institute of Management. The 2000 results are based on 1,516 respondents.

54   Jeremy Rifkin, *The End of Work: The Decline of the Global Labor Force and the Dawn of the Post-market Era* (New York: Tarcher/Putnam, 1995).

55   These figures are an approximation because we are mixing sources. Figures from 1970 to 1993 are from *The Financial Post*, January 22, 1993, and 1993 to 2000 are from Glenn Starnes, Systems Manager at the Northeast Midwest Institute.

Chapter 4

1   Robert H. Waterman, Jr, "Structure is not Organization," McKinsey & Company staff paper, June 1979, p. 5.

2   Presentation by Jon Fay, vice-president, Mercer Management Consulting at the National Association of Recording Merchandisers conference, March 11-14, 2001, Orlando, Florida, as reported in *Billboard*, March 31, 2001, "SITES + SOUNDS: Napster, CD Burning, Internet Retail Are Hot NARM Confab Topics."

3   Colin Freeze, "Canada Hits Coke with Huge Tax Audit: Soft-drink Giant Could Owe Ottawa more than $100-million in Back Taxes," *Globe and Mail*, June 23, 2001.

4   *Yomiuri Shimbun*, February 24, 1998, p. 1.

5   In fact it was not Frank Lloyd Wright who originally coined this phrase. In 1888 he moved to Chicago where he quickly became the chief protégé of architect Louis Sullivan, who coined the phrase.

6   Waterman, "Structure is not Organization," , p. 6.

7   The W. Edwards Deming Institute, PO Box 59511, Potomac, MD 20859-9511. Voice: (301) 294-8405; fax: (301) 294-8406; staff@deming.org.

8   Michael Rogers and Jennet Conant, "It's the Apple of His Eye," *Newsweek*, January 30, 1984, p. 54.

9   From an interview with Hank Berry, August 7, 2001.

10   Baldwin and Ford, "Transfer of Training: A Review and Directions for Future Research," *Personnel Psychology*, 1998.

11   Don Tapscott, *The Digital Economy: Promise and Peril in the Age of Networked Intelligence* (McGraw-Hill: New York, 1996), p. 3.

12   Michael Pellecchia, "Book about GE Restructuring Offers Insight into Search for New Big Blue CEO," *Dallas Morning News*, March 14, 1993.

13   Six Sigma statistics provided by Corporate GE Six Sigma department, October 24, 2001

14   Jack Welch with John A. Byrne, *Jack: Straight from the Gut* (Warner Business Books: New York, 2001), p. 335.

15   Ibid., pp. 331–332.

16   This program assumes that the people closest to the work know it best. During a 2-3 day retreat, employees share their views on the bureaucracy that takes place in their department – approvals, reports, meetings and measurements – away from managers. At the end of the session, the employees present their ideas to the manager who must make decisions on the spot or set a date for a decision. Managers must respond to their employees suggestions. They can't bury the report. For more information about this program, read Jack Welch, *Jack: Straight from the Gut*.

17   Alfred, Lord Tennyson, "Charge of the Light Brigade."

18   There is a counter-argument that could be made here that some of the brightest programmers will not be lured away by Microsoft because they want to pursue their own interests and work on their own start up.

19 US Department of Commerce, Economics and Statistics Administration, *Establishment and Firm Size 1997 Economic Census Retail Trade*.

Chapter 5

1 Andrew Sawers, "The Financial Director Interview; I'm Not Worried About our Share Price," *Financial Director*, April 10, 2001.

2 David Cay Johnston, "Study Finds That Many Large Companies Pay No Taxes," *The New York Times*, October 20, 2000, p. 2.

3 Graph provided by Cisco Systems Inc. CEO John Chambers presented this graph at Comdex 2001 in Los Vegas, NV.

4 Matt Krantz, *USA Today*, May 2, 2001.

5 CNNFN-Street Sweep, December 4, 2001.

6 Joanne Lee-Young and Megan Barnett, "Furiously Fast Fashions," *Industry Standard*, June 11, 2001.

Chapter 6

1 Frederick F. Reichheld. *The Loyalty Effect* (Boston, MA: Harvard Business School Press, 1996), p. 14.

2 Don Peppers and Martha Rogers, "Customer Value," *CIO Enterprise Magazine*, September 15, 1998.

3 Cindy Perper, President of the National Business Travelers Association in a statement to the Hearing of the Aviation Subcommittee of the House Transportation and Infrastructure Committee Panel. October 11, 2000. Federal News Service.

4 Don Peppers and Martha Rogers. *The One to One Future* (New York: Currency Doubleday, 1993), p. 52.

5 Don Peppers at a seminar on CRM May 27, 2001 in Toronto, Canada.

6 This term was coined by Jan Carlson, the former president of SAS airlines.

7 Frederick R Reichheld, *The Loyalty Effect* (Boston, MA: Harvard Business School Press, 1996), p. 1.

8 Frederick R Reichheld and W. Earl Sasser, "Zero Defections: Quality Comes to Services," *Harvard Business Review*, September–October 1990, p. 1.

9 Reichheld, *The Loyalty Effect*, p. 51.

10 Peppers and Rogers, *The One to One Manager*, p. 78.

11 Booz, Allen & Hamilton Inc., *Internet Banking: A Survey of Current and Future Development*, February 1996.

12 FedEx Corporation.

13 Joseph Nocera, "Banking Is Necessary – Banks Are Not," *Fortune*, May 11, 1998, p. 84.

14 Interview with Dennis Jones, former CIO, FedEx.

15 James Watson, Gail Donnelly and Joshua Shehab, *The Self-Service Index Report*, Doculabs, First Quarter 2001, Table 2.

16 Larry Selden and Geoffrey Colvin, "Will Your E-Business Quick Leave You or Dead?," *Fortune*, May 28, 2001.

17 Hal Steiger and Michael Smith, "Evaluating the Stick Finger in E-Commerce, Phase II," Broadbase Software Inc., 1999.

18 Watson *et al.*, *The Self-Service Index Report*, p. 7.

19 This report is available for download at www.rightnow.com/news/doculabs.html.

20 Tom Spring, "Dell Ditches Live Online Support," *Network World*, June 18, 2001.

21 Scott Strumello of Auriemma Consulting Group. Contact (516) 333-4800.

22 Peppers and Rogers, *The One to One Future*, p. 52.

23 Business Wire, *Presenting: The Class of 2001*, May 18, 2001

24 Microsoft Inc., "Microsoft Acquires Hotmail," Press Release, December 31, 1997.

Chapter 7

1　Laura Spinney, "Blind to Change," *New Scientist*, November 18, 2000, p. 28.

2　Ibid.

3　At the time the company was known as Smith Kline & French Laboratories.

4　IMS Health, a leading provider of healthcare and pharmaceutical information and analysis. Their data on antiulcerants can be viewed on the Web at www.imshealth.com.

5　Kandice L. Knigge, MD, "The Role of *H. pylori* in Gastrointestinal Disease," *Postgraduate Medicine*, September 2000, p. 71.

6　According to the Netcraft Web Server Survey. Red Hat Press Release, "Red Hat Leads Global Linux Use in New Surveys," July 25, 2000.

7　According to Gartner Group.

8　Luke 12:49–53.

9　The origin of the Serenity Prayer is obscure. It may date back to Boethius, a philosopher who lived about A.D. 500 and was martyred by Christians. It is usually credited to Reinhold Niebuhr, a 20th-century theologian who in turn credited an 18th-century theologian, Friedrich Oetinger.

Chapter 8

1　Christopher Cerf and Victor Navasky, *The Experts Speak: The Definitive Compendium of Authoritative Misinformation* (New York: Pantheon Books, 1984; republished Villard Books, 1998). Check it out for more great "expert wisdom".

2　The Myers–Briggs Type Indicator is a questionnaire, which determines an individual's personality type. Personality type varies based on how people process information, make decisions and communicate.

3　Legendary investor Jesse Livermore, whose exploits are detailed in *Reminiscences of a Stock Operator*, coined the phrase "never fight the tape" – i.e. always align with market movements: buy in a rising market and sell in a falling one.

4　George A. Miller, "The Magical Number Seven, Plus or Minus Two: Some Limits on our Capacity for Processing Information," *Psychological Review*, vol. 63(2), March 1956. A psychologist studies human short-term memory.

5　Henry Albert's work in helping to redesign the US Defense Acquisition System.

6　Owen Harrison, *Open Space Technology: A User's Guide*, 2nd edn (Berrett-Koehler, 1997).

Chapter 9

1　In 1997 IBM's Deep Blue, which beat Gary Kasparov, the best chess player in the world, could analyze 200–300 million moves a second, analyzing up to 74 moves ahead, compared to chess masters who typically think 10 moves ahead.

2　Paul Leavitt and Pat O'Driscoll, "Million Tons of WTC Debris Removed So Far," *USA Today*, January 11, 2002.

3　Kevin Done, "Long Struggle to Put People Back on Board," *The Financial Times*, November 30, 2001.

4　Susan Pigg, "Wide-body Graveyard," *Toronto Star*, February 2, 2002, p. E5.

5　Done, "Long Struggle," Surveys BTR1.

6　Pigg, "Wide-body Graveyard," p. E5.

7　Ibid.

8　Prior to September 11, 2001 $200 billion of airport expansion was planned in the US. Over $150 billion of this was cancelled after the attacks.

9　Pigg, "Wide-body Graveyard," p. E5.

10 Associated Press, "AMR Reports $414 Million Loss in Third Quarter - $525 Million Shortfall Before Special Items," October 24, 2001.

11 "Attacks Just Part of Reason Insurance Rates Are Rising," *The Business Journal (Central New York)*, vol. 15(51), p. 8, December 21, 2001. Notes Ellen D. Kiehl, executive assistant director of government and industry affairs for the Professional Insurance Agents of New York, New Jersey, Connecticut, and New Hampshire.

12 Ibid.

13 Dana Hedgpeth, "Hotels Fail to Win Direct US Aid; Congress, White House View other Industries as Being More Needy," *Washington Post*, December 18, 2001, p. E01.

14 Ibid.

Chapter 10

1 Lewis Carroll, *Alice Through the Looking Glass*, chap. 2 (1872).

2 Peter Drucker, *Management Tasks, Responsibilities, Practices* (1974), chap. 2.

3 Webber is also the former editor of the *Harvard Business Review*. From a paper called "The LOGIC of the New Economy."

4 Visit the Shambhala Institute at www.shambhalainstitute.org. Shambhala was a legendary Asian kingdom, whose culture was characterized by a high degree of wisdom and compassion. Shambhala teachings have been handed down in Tibetan Buddhist traditions.

5 Dr Fred Kofman founded Leading Learning Communities as a joint venture between MIT's Organizational Learning Center and EDS while he was a professor at the MIT Sloan School of Management. The curriculum integrates the latest research in economics, strategy, philosophy, cognitive science, systems thinking and organizational learning. Clients include Chrysler, Shell Oil, General Motors, EDS, Xerox, Intel, Phillips and others to create effective learning environments. Dr Kofman has published numerous papers in books and journals including *The Fifth Discipline Handbook*. His new book *Metamanagement* was published in Spanish by Editorial Granica in 2001 and will be released in English in 2002. Dr Kofman has been named "Teacher of the Year" by the Sloan School of Management at MIT. He has given seminars to thousands of people in the USA, South America and Europe.

6 General Dwight D. Eisenhower, *Reader's Digest*, May 1957, p. 27 (provided by Herb Pankratz at the Eisenhower Library).

7 Harold S. Kushner, *When Bad Things Happen to Good People* (New York: Avon Books, 1983), pp. 61-62.

8 Ibid., p. 63.

9 J. E. Hunter and R. F. Hunter, "Validity and Utility of Alternative Predictors of Job Performance," *Psychological Bulletin*, vol. 76(1), pp. 72-93, 1984.

10 Richard Bandler and John Grinder, *ReFraming* (Utah: Real People Press, 1982), p. 1.

Bibliography

Allee, Verna. *The Knowledge Evolution: Expanding Organizational Intelligence*. Boston, MA: Butterworth Heinemann, 1997.

American Management Association. *Blueprints for Service Quality: The FedEx Approach*. New York: American Management Association Briefing, 1991.

Argyris, Chris. *Overcoming Defensive Defenses: Facilitating Organizational Learning*. Englewood Cliffs, NJ: Prentice Hall, 1990.

Bandler, Richard and Grinder, John. *Reframing: Neuro-linguistic Programming and the Transformation of Meaning*. Moab, UT: Real People Press, 1982.

Bank, David. *How Bill Gates Fumbled the Future of Microsoft*. New York: The Free Press, 2001.

Bardwick, Judith. *Danger in the Comfort Zone*. New York: American Management Association, 1991.

Bardwick, Judith.*The Plateauing Trap*. New York: Bantam, 1988.

Barker, Joel Arthur. *Paradigms: The Business of Discovering the Future*. New York: HarperBusiness, 1993.

Beck, Nuala. *Shifting Gears: Thriving in the New Economy*. Toronto: HarperCollins, 1992.

Bergman, Michael K. *The Deep Web: Surfacing Hidden Value*. White Paper, Bright Planet, 2001.

Bond, Jonathan and Kirshenbaum, Richard. *Under the Radar: Talking to Today's Cynical Consumer*. New York: John Wiley & Sons, 1997.

Booz, Allen & Hamilton Inc. *Internet Banking: A Survey of Current and Future Development*. February 1996.

Broadhead, Rick and Carroll, Jim. *Get a (Digital) Life: An Internet Reality Check*. Toronto: Stoddard, 2001.

Carlzon, Jan. *Moments of Truth*. New York: Harper & Row, 1987.

Cerf, Christopher and Navasky, V. *The Experts Speak*. New York: Pantheon, 1984.

Christensen, Clayton M. *The Innovator's Dilemma: When New Technologies Cause Great Firms to Fail*. Boston, MA: Harvard Business School Books, 1998.

Paul Churchland, *The Engine of Reason, the Seat of the Soul*. Cambridge, MA: MIT Press, 1996.

Clark, Jim with Edwards, Owen. *Netscape Time: The Making of the Billion-dollar Start-up that Took on Microsoft*. New York: St Martin's Press, 1999.

Covey, Stephen. *The Seven Habits of Highly Effective People*. New York: Fireside, 1989.

Covey, Stephen. *Principle Centered Leadership*. New York: Summit Books, 1990.

Covey, Stephen. *How to Succeed with People*. Salt Lake City, UT: Deseret Book Company, 1971.

Csikszentmihalyi, Mihaly. *Flow: The Psychology of Optimal Experience*. New York: Harper & Row, 1990.

Csikszentmihalyi, Mihaly. *Finding Flow: The Psychology of Engagement with Everyday Life*. New York: Basic Books, 1997.

Csikszentmihalyi, Mihaly. *Creativity: Flow and the Psychology of Discovery and Invention*. New York: Harper Perennial, 1997.

Cusumano, Michael A. *Japanese Software Factories: A Challenge to US Management*. New York: Oxford University Press, 1991.

Cusumano, Michael A. and Selby, Richard W.. *Microsoft Secrets: How the World's Most Powerful Software Company Creates Technology, Shapes Markets and Manages People*. New York: Free Press (Simon & Schuster), 1995.

Cusumano, Michael A. and Yoffie, David B.. *Competing on Internet Time: Lessons from Netscape and its Battle with Microsoft*. New York: The Free Press, 1998.

Davis, Wade. *One River: Explorations and Discoveries in the Amazon Rain Forest*. New York: Simon and Schuster, 1996.

De Geus, Arie. *The Living Company*. Boston, MA: Harvard Business School Press, 1997.

De Geus, Arie. "Planning as Learning," *Harvard Business Review*, March/April 1988.

Delphi Group. "Need to Know: Integrating e-Learning with High Velocity Value Chains," White Paper, December 2000.

Deming, W. Edwards. *Out of Crisis*. Cambridge, MA: MIT Center for Advanced Engineering Study, 1982.

Drucker, Peter F. *New Realities*. London: Butterworth-Heinemann, 1989.

Drucker, Peter F. *Management Tasks, Responsibilities, Practices*. Perennial Library, 1974.

The Economist, "Serious Games," July 8, 2000.

Eden, Colin, Jones, Sue and Sims, David. *Messing About in Problems: An Informal Structured Approach to their Identification and Management*. Oxford: Pergamon Press, 1983.

Fisher, Roger and Ury, William. *Getting to Yes: Negotiating Agreement Without Giving In*. New York: Penguin, 1981.

Frank, Andrew. "The Copyright Crusade,".White Paper, Viant Corporation, 2001.

Frappaolo, Carl. *Ushering In the Knowledge-Based Economy*. The Delphi Group (Forbes Magazine Special Advertising Section), April 1998.

Friend, John and Hickling, Allen, *Planning Under Pressure: The Strategic Choice Approach* Oxford: Butterworth-Heineman, 1987.

Gerlach, Charles. "The ASP Revolution: Why Hosting Applications Will Transform Business," *Mainspring*, January 2000.

Gianforte, Greg. *Self-learning Knowledge Bases: A Revolutionary Approach to Knowledge Management*, White Paper, RightNow Technologies, 2001.

Gilder, George. *Telecosm: How Infinite Bandwidth Will Revolutionize Our World*. New York: The Free Press, 2000.

Thomas Gilovich, *How We Know What Isn't So: The Fallibility of Human Reason in Everyday Life*. New York: The Free Press, 1991.

Gleick, James, *Chaos: Making a New Science*. New York: Penguin Books, 1988.

Godin, Seth. *Permission Marketing*. New York: Simon and Schuster, 1999.

Godin, Seth and Gladwell, Malcolm. *Unleasing the Ideavirus*. Do You Zoom, Inc. September 2001.

Graff, James. "Left Behind: Europe's Labor Force is Out of Date . . . And Out of Work," *Time Magazine*, May 8, 2000.

Grove, Andrew. *Only the Paranoid Survive*. New York: Bantam Doubleday Dell, 1996.

Hamel, Gary and Prahalad, C.K.. *Competing for the Future: Breakthrough Strategies for Seizing Control of Your Industry and Creating the Markets of Tomorrow*. Boston, MA: Harvard Business School Press, 1994.

Hammer, Michael. "Reengineering Work: Don't Automate, Obliterate," *Harvard Business Review*, July/August 1990.

Hammer, Michael and Champy, James. *Reengineering the Corporation: A Manifesto for Business Revolution*. New York: HarperBusiness, 1993.

Harris, Jim, *The Learning Paradox*. Oxford: Capstone, 2001.

Harrison, Owen, *Open Space Technology: A User's Guide*, 2nd edn. Berrett-Koehler, 1997.

Innes, Eva, Lyon, Jim and Harris, Jim. *The 100 Best Companies to Work for in Canada*. Toronto: Harper-Collins, 1990.

Janes, F.R. "Interpretive Structural Modeling: A Methodology for Structuring Complex Issues," *Trans. Inst. Mech. Engrs. C*, vol. 10(3), August 1988.

Kleiner, Art. *The Age of Heretics: Heroes, Outlaws and the Forerunners of Change*. New York: Doubleday, 1996.

Krasilovsky, M. William and Shemel, Sidney. *This Business of Music: The Definitive Guide to the Music Industry*, 8th edn. New York: Billboard Books, 2000.

Kuhn, Thomas S. *The Structure of Scientific Revolutions*. Chicago: University of Chicago Press, 1970.

Kushner, Harold S. *When Bad Things Happen to Good People*. New York: Avon Books, 1983.

Levering, Robert. *A Great Place to Work: What Makes Some Employers So Good (and Most So Bad)*. New York: Random House, 1985.

Levering, Robert and Moskowitz, Milton. *The 100 Best Companies to Work for in America*. New York: Doubleday/Currency, 1993.

Miller, George A. "The Magical Number Seven, Plus Or Minus Two: Some Limits On Our Capacity For Processing Information," *Psychological Review*, vol. 63(2), March 1956.

Mintzberg, Henry "That's Not Turbulence, Chicken Little, That's Real Opportunity," *Planning Review*, 22(6), 1994.

McMurrer, Daniel P., Van Buren, Mark E. and Woodwell, William H., Jr. *The 2000 ASTD State of the Industry Report.* American Society for Training and Development, 2000.

Moore, Geoffrey and McKenna, Regis. *Crossing the Chasm: Marketing and Selling High-tech Products to Mainstream Customers.* New York: Harper Business, 1997.

Moore, Geoffrey. *Inside the Tornado: Marketing Strategies from Silicon Valley's Cutting Edge.* New York: Harper Collins, 1999.

Moore, Geoffrey. *Living on the Fault Line: Managing for Shareholder Value in the Age of the Internet.* New York: Harper Business, 2000.

Moe, Michael T. and Blodget, Henry. "The Knowledge Web: People Power – Fuel for the New Economy." Merrill Lynch & Co., May 2000.

Negroponte, Nicholas. *Being Digital.* New York: Alfred A. Knopf, 1995.

Nolan, John. *Confidential: Uncover Your Competitors' Top Business Secrets Legally and Quickly – and Protect Your Own.* New York: Harper Business, 1999.

Osborne, David and Gaebler, Ted. *Reinventing Government.* Reading, MA: Addison-Wesley, 1992.

O'Toole, James. *Leading Change: The Argument for Values-based Leadership.* New York: Random House, 1995.

Perkins, Anthony and Perkins, Michael C. *The Internet Bubble: The Inside Story on Why It Burst and What You Can Do To Profit Now,* rev. edn. New York: HarperBusiness, 2001.

Peppers, Don and Rogers, Martha. *The One to One Future.* New York: Currency Doubleday, 1993.

Peppers, Don and Rogers, Martha. *The One to One Manager.* New York: Currency Doubleday, 1999.

Peppers, Don and Rogers, Martha. *CRM in a Down Economy.* White Paper, Peppers and Rogers Group, February 8, 2001.

Porter, Michael. *Competitive Advantage: Creating and Sustaining Superior Performance* (June 1998)

Pritchett, Lou. *Stop Paddling and Start Rocking the Boat.* New York: Harper Business Books, 1999.

Pugh, Stuart. "Concept Selection – A Method that Works," paper delivered to the International Conference on Engineering Design, March 9–13, 1981

Rebello, Kathy. "Inside Microsoft: The Untold Story of How the Internet Forced Bill Gates to Reverse his Corporate Strategy," *Business Week,* July 15, 1996, pp. 56–67.

Reichheld, Frederick F. *The Loyalty Effect: The Hidden Force Behind Growth, Profits, and Lasting Value.* Boston, MA: Harvard Business School Press, 1996.

Reichheld, Frederick F. and Sasser, W. Earl. "Zero Defections: Quality Comes to Services," *Harvard Business Review,* September/October 1990.

Reilly, D. L. "Neural Network Fraud Control in the Bank Card Industry," in R. Freedman, R. Klein and J. Lederman (eds), *Artificial Intelligence in the Capital Markets.* Probus, 1995.

Rifkin, Jeremy. *The End of Work.* New York: Tarcher/Putnam, 1996.

Ringland, Gill. *Scenario Planning: Managing for the Future.* Chichester, UK: John Wiley & Sons, 1998.

Rosenberg, Marc J. *e-Learning: Strategies for Delivering Knowledge in the Digital Age.* New York: McGraw-Hill, 2001.

Schwartz, Peter *The Art of the Long View: Planning for the Future in an Uncertain World.* New York: Currency Doubleday, 1991.

Senge, Peter. *The Fifth Discipline: The Art and Practice of the Learning Organization.* New York: Doubleday/Currency, 1990.

Souque, Jean-Pascal. "Training & Development Practices, Expenditures and Trends," Conference Board of Canada, 1996.

Steiger, Hal and Smith, Michael. "Evaluating the Stick Finger in E-Commerce, Phase II," Broadbase Software Inc., 1999.

Stein, Daniel, "All Systems Slow: How Everything from Glass to the Economy Takes Shape," *The Sciences,* September/October 1988.

Tapscott, Don and Caston, Art. *Paradigm Shift: The New Promise of Information Technology.* New York: McGraw-Hill, 1993.

Tapscott, Don. *The Digital Economy: Promise and Peril in the Age of Networked Intelligence.* New York: McGraw-Hill, 1996.

Toffler, Alvin. *The Third Wave.* New York: Bantam Books, 1981.

Torvalds, Linus. *Just for Fun. The Story of an Accidental Revolutionary.* New York: Harper Business, 2001.

Treacy, Michael, and Wiersema, Fred. *The Discipline of Market Leaders.* Reading, MA: Addison-Wesley, 1995.

Tsai Chih Chung, *Zen Speaks*, trans. Grian Bruya. New York: Anchor Books, Doubleday, 1994.

Van Der Heijden, Kees. *Scenarios: The Art of Strategic Conversation.* Chichester, UK: John Wiley & Sons, 1996.

Varian, Hal R. and Lyman Peter. *How Much Information?* School of Information Management and Systems, University of California at Berkeley, 2000

Wack, Pierre. "Scenarios: The Gentle Art of Reperceiving," Harvard Business School working paper, 1984.

Wack, Pierre. "Scenarios: Shooting the Rapids," *Harvard Business Review*, vol. 63(6), 1985.

Wack, Pierre. "Scenarios: Uncharted Waters Ahead," *Harvard Business Review*, 63(5), 1985.

Waldrop, M. Mitchell, *Complexity: The Emerging Science at the Edge of Order and Chaos*, New York: Touchstone (Simon & Schuster), 1992.

Wallace, James and Erickson, Jim. *Hard Drive: Bill Gates and the Making of the Microsoft Empire.* New York: HarperBusiness, 1992.

Warfield, John N. *Societal Systems: Planning, Policy, and Complexity.* New York: Wiley Interscience, 1976

Warfield, John N. *A Science of Generic Design: Managing Complexity through Systems Design*, 2 vols. Salinas, CA: Intersystems, 1990; 2nd edn published Ames, IA: Iowa State University Press, 1994.

Warfield, John N. and Cárdenas, A. Roxana, *A Handbook of Interactive Management.* Ames, IA: Iowa State University Press, 1994.

Waterman, Robert H., Jr. "Structure Is Not Organization," McKinsey & Company staff paper, June 1979.

Watson, James, Donnelly, Gail and Shehab, Joshua. *The Self-service Index Report.* Doculabs. First Quarter 2001.

Wheatley, Margaret J. *Leadership and the New Science: Learning about Organization from an Orderly Universe.* San Francisco: Berrett-Koehler, 1992.

Wilson, Larry and Wilson, Hersch. *Stop Selling and Start Partnering: The New Thinking about Finding and Keeping Customers.* New York: John Wiley & Sons, 1996

Wilson, Larry and Wilson, Hersch. *Play to Win!: Choosing Growth over Fear in Work and Life.* Bard Press, 1998.

Yankelovich, Daniel. *The Magic of Dialogue: Transforming Conflict into Cooperation.* New York: Touchstone, 1999.

Young, Bob and Goldman Rohm, Wendy *Under the Radar: How Red Hat Changed the Software Business – and Took Microsoft by Surprise.* Scottsdale, AZ: Coriolis Group, 1999.

Acknowledgments

B*lindsided!* began with a question, "How can individuals and organizations better respond to the rapid change?" The process of writing the book has been a profound journey of discovery.

I would like to thank the business leaders who gave so generously of their time to be interviewed in preparing this book.

I am really excited to be working with Capstone: Mark Allin and Richard Burton the founders of Capstone and co-Publishers, and Katherine Hieronymus and Sue McCormick who are responsible for marketing and promotion, Nick Allen for editing and his attention to details, Mark Essen for text design and Darren Hayball for the elegant, fun and provocative cover design. Capstone is an imprint of John Wiley & Sons, a global publisher of print and electronic products. In addition to offices in the US, Wiley has operations in Europe (England and Germany), Canada, Asia and Australia. It is exciting that *Blindsided!* will be released in 80 countries simultaneously.

I am especially grateful to my literary agents, Robert Mackwood and Perry Goldsmith of Contemporary Communications, who are diligent, professional, skilled and delightful to work with.

At Strategic Advantage there was a team transcribing interviews, researching and writing. Transcribing over 60 interviews were Sue Carr, Karen Emery, James O'Hearn and Alyson Waite. Victoria Musgrave headed the research team, which focused on fact checking and case study background, with assistance from Mike Cormack, Lindsay Bruce, Sue Carr, and James O'Hearn. Victoria Musgrave and Michael Cormack also helped write cases and Cathy Harris and John Hockin each prepared a case study.

The entire researching team used *Lexis-Nexis* to research *Blindsided!* and I found it to be an invaluable tool. It is truly an amazing product.

I also want to thank Shawnessy Johnson who served as the office manager during this period.

Thanks to my friends, colleagues and clients who have greatly enriched the text through their insights in reviewing the manuscript: Marsha Anevich, Everett Anstey, Tina Boudreau, Rick Broadhead, Lindsay Bruce, Wayne Burgess, Michael Cormack, Graham Crawford, Art Daniels, Linda Davidson,

Joanne Downey, Richard Elmes, Jim Estill, Barb Frances, Jim Gannon, Chris Gibson, Roberta Kelly, John Kempster, Alyson Latimer, Lee-Anne McAlear, Robert Mackwood, Karen Mason, Susan McLarty, Mike Millhaem, Belinda Miller Foey, Victoria Musgrave, Laurie Peck, Wayne Roberts, John Schumacher and Bill Scott.

Parts of chapters 2, 8 and 9 were written in collaboration with Dr Cliff Saunders.

I am *truly* grateful to my global agents at Can*Speak: Linda Davidson, Tina Boudreau, Sheree McGarrity, Belinda Miller-Foey, Lesley Rizvi, Laurie Peck, Christine Christianson, Mary Bray and Amy Duquette. Life is short so it had better be fun, and the team certainly has made it fun. They are a joy to work with!

I am excited to be working with Celebrity Speakers representing me in Europe and the Middle East: Alex Krywald and Dagmar, Sylvie Guenier, Dave Daniel, Michael Ford, Trevor Marsden, Cosimo Turroturro, Susan Wiltshire, Deirdre Edwards, Corinna, Hazel, Britta Lams, Helen Lacey, Jason O'Sullivan. I am also excited to be working with CSA's wider group of associates throughout Europe: Joe Albayati, Milena Amvrazi-Diamantopoulou, Lutz Beutling, Barbara Beutling, Oliver Beutling, Fred Brauer, Handan Demiroz, Torsen Fuhrberg, Eithne Jones, Jan Marlier, Noel Marlier, Leila Proud, Bernd Riekenbrock, C.-J. Spies and Judy Hill's team in Andorra: Fabienne Dubois, Felipe Gallardo, Lynda Livett, Peter Lucas, Ben Myatt, Marije de Ruiter, Enrique Vessuri, Saskia Willets.

About the author

Blindsided! Strategies for Accelerating Recognition and Response in a Fast Changing World is Jim Harris' third book.

Mr Harris is the principal of Strategic Advantage, a management consulting firm providing strategic planning and leadership development to leading organizations. His second book, *The Learning Paradox*, was nominated for the Canadian National Business Book Award, and has appeared on numerous bestseller lists. There are now over 40,000 copies in print and it has been published in over 80 countries.

Mr Harris co-authored the second edition of *The Financial Post's* bestseller, *The 100 Best Companies to Work for in Canada*, which sold 50,000 copies. Between 1992 and 1996 he represented the Covey Leadership Center of Utah in Canada by teaching Dr Stephen Covey's work *The 7 Habits of Highly Effective People*.

Presentations by Jim Harris

Passionate, inspirational, fun, describe Jim Harris. He speaks internationally at over 50 conferences a year on issues of most concern to executives:

- Customer relationship management
- eLearning
- Leadership amid change
- Creativity and innovation
- Customer intimacy
- Time management

Interactive workshops on:
- Strategic planning
- Mission and vision
- Teamwork

International clients representing all industries

Arthur Andersen · Association of College and Research Libraries · Barclays Bank · Bell Canada International · CSAE · Connaught Laboratories & Pasteur Mérieux · Credit Union Executives Society · CXY Chemicals · Deloitte & Touche · Ernst & Young · The Executive Committee (TEC) · European Snack Food Association · General Motors · George Weston · Glaxo-Welcome · IBM · IABC · International Council of Shopping Centers · International Meeting Planners & Incentive Travel · LEGO

For more information on booking Jim Harris, visit www.jimharris.com

Index